THE
COMMONWEALTH
GAMES

THE
COMMONWEALTH
GAMES

EXTRAORDINARY STORIES
BEHIND THE MEDALS

BRIAN OLIVER

BLOOMSBURY
LONDON • NEW DELHI • NEW YORK • SYDNEY

Published by Bloomsbury Publishing Plc
50 Bedford Square
London WC1B 3DP
www.bloomsbury.com

Bloomsbury is a trademark of Bloomsbury Publishing Plc

First edition 2014
Copyright © 2014 Brian Oliver

ISBN (print): 978-1-4729-0732-5
ISBN (ePdf): 978-1-4729-0844-5
ISBN (EPUB): 978-1-4729-0843-8

Acknowledgements
Cover photograph © PA Archive/PA Images
Inside photographs, see the picture credits, page 197
Commissioned by Charlotte Croft

This book is produced using paper that is made from wood grown in
managed, sustainable forests. It is natural, renewable and recyclable.
The logging and manufacturing processes conform to the
environmental regulations of the country of origin.

Typeset in 11 on 13 Bembo by Saxon Graphics Ltd, Derby
Printed and bound in Great Britain by CPI Group (UK) Ltd, Croydon, CR0 4YY

10 9 8 7 6 5 4 3 2 1

Contents

Acknowledgements

My thanks go to all the athletes, past and present, who have given interviews for this book, who are too numerous to list. Special mention must be made of Brendan Foster for his enthusiasm in writing the foreword, and to Precious McKenzie, Ron Hill and Roy Williams, who helped not only with recollections of their own achievements but also in putting me in touch with other athletes and individuals involved in the Games. As for the distressing story about Emmanuel Ifeajuna, his widow Rose and son Emmanuel were most helpful in difficult circumstances. At the Commonwealth Games Federation (CGF), Peter Murphy and Mike Hooper gave early impetus and encouragement to the project.

Thanks also to the many journalists, academics, writers, business executives and enthusiasts who helped with advice, contact information, research and general knowledge about the Games. Among these are: Stan Greenberg, Peter Matthews, Bob Phillips, Louise Martin, Alex Wood, David Webster, Doug Gillon, Mike Maloney, Athole Still, Norman Harris, Bruce Kidd, Frank Foy, Mike Fleet, Chris Carter, Steve Bunce, Neil Wilson, Duncan Mackay, Pat Butcher, Neil Shuttleworth, Travis Cranley, Jacqueline Magnay, Dave Stubbs, James Lawton, Matthew Curtain, Chris Akers, Patrick Nally, Malcolm Beattie, Peter Radford, Prof Alan Tomlinson, Prof Marc Keech, Mel Davis, Stuart Falla, Chief Emeka Anyaoku, Prof Cyril Enwonwu, Adeyinka Makinde, Richard Bourne and Richard Dowden.

Above all, my thanks go to my wife Marlene, daughter Bonita and son Victor for putting up with an obsessive author for a year. This book is dedicated to them.

Introduction

The Commonwealth Games are something of an oddity in the world of modern sport. They do not make a fortune, nor do they expect to. They do not have an array of commercial backers and sponsors, or an army of multilingual executives carrying out their business in a bustling headquarters. The Games do not fill the sports pages in the way they did half a century ago. They do not even appear to have any clearly defined purpose other than that ascribed to them by their founder, Melville Marks 'Bobby' Robinson, back in 1930, when he had become thoroughly fed up with the extreme nationalism and intensity of the Olympic Games. The Americans, especially, irked him. 'The event will be designed on an Olympic model,' Robinson said, 'but these Games will be very different. They should be merrier and less stern, and will substitute the stimulus of a novel adventure for the pressure of international rivalry.' The British sense of fair play and sportsmanship would be paramount.

This was all very well in the days of amateur sport. The British newspapers were very supportive of the British Empire Games, as they were then known. They gave them far more coverage than the football World Cup, which also started life in the summer of 1930 and that has been staged, like the Games, every four years since then, wars permitting. But how does it sound in the twenty-first century? What, exactly, is the purpose of the Commonwealth, never mind the Commonwealth Games? 'There hasn't been any meaningful debate about the Commonwealth Games in the past 20 years,' was one view put forward by a leading sports sponsorship executive ahead of the Glasgow 2014 Games. That much is true, but there was no debate in the 20 years before that, either. Or in the 20 years before that. Has there ever been any debate since the Games started in the 1930s? The Games have just carried on regardless of the political and cultural transformation of what was once the British Empire, and of all the changes sweeping through the sporting world. That is a great achievement in itself.

A pertinent interpretation of Bobby Robinson's statement may be: 'These Games will be fun.' They were then and they still are now. There has been one constant throughout those 80-plus years of rich sporting history: the athletes love the Commonwealth Games. There is room for a bit of fun in everybody's life. The competitors spoke glowingly of their 'novel adventure' back in the 1930s when many of them had to take months off work to compete. They have enjoyed the Games just as much in more recent years, a point made in the enthusiastic comments of, among others, Dame Kelly Holmes, Sally Gunnell, Paula Radcliffe, Jonathan Edwards and Ian Thorpe, all of them Olympic champions and/or world record holders. 'The Friendly Games' have clearly earned that title on merit.

Why write a book about the history of these Games? Because it was a challenge, because nobody in Britain had done so before and because it soon became clear, in researching the project, that there were a great many untold stories worth telling. Like the Games themselves, the research has been fun. The willingness of those involved to talk about their experiences has helped; so, too, has the quite remarkable array of resources at the British Library.

Selecting the best stories was not easy. The idea was not to record a chronological list of achievements, but to highlight the heroes, the people who made the Games what they are, and what they were. These stories, it is hoped, provide a portrait of the Games, a human history rather than a statistical one. If some of the chapters appear more biographical than others it will be because it works better that way, and adds colour to the portrait.

This selection process has led to two chapters on weightlifting, and none specifically on boxing: but how could Precious McKenzie and Marcus Stephen be left out? There is no chapter dedicated to a champion from the Indian subcontinent or the Caribbean – Marilyn Neufville and Don Quarrie would have been obvious candidates. Maybe these will be covered in the next edition: there is not room for all of them here. For a touch of drama, every chapter has been given the title of a film. Several of the stories would be ideal for dramatisation on the big screen. It was almost a guilty pleasure at times to look back over so many years of 'Britishness' and find a level of respect and admiration for the Queen and the royal family that had not been there before. The chapter on Emmanuel Ifeajuna led me to read eight books about the Biafran War (Nigerian Civil War) and the first Nigerian coup of 1966, and a good deal besides. It was rewarding and worthwhile. I can honestly say my life has been enriched by having spent a year researching the heroes and history of the Commonwealth Games.

Host cities and athlete numbers

Year	Host city	Nations	Sports	Competitors
1930	Hamilton, ON	11	6	400
1934	London	16	6	500
1938	Sydney	15	7	464
1950	Auckland	12	9	590
1954	Vancouver	24	9	662
1958	Cardiff	35	9	1122
1962	Perth, Australia	35	9	863
1966	Kingston, Jamaica	34	9	1050
1970	Edinburgh	42	9	1383
1974	Christchurch	38	9	1276
1978	Edmonton, AB	46	10	1474
1982	Brisbane	46	10	1583
1986	Edinburgh	26	10	1662
1990	Auckland	55	10	2073
1994	Victoria, BC	63	10	2557
1998	Kuala Lumpur	70	15	3633
2002	Manchester	72	17	3679
2006	Melbourne	71	16	4049
2010	Delhi	71	17	4352
2014	Glasgow	—	17	—
2018	Gold Coast	—	17	—

1930–50: British Empire Games
1954–66: British Empire and Commonwealth Games
1970–4: British Commonwealth Games
1978 to present day: Commonwealth Games

Foreword

Brendan Foster

My favourite memory from my running days – the most exciting race I ever ran in my life – was at the Commonwealth Games in Edinburgh in 1970. Earlier in the year I hadn't even made the Northumberland and Durham team for the inter-county championships. I'd never run internationally and here I was at the Commonwealth Games. I won a bronze medal behind the great Kip Keino and my wife still says it was her favourite of all my races. Her mother was even more impressed – not with the race, but because my medal was presented by the Queen. I was delighted to finish third. My parents were there, as were a group from the school where I was working as a teacher at the time. Nothing has ever meant more to me. Ever since then I have loved the Commonwealth Games.

Kip Keino was my hero at the time. I remember when I was a student in 1968, and money was tight. I was sharing a house where we had a television but it was locked away in a bedroom because we couldn't afford a TV licence. We brought it out for the Olympic Games in Mexico City in October – we thought that if we got caught they wouldn't fine us just for watching the Olympics.

The highlight for me was watching Kip Keino winning the 1500m. Those Games were called the 'Cardiac Olympics' because so many distance runners collapsed – they couldn't cope with the high-altitude atmosphere. Kip Keino was amazing. He ran six races in eight days. He had stomach cramps in the 10,000m final and dropped out, and he was just beaten in the 5000m. A doctor told him he shouldn't risk running in the 1500m but he made a late decision to go for it and boy, what a run it was. He beat the world record holder Jim Ryun, from America. When he came to Edinburgh I was in awe of him – he was the Olympic champion and the defending Commonwealth champion.

I'll always remember the first time I saw him. It was freezing cold and blowing a gale, and when we got to the warm-up track before the race there he was in an overcoat. Can you imagine it? Kip Keino jogging around in a coat before he won that gold medal...

Not many people know that. There are so many stories people don't know about 'The Friendly Games', which is why it's so good to have a book such as this to tell some of those unknown or forgotten tales. For example, here are three things that exist solely because of the Commonwealth Games: medal ceremonies at the Olympics, Nike sportswear and the London Marathon. Maybe I'm stretching a point on the last two, but the first we know for sure. The idea of a podium and a ceremony for presenting the medals was dreamed up at the first British Empire Games in Canada in 1930 and pinched by the Olympics.

Back in Canada again, in Vancouver in 1954, the 'mile of the century' race between Roger Bannister and John Landy was a huge event – the biggest race in history. I used to work with Phil Knight, the co-founder of Nike, and he proudly told me he was at that race. His father took him up to Vancouver from Oregon and he was hooked; it was Bannister v Landy that started his interest in running, and that interest eventually led to the creation of Nike.

Of course you could argue that the 1500m race between Filbert Bayi and John Walker in Christchurch in 1974 was even better than the 'mile of the century'. I would have to agree, because I ran in that race. I didn't win a medal but I broke the British record, and it was one of the all-time great races. John Walker, who became a great friend of mine, beat the world record but it still wasn't enough. Filbert Bayi, from Tanzania – another good friend – led all the way and beat him. It was phenomenal. The quality of the athletics at those games in Christchurch was unbelievable.

And the London Marathon? Back to Canada again, in Edmonton for the 1978 Games. I was very friendly with Chris Brasher, who was sports editor of the *Observer* at the time. I had won the 10,000m and I was telling him he should follow the marathon. He wasn't much interested but we ended up in the lead vehicle following the race together and he loved it. It was a fantastic race. I was cheering on the eventual winner Gidamis Shahanga, shouting at him to 'run like Filbert' because he was from Tanzania, too. I had a bit of a soft spot for the Africans – I ran in five Commonwealth races and every time I lost I was beaten by an East African. We got talking about marathons after that, Chris and I, and the following year he was off to New York to run in their race. Marathons were beginning to take off, and it was after that visit to New York that Chris and John Disley had the idea of setting up a London Marathon. It started in 1981, the same year as our first Great North Run in Newcastle.

The thing that sets the Commonwealth Games apart is that everybody speaks English, so you can have a chat with your rivals and sink a beer after the race. Kip Keino came and congratulated me when I won that medal in 1970 – that would never have happened in the Olympics, and not just because the other runners didn't necessarily speak English. When your rivals were from the Soviet Bloc they weren't even allowed to be friendly. Nationalism is not such a big thing as it is at the Olympics. Calling them 'The Friendly Games' is absolutely spot on. It's always great to see the Queen at the Games. She has held them together fantastically well, has always been really enthusiastic, and, it is to be hoped, the next generation of the royal family will hold the Games as close to their hearts as she has done.

Of course it was all so different back in the 1950s, 60s and 70s when the Commonwealth Games were so strong. There were no world championships in athletics or swimming then. There were so many big names competing – people such as Herb Elliott, Peter Snell, Dawn Fraser, Kip Keino. Nowadays it's tougher – a lot of the big stars don't compete in the Games. You look at it sometimes and worry about the Games' place in the modern world of sport.

That's why my Commonwealth Games hero is not one of those great athletes from the past. It's the city of Glasgow. They have timed it perfectly as hosts. You couldn't really say the 2010 Games in Delhi were a great success but the 2014 Games will be: look at the ticket sales for a start. The success of the London Olympics has been a big help, too. It's good to have the Games here in Britain, and I hope they are around for a long while to come.

Brendan Foster, BBC athletics commentator and founder of the Great North Run, ran in the Commonwealth Games three times. He won a 1500m bronze in 1970; a 5000m silver in 1974, when he finished seventh in the 1500m; and a gold at 10,000m and a bronze at 5000m in 1978. He has attended eight Games with the BBC and will be part of the team in Glasgow.

1

The Empire strikes back

Bigger than the World Cup – how it all started

There were huge crowds and great drama at the first Games, brought to life in 1930 by Canadian 'Bobby' Robinson after he had a bellyful of American arrogance at the Olympics.

If there were two words an exhausted Billy Savidan did not want to hear after slogging his way through six miles in searing heat in the hardest race of his life, they were the very ones that were shouted at him as he staggered over the finish line and stopped: 'Another lap!'

No, they must be wrong. The steward had clearly indicated one lap to go when Savidan was last here a minute or so back. But several men in blazers were waving their arms frantically and yelling at him. 'Another lap!'

The full house of nearly 20,000 spectators could hear it all too clearly, too. The New Zealander was a long way clear but he had run 23 laps, not 24. The official who was there to show the runners how many laps remained, by holding up a big figure printed on a sheet of paper, had turned over two sheets instead of one. He should have shown Savidan a figure 2: instead he held up a 1. Savidan would have to go around again to hold off the challenge of the Englishman Ernie Harper. The crowd roared him on.

This was the opening day of the first British Empire Games in Hamilton, Ontario. Savidan had been in the new Civic Stadium for hours and was hot – very hot. Before the race he had stood in the open with 400 other athletes listening to the worthies make their speeches on this famous day: 16 August 1930.

There were no races in New Zealand longer than three miles, nor was there yet a cinder track – the favoured surface for athletics until the 1960s. Savidan had never raced on cinders, nor over this distance, the imperial version of the 10,000m. He had plenty of stamina, built up not just by running but by his daily walks of at least five miles. A tough stonemason, he loved training in the sun: his preparations had featured a time-trial over six miles when it was 100°F in the shade. He was, he said later, 'all bone and muscle' by the time of the Games. But this 'extra' lap was proving too much for him.

His legs felt like jelly, his shoes like they had lead weights in them, his mind was frazzled and he could not keep to a straight line as the noisy spectators urged him through another circuit. 'Come on!' they yelled at Savidan. Harper was gaining and he too knew how to handle the heat. He had been Britain's only finisher, in fourth place, in a punishing Olympic cross-country race in 1924 in which 23 runners stopped or collapsed. Already four-time national champion over 10 miles, he would win a silver medal in the 1936 Olympic marathon.

Savidan desperately wanted to win this and the three-mile race to prove the New Zealand selectors wrong. They had overlooked him for the 1928 Olympics despite his being national champion at a mile and three miles: that had hurt. The New Zealand Amateur Athletic Association (NZAAA) had snubbed him again in selecting the team for these Games. First, they insisted that he or his Auckland club pay all his expenses; second, they did not confirm his place in the team until 24 hours before their boat left for Canada.

Victory would mean so much, but he felt 'like a drowning man in heavy surf, gulping for air,' and began to veer and wobble all across the track on the home stretch, struggling to stay on his feet. Some frenzied spectators jumped over the trackside fence and ran alongside Savidan at the edge of the track, shouting themselves hoarse to encourage him. He almost stopped at one point; then, to the crowd's delight, he found more energy from somewhere. As Harper's challenge failed to materialise Savidan made it home to 'win' for a second time, earning one of the biggest cheers of the week.

The drama was not over yet. There were only four in the New Zealand athletics team, two of them gold medallists in Hamilton: Savidan and javelin thrower Stan Lay, who amazingly competed again 20 years later in the Auckland Empire Games, finishing sixth. The other two Kiwis, sprinter Alan Elliott and triple jumper Ossie Johnson, were there to support Savidan at the end of his ordeal. This was a close-knit team, who had arrived a month early to acclimatise.

Savidan was clearly distressed as he crossed the winning line. His team-mates helped him around the track to have his photo taken with Harper and Tom Evenson, the Englishmen who finished second and third, and supported him at the medal ceremony. 'Amid great enthusiasm,' reported

The Times in England the following day, 'Savidan took his place on the dais while the band played and the winners' flags fluttered in the breeze to close a memorable day.'

Savidan, in shock, remembered nothing of this. He had to be walked around the track again by his teammates, this time for half an hour before he was able to sign the paperwork confirming his Canadian and Empire Games six-mile records. 'I can remember heading for the tape…,' he said, but that was all, and he even asked later if he had won. After briefly losing consciousness in the dressing room he recovered and said, 'I think I'm going mad.'

That race took its toll. In the three miles, for which he was favourite, Savidan was unable to finish. When he did make it to the Olympic Games two years later, in Los Angeles, he suffered the disappointment of finishing fourth in both the 5000m and 10,000m, an admirable effort given that he was still unable to train on cinders. The New Zealanders did not arrive home from Canada until October. Savidan's story was not told in detail until the writer Norman Harris spoke to the men from the 1930 Games more than 30 years later for *Lap of Honour*, a book on New Zealand's athletics heroes.

'From being one of my easiest races it turned into my hardest,' said Savidan. 'I collapsed for the first time in my life.' He won, however, and the crowd loved it.

The Empire Games were the second of two major sporting events, both still with us, that were conceived at the Amsterdam Olympics in 1928 and born two years later. First was football's World Cup. Uruguay, the driving force of the international game, had been watched by a crowd estimated at 1000 in their opening-round victory in the 1924 Paris Olympics. Just over four years later a quarter of a million people from all over Europe applied for tickets to watch them retain their title in Amsterdam.

Despite its booming appeal to the public, international football was being strangled by the constraints of amateurism, and its players earned either very little or nothing at all. On the eve of the Amsterdam tournament a new body was formed to govern football and ensure that Olympic gold would no longer be the pinnacle of a player's career. The Fédération Internationale de Football Association (FIFA) were now in charge, and the first World Cup kicked off in Uruguay on Sunday 13 July 1930.

Five weekends later, in Canada, a parade of nations was followed by the first contests in the Empire Games. In contrast to football, this addition to the sporting calendar was a fierce defender of amateurism. It also championed the 'glorious traditions of British sportsmanship', the perceived absence of which, in Amsterdam, had infuriated the Canadians and spurred them into action. A direct result was the creation of the British Empire Games.

There is little doubt which of the two was more important to the British media. England disdained the World Cup and apart from a mention before it started, in a report about Uruguay's centenary celebrations, it merited no coverage whatsoever in London's most respected newspaper, *The Times*. On 31 July the *Guardian* recorded the winning of the tournament by Uruguay in one paragraph, and got the score wrong. The World Cup was a 'foreign' concept to the British: no home nation would enter it until 1950. The Empire Games, far more newsworthy, were reported at length by special correspondents in Canada.

Any criticism from abroad would be sharply felt by the Canadians, not least because one of their own, the national athletics team manager Melville Marks 'Bobby' Robinson, had done more than anybody else to make the Games happen. This was a risky enterprise at a time of global economic recession and there was more than civic pride at stake for Hamilton, which had a population of 151,000. They wanted to show the world that they were capable, welcoming and efficient hosts – without going broke in the process.

Unsurprisingly, given that Robinson worked for the *Hamilton Spectator*, local press coverage was highly favourable. For an unbiased, independent view Bevil Rudd is a good name to turn to. Rudd was a decorated soldier, Olympic champion and respected writer. His grandfather Charles, Cecil Rhodes's business partner, co-founded the De Beers diamond mining company in South Africa, where Rudd grew up before taking a scholarship at the University of Oxford. He was awarded the Military Cross for bravery in the First World War, and won the 400m Olympic gold medal for South Africa at the 1920 Games in Antwerp. He became a prolific correspondent for British newspapers and, later, an editor at the *Daily Telegraph*.

Rudd travelled to Hamilton, from where he sent dispatches to newspapers in London and Manchester. There had been worries about the city's ability to stage the Games, he acknowledged. Would the costs be too much of a burden? Would the public buy tickets? The organisers should have given the athletes more notice of the event schedules, Rudd said, but otherwise all the challenges were met. He overlooked the lap-counting incident and the absence of medical help for runners, and declared the Empire Games 'without a doubt an unqualified success ... a significant beacon in Empire relations'. They must be repeated, he said. They have been, many times: 84 years later they head for Glasgow as the twentieth Commonwealth Games.

Rudd, like the capacity crowd in the stadium on the first day, was enthralled from the start. He saw an impressive opening ceremony with a parade by those 400 athletes, and scores of officials, from 11 nations, then watched a Canadian take the first gold medal of the Games. Gordon 'Spike' Smallacombe, from the West YMCA club in nearby Toronto, won the hop, step and jump, later renamed the triple jump, setting a national record in the process.

The speeches preceding Smallacombe's small leap into sporting history were 'picked up by microphones and relayed by means of loud-speakers not only to the thousands of Canadians actually in the stadium, but all over the Dominion,' reported the *Guardian*'s special correspondent. 'In an atmosphere of athletic loyalty which has never been possible of achievement before, the great gathering of English-speaking athletes took the oath, a squad of soldiers fired a volley over the heads of the competitors, and in strict conformity with Athenian tradition, carrier pigeons were released.' There were fireworks and a huge display of flags.

The Canadian prime minister, R. B. Bennett, spoke of the 'happy occasion of such a family gathering' and read messages from King George V, the Prince of Wales, the Duke of Connaught and Lord Derby. The Games were officially pronounced open by Viscount Willingdon, Canada's Governor-General, who said, 'The greatness of the Empire is owing to the fact that every citizen has inborn in him the love of games and sports.' In keeping with the times there was no mention of 'her'. Willingdon was sent to India the following year to try to counter the growing popularity of Mahatma Gandhi and the Indian nationalists.

When Smallacombe was presented with his medal he stood on a raised platform, with the other medallists on a lower level. He saluted as Canada's flag was raised and as the anthem was played by the band of the Argyll and Sutherland Highlanders. Rudd was not alone in admiring this spectacle. R. J. Hobbs, the New Zealand team manager, described the ceremonies as 'a tremendous thrill' for athletes and spectators. Among the distinguished guests in Hamilton were the Belgian aristocrat Count Henri de Baillet-Latour, and the American Avery Brundage, present and future presidents of the International Olympic Committee (IOC). Baillet-Latour ordered that the podium ceremony, never before seen at the Olympics, must feature at future Games, starting in 1932. Indeed the IOC men adopted more ideas from these first Empire Games, among them the billeting of competitors in an athletes' village, and recruitment of volunteers to help with the efficient day-to-day running of the Games.

The most famous athlete who took part on the first day of competition was, like Count de Baillet-Latour, an aristocrat. The popular Olympic 400m hurdles champion David Cecil, better known as Lord Burghley, carried England's flag at the opening ceremony. He then breezed through the heats of the hurdles on his way to glory later in the week. 'The glamour of his reputation captured the public imagination,' wrote Bevil Rudd, the influential correspondent for the British newspapers. Another report predicted on the morning of the Games that the Canadians would see Lord Burghley as the star attraction and would 'regard it as a great novelty to see the heir of one of Britain's old aristocratic families skipping over the hurdles'.

Lord Burghley won three golds, the hurdles at 120 and 440 yards, and the 440-yard relay. Rudd was effusive after Burghley's 'race of his life' in the sprint hurdle, for which two South Africans had been strong contenders. Howard Davies, fastest in qualifying, was beaten by a tenth of a second, while the indefatigable Johannes Viljoen was fourth. Viljoen competed in the high jump, which he won, the long jump (bronze), hammer, a sprint relay and both hurdles races. When Burghley saw off his challengers, wrote Budd, 'the spectators were wild with excitement. Burghley was flinging his whole energy into the scale. At the ninth hurdle he had a good yard's lead and the race was as good as won. For sheer racing genius it was the greatest race of Burghley's life.'

Burghley, who later took the grander title of Marquess of Exeter, became one of the most influential figures in amateur sport in the twentieth century. He was the figurehead of the 1948 London Olympics, and served on the International Olympic Committee for 48 years. He drove a Rolls-Royce with the number plate AAA1, a reference to his 30-year presidency of the Amateur Athletic Association (AAA).

A far more down-to-earth runner, the Yorkshireman Stanley Engelhart, won the first track final over 220 yards. It was a proud victory both for Engelhart and his home town of Selby, where a road was later named after him: 5000 well-wishers cheered him at a civic reception on his return, when the church bells were rung and he was flown around in a biplane. Empire gold, clearly, was highly valued.

After a 'home' win for Smallacombe, Burghley's success in the heats and Savidan's exciting victory at the close of day one, news quickly spread of the drama. 'Perhaps those who dedicated the Games earlier in the day could regard these results, namely the victories of a nobleman and a builder, as typical examples of the spirit and the interest which they hope will pervade these contests,' wrote one correspondent.

Crowds grew at all sports as the days went by. A thousand extra seats were installed at the Civic Stadium. Cars flooded into the city, many of them bringing visitors who were on their way to the Canadian National Exhibition, which was due to open in Toronto the day before the Games finished. Thousands were locked out of the stadium for the last two days of athletics.

Rudd wrote of spectators being 'frantic' and 'in a frenzy' throughout the Games. 'Even the field events were watched with an excited scrutiny that must have been a novel experience for the performers.' The arenas for swimming and boxing were packed, and free viewing up above the course meant that 'great rowing was watched by crowds that at times swelled to nearly 100,000'. These were enormous numbers for a fledgling sports event.

When the rain came there was 'no lessening of enthusiasm'. The streets of Hamilton were bedecked with flags, and when Percy Williams was due to run 'all the shops and most of the offices in the city closed at one o' clock and even the local paper had a half-holiday'.

Williams was Canada's great sporting hero. Winner of the sprint double at the 1928 Olympics, he set a world record in Toronto a week before the Empire Games opening ceremony, at which he had the honour of pledging the athletes' oath of sportsmanship. The American press said Williams had been a lucky winner in Amsterdam, suited by the new, soft surface. He proved them wrong by winning 21 of 22 races in the four months after his return, all of them in the United States.

Williams restricted himself to the 100 yards in Hamilton, where he looked set for another world record on the final day of competition. Soon after halfway, however, Williams tore a thigh muscle. Although he stumbled home to victory he would never fully recover, not least because the Canadian team did not have a doctor on duty. An embittered Williams was told before the 1932 Olympics, where he failed to reach the final, that only an immediate operation in Hamilton would have saved his running career.

Percy Williams was named Canada's greatest ever Olympian later in his troubled life. He helped to promote the 1954 British Empire and Commonwealth Games in his home town of Vancouver. He ran an insurance company, became reclusive, said he 'hated running' and declined an invitation to attend the 1976 Olympics in Montreal. He lived alone after his mother died in 1977, and suffered severe pain from arthritis. In November 1982 he blew his head off with a shotgun.

There may have been other Olympic champions for the crowd to cheer in Hamilton but, sadly for Canada, there were no women's athletics events. Two years earlier in Amsterdam, when women had first been invited to compete on the Olympic track, Canadians had won five medals, more than any other nation. The 'Matchless Six', as Canada's female Olympic athletes were known, were cheered by 200,000 at a reception in Toronto on their return. There was nobody for them to race against in Hamilton: Britain's best were competing in the Amateur Athletic Association championships, watched by only 3000, at Stamford Bridge in London while the Empire Games took place. They had already committed, along with 16 other countries, to the Women's World Games in Prague in September.

Women had a chance to make their mark in only two sports: swimming and diving. Cecelia 'Cee Cee' Wolstenholme, a 15-year-old schoolgirl from Manchester, made sure they did so without delay, setting the first world record of the Empire Games on the first day in the 200 yards breaststroke. All the other women's swimming races were won by the Games' first quadruple-gold medallist, Joyce Cooper. The Englishwoman, daughter of a wealthy tea planter, had been raised in what was then Ceylon and is now Sri Lanka. Like the Olympic champion David Wilkie many years later, she had learned to swim in Ceylon. Cooper won all of her four races, benefiting enormously, as the *Guardian* pointed out, from the weakness of the opposition. Australia, which later became the strongest swimming nation in the Commonwealth, sent two men and no women.

Never mind that the competition may have been stronger, the public wanted to be there. Bevil Rudd reported on another problem at the pool: there were not enough seats. The 'zest of the crowd was unabated' at the rowing despite poor weather, and the boxing was keenly contested before an appreciative audience, he said. 'The atmosphere throughout was one of genuine comradeship and enthusiasm.' Before the week was out an Empire Games Federation had been formed, New Zealand and South Africa had applied to be the hosts in 1934 and the future of the British Empire Games (1930–50), the British Empire and Commonwealth Games (1954–66), the British Commonwealth Games (1970–4) and the Commonwealth Games (from 1978), was assured.

When many of the visiting track-and-field athletes left as a single group, on their way to a match between the United States and the British Empire that would attract 50,000 to a floodlit stadium in Chicago five days later, a huge crowd gathered at Hamilton's railway station. The band of the 91st Highlanders piped them aboard the train and played a farewell. Praise rained down on Hamilton from all quarters: from athletes, officials, the media, and spectators lucky enough to have been there. For one man, above all others, Hamilton had been a magnificent triumph. That man, as Bevil Rudd acknowledged, was the founding father of the Commonwealth Games: 'Bobby' Robinson.

Robinson was born in Peterborough, Ontario in 1888. He left school at 13 to work his way up through local newspapers in Toronto and Hamilton, from office boy to assistant editor to sports editor of the *Hamilton Spectator*. He served in the First World War, became manager of the national athletics team, a post he held until 1938, was well connected in local business and commerce, and was 'known throughout Canada' – according to the slim surviving documents about the Hamilton Games – as an aggressive campaigner in the world of agriculture. Having lived on a farm, he negotiated fiercely on behalf of fruit and vegetable growers who were victims of price-cutting by wholesale buyers. He was a man who did not like to take 'No' for an answer. 'Bobby is known from coast to coast as a great organiser,' said the *Toronto Daily Star* in 1929, the year when Robinson set out his plans for Hamilton to host the Empire Games.

The idea had first taken hold two years earlier. Robinson and Howard Crocker, an important figure in Canada's early Olympic history, were discussing ways of giving the nation's best athletes stronger competition. Crocker mentioned the Festival of Empire, hosted by London in 1911 at the time of the coronation of King George V and featuring an international sporting championship. He also told Robinson of an earlier suggestion, from the Englishman J. Astley Cooper in the early 1890s, to stage a 'Pan-Britannic Festival' of culture and sport. Robinson liked what he heard; he began planning immediately, little knowing that Astley Cooper would later appear to claim the credit. The events of the 1928 Olympics made him more determined than ever that the Empire Games should take place.

Robinson was so incensed by the perceived lack of respect shown to his team in Amsterdam, and by the domineering attitudes of others that he threatened to withdraw Canada from the 1932 Olympics in Los Angeles. The Americans were largely to blame, he felt, and he made his views known. Lou Marsh was Canada's best-known sports writer at the time, as well being an Olympic ice hockey referee who, on his death in 1936, gave his name to the trophy awarded annually to Canada's top sports performer. In the *Toronto Star* Marsh reported that meetings to discuss the Empire Games were held in Amsterdam 'as a direct result of the dominance, real or attempted, by Germany and the United States at the Olympic meet … Robinson finally boiled over and, after consultation with other Canadian officials, met representatives of the other British teams'.

Among Robinson's gripes at the Olympics, where Canada made an official complaint, were: the absence of a Canadian flag when Percy Williams received his 100m gold medal; the fact that Americans were allowed to train on the track but Canadians were not; a disputed judges' decision in the women's 100m that went in favour of an American when the Canadians thought their runner had won; and a direct insult by Avery Brundage, then the most influential American in the Olympic movement, to a Canadian team official.

These confrontations fuelled the anti-American fire. The *Toronto Star* wrote of 'serious trouble brewing between the Canadian and US teams and between the Canadian representatives and the IOC'. At one point Robinson vented his anger at Sigfrid Edstrom, the IOC official who would bridge the presidency between Baillet-Latour and Brundage. 'We know the Canadians are getting the run-around here and we don't like it!' he said.

Robinson was worried about the Olympics, in which the participants were too often hostile and antagonistic to one another. The Canadians even had a dispute among themselves, which would fester for months, over the making of that official complaint. He wanted the Empire Games to be more relaxed and friendly, to be 'sport for sport's sake, devoid of petty jealousies and sectional prejudices'. The organisers made clear their aims. 'The event will be designed on an Olympic model, but these Games will be very different. They should be merrier and less stern, and will substitute the stimulus of a novel adventure for the pressure of international rivalry.'

Robinson was loyal both to the Union Flag and the British sense of fair play and sportsmanship. Fair play had been absent at the Olympics, he felt, and he was delighted when the new Games in Hamilton provided a moment of great contrast in the heats for the 100 yards. Alan Elliott was one of those four New Zealanders who spent four months away from home. He had already been eliminated from the 220 yards heats when he lined up for the shorter sprint. He jumped the gun at the start, twice: he was disqualified. Robinson knew how he must have felt. He had watched an inconsolable Myrtle Cook, the Canadian favourite, sit in tears at the trackside for half an hour when the same thing had happened to her before the Olympic women's final in Amsterdam.

But the Hamilton crowd would not have it. They wanted Elliott reinstated regardless of the rules; they made so much noise that officials could not start the race. When Percy Williams had taken the athletes' oath he had pledged on their behalf 'to uphold the glorious traditions of British sportsmanship'. Elliott's rivals were happy to go along with that, so there were no complaints from them when Elliott, to huge cheers from the crowd, was called back to the start. He finished third and failed to qualify for the final but, as the incident showed, the organisers, competitors and spectators alike agreed that 'it's the taking part that counts'.

There was a far more serious, non-sporting falling-out between Canada and the United States at the time of the Games. In June the Americans, suffering in the Great Depression, had announced tariffs on goods imported from Canada and elsewhere. This started a trade war between the two countries: while relations with their neighbours soured badly, Canada's bond with the Empire was strengthened.

The Games were a significant political success. At the time of that Empire Festival in 1911 there had been talk, led from Australia, of an all-in-one British Empire team competing in the Olympics, featuring athletes from Britain and the four main dominions – Australia, New Zealand, Canada, and South Africa. By the middle of the 1920s such a suggestion would have been unthinkable. At the 1926 Imperial Conference, held in London, South Africa asked for a constitutional definition of the British Empire. There was 'fundamental political and economic change' and the Commonwealth had become 'a fragile and problematic coalition of interests', wrote the historian R. F. Holland. Members of the Empire, most notably the dominions, sought to find their own identities.

'Political domination in the world by Great Britain was a rapidly fading memory and it was no longer the premier sporting power either,' wrote the sports historian Katharine Moore. 'The Empire needed the Games in 1930 to reconfirm and redefine its unity. They could be seen as one step towards re-establishing its sagging prestige … as the various Empire countries matured and blossomed in their own right.'

At its height the British Empire ruled nearly a quarter of the world's population and a third of its land mass. Its most populous territories, in Africa and Asia, were not represented in Hamilton. India was invited but chose instead to send a team of three athletes to the Far Eastern Championship Games in Tokyo three months before the Empire Games. They were outclassed by opponents from China, the Philippines and Japan. Although the Indians, according to an IOC observer in Tokyo, felt they were not yet ready for a higher level of international competition they improved quickly enough to send a team to the second Empire Games in London in 1934. African countries competed in the 1930s, when the medallists from South Africa and Rhodesia had names such as Edwin, Hendrik, Cynthia and Dorothy. Black Africans would not feature in the Games until Nigeria competed in 1950, followed by Kenya, Ghana, Zambia and Uganda four years later.

The Games were not all-white in Hamilton. One of Percy Williams's teammates in the 1928 Olympics, Phil Edwards, ran in the one-lap, two-lap and mile races under another flag. He represented Canada in the Olympics and his homeland, Guyana, which did not have an Olympic association, in the Empire Games. Edwards, Canada's first successful black athlete, was known as 'the man of bronze' because he finished third five times in three different Olympiads. His only gold, at 880 yards, was for Guyana in the London Empire Games in 1934. Those Games had been awarded to Johannesburg but were moved to London because of South Africa's racial policies.

Whether Bobby Robinson was aware of the wider political significance of the Empire Games is unclear. There are barely any documentary records of the topics discussed by the organising committee. An IOC report laments, 'It is a pity that the original minutes of the Hamilton Organising Committee have disappeared, probably forever. They are not in the Hamilton archives, nor in the archives of the Canadian Commonwealth Association, nor in those of the British Empire Games headquarters in England.' What happened to them, nobody knows, although newspaper reports make clear that the biggest concern for the organisers was finance.

When he first met the city's leaders in January, 1929, Robinson asked for $25,000 to run the Games and for a further $160,000 to build the stadium and other facilities. He organised a 'test event' in July 1929, when the Hamilton Olympic Club hosted a match against a combined Oxford and Cambridge team. Everything was going well until late October when the American stock market crashed, heralding the start of the Great Depression.

The Australians, having agreed to travel to Canada, decided in January that it was too expensive. Robinson's telegram offering $5000 towards expenses made them change their minds. Expenses were also paid to other nations: New Zealand awarded their entire sum to the rowing team, which was hardly fair on long-distance hero Billy Savidan and his fellow track and field athletes who spent so much time away from their jobs. Eight more teams accepted but, to Robinson's consternation, England did not. The governors of English amateur sport were not only short of money, they were worried that the Empire Games may overshadow the Olympics.

Gaining public support for Britain's Olympic team had been extremely tough after the First World War. The working man and his family felt excluded from Olympic sport by the 'toffs' who ran it; there were more important things to worry about than the frivolity of amateur sport. Fundraising efforts to send a team to the first post-war Games in 1920 fell so far short that there were fears for Britain's participation. The target was lowered from £30,000 to £13,000 to £5500, and even when Britain sent a team there were comments in the top newspapers saying that the Games were 'entirely alien to British thought and character'. The British Olympic Association (BOA) eventually won over the public. A decade later the English did not unanimously agree that it would be a good idea to send a team to a new international event on another continent. So Robinson travelled to England to meet Lord Desborough, chief organiser of the 1908 London Olympics, Lord Derby and the other gentry who ran amateur sport. He argued his case and, in the words of the Canadian author Cleve Dheensaw, 'the ebullient Robinson just kept on pushing and pushing. If they would not accept willingly, he decided he would just wear them down with his sheer persistence and enthusiasm for the project'. It worked: England eventually said 'Yes' a month before the opening ceremony. They raised £8000 through a public appeal.

By that time New Zealand had already arrived, benefiting from Robinson's legendary organisational skills. They were given a civic reception when the *Aorangi*, carrying their own team and the nine men of Australia, docked at Vancouver. On the 2700-mile train journey across Canada they were 'similarly welcomed at every town' according to their team manager.

Hamilton recouped much of its huge outlay from donations and ticket sales, and made a loss of only a few thousand dollars. Afterwards Robinson wrote:

> During the organisation period a few of us had the opinion we would be able to put the British Empire Games over but few ever dreamed the Empire would rally so strongly. We had our moments of anxiety, but we always had a sensational ace in the hole, loyalty to the British Empire, and we felt that we could wave the good old flag and all would gather round. From all corners of the world, competitors have come, eager of course to reflect credit on their respective colonies, but proud of the blood ties that bind them in a great entity.

In the build-up to the Games, the Reverend J. Astley Cooper had appeared to claim much of the credit for their existence. True, Astley Cooper, a well-travelled man of the cloth who lived in Africa and was a friend of Cecil Rhodes, had been the first to suggest the holding of a Pan-Britannic Festival. True, his ideas – set out in letters to *The Times* and *Nineteenth Century* magazine in 1891 and 1892 – pre-dated those raised elsewhere in Europe to revive the ancient Olympics. His aim, however, was to show through a festival of sport and culture that Anglo-Saxons ruled the world. Americans would have been invited; there would have been cricket matches and an 'Imperial Holiday'.

Robinson, three years old when Astley Cooper wrote to *The Times* to set out his plans, would have been intrigued by a report in the *Observer* in 1929, looking ahead to the Games in Hamilton. 'Mr J. Astley Cooper is known in different parts of the Empire as the pioneer of this project,' wrote the correspondent after interviewing Astley Cooper, then in his seventies. Astley Cooper said, 'I am satisfied with indirect results, as far as they have been obtained. Though my scheme did not attain its fulfilment as I planned … I have done some spade work for the idea of the Imperial Games for the British peoples.' He made no mention of Canada or Bobby Robinson.

British newspaper readers were left in no doubt after the Games. Canada had 'cut herself loose from the American orbit and given a lead to the Empire that should inspire British sportsmen all around the globe'. Harold

Abrahams, the British sprinter who won Olympic gold in 1924 before becoming one of the most influential voices in athletics in the first half of the twentieth century, put the record straight. 'But for the unbounded enthusiasm and persistency of Mr Robinson,' he wrote, 'the whole thing would never have started.'

2

Precious

The amazing, uplifting story of the
Queen's favourite strongman

He suffered horrific abuse as a child and racial discrimination as an adult, yet the 4ft 10in weightlifter Precious McKenzie is a giant character who can stand tall as one of the Queen's favourite sportsmen.

The first of Precious McKenzie's many memories of the royal family is a sad story of heartbroken children and an unwanted, hands-on appointment with a big pile of cow dung. His later encounters with the Queen, Princess Anne and the Queen Mother are among the proudest and happiest moments of this great royalist's utterly amazing life. Precious suffered horribly as an infant, was brutally abused as a child, discriminated against as an adult and never grew taller than 4ft 10in. Yet he became a sporting giant whose belated, record-breaking success came with royal approval. He is not only one of the most remarkable characters in Commonwealth Games history – arguably Precious is *the* defining character – he is one of the Queen's favourite sportsmen, an entertaining strongman whose life story would make a Hollywood film.

The script would feature a gruesome death by crocodile; a dramatic hospital scene in which Precious, then a South African infant, clings on to life; a mother with a drink problem; wicked foster parents who tie up and beat young Precious and his sister; a shocking visit to a witch doctor in which both children are cut and scarred for life; an unimaginably horrific near-death experience in a cesspit; a brilliant young acrobat who is turned away by the circus because of his colour; escape from apartheid to a new life in Britain, helped by a senior government minister; gold medals and glory in Commonwealth weightlifting; a famous encounter with Muhammad Ali; many memorable meetings with the royals; and a final record-breaking achievement at the Commonwealth Games for his second adopted country, New Zealand, where Precious and his family live happily ever after.

His survival through serious illness as an infant prompted his mother, Christina, to name her youngest son Precious. She chose well. Whatever his age, whatever the exalted company he may be keeping, he has forever since been known simply as 'Precious'. Just like Serena in tennis, Tiger in golf and Pele in football, Precious is a one-word wonder. McKenzie just will not do.

Of all his many stories, so enthusiastically told, perhaps the best is his recollection of his fourth and final Commonwealth Games appearance in Canada in 1978. He was born and raised in South Africa, became a British citizen and eventually settled in New Zealand, the nation he represented in Edmonton at the age of 42. His record-breaking victory was watched by the Queen, who called the local police into action the following day to find Precious and deliver him to her garden party. He had a photo taken with the Queen and later sent it to Buckingham Palace, asking if she would be so kind as to autograph it: she did.

The foreword to his 1975 biography, *The Precious McKenzie Story* by Marion Connock, is a good place to find a lasting verdict on this remarkable man. Denis Howell, the former government minister who remained a friend to Precious until his death in 1998, wrote: 'The story of Precious McKenzie is one of the most incredible in the history of sport … No world-class sportsman could have emerged from greater personal adversity than he faced in his childhood. I have never heard anyone talk about Precious McKenzie except in the most appreciative and affectionate terms.'

Precious McKenzie came into the world in June 1936. Christina McKenzie did not record the birth, in a Durban hospital ward for 'coloured' mothers, as the white rulers of South Africa had decided it was not compulsory to register non-white children. The boy never knew his father, Joseph, who was away hunting crocodiles on the Limpopo River when his son was born. He never knew Joseph's surname either and he became a McKenzie, named after a Scottish immigrant, Christina's grandfather, who had managed an off-licence in Pietermaritzburg.

Double pneumonia almost claimed his infant life. Christina took him in her arms and ran to the nearest hospital, just in time for doctors to save him. The pneumonia would not abate, so a plaster cast was put on his chest. It was left on for too long, burning a hole in his skin that became so bad over the next five months that Christina could see his internal organs. She thought Precious would die. Joseph returned from his hunting to visit the boy: Precious survived, and weeks later it was Joseph who died a horrible death. Hunters shooting from an open boat on the Limpopo wounded a crocodile, which knocked them into the water when it thrashed its tail. The crocodile bit off Joseph's leg at the thigh. He bled to death on the riverbank.

Christina, a heavy drinker, was devastated and penniless, unable to cope with raising her family. After Precious was discharged from hospital as 'incurable', all further treatment throughout his early years failed. His nightly wailing caught the attention of a German neighbour in Pietermaritzburg who suggested placing herbal leaves on his wound, to be left until they withered. It worked. The wound healed, Precious was out of bed at last and, and at the age of three and a half, he had to learn to walk again. He went with his younger sister, Gloria, to live with an aunt in the countryside for a year, their only extended happy time together in their early childhood, before moving back in with their mother when the aunt changed jobs. Christina spent much of her time drinking in a local shebeen where she met a Dutchman, a Nazi sympathiser, who was more than 20 years older than her. For a while the McKenzies lived with him, only to be kicked out because Christina did not support the Germans in the war. Precious and Gloria were by now inseparable. Left to their own devices as they moved to a succession of rooms with Christina, they would perform on the streets for food and coins, singing or practising acrobatics.

Christina had two older boys, Laurence and Leslie, who were brought up by their grandfather until they were signed over to the welfare system. Precious idolised Leslie, who was four years his senior, although they rarely met after Precious and Gloria were also sent out to a succession of foster parents. They attended school only occasionally: they remained illiterate until their teenage years.

Precious and Gloria were first fostered by a kindly African couple for a few months. They thought highly of their next foster mother, Alice, too, for a short while, little knowing that she was known locally as 'the hated one'. When they had learned how to carry water drums and firewood on their heads, balanced on rope plaits, these tiny children were forced to take four-gallon drums and ever-increasing loads. If they fell then Alice would beat them with sticks so severely that, on one occasion, Precious had to go to hospital. He was too frightened to tell anyone what had happened, and would soon be even more terrified. Alice, having decided that the children were possessed by devils, took them to a witch doctor who made inch-long cuts on their shoulders, elbows, wrists, groins, knees, ankles, toes and necks and on top of their heads, rubbing in a foul black mixture when they bled. The week after this visit, Alice threw a knife at Precious that stuck in his calf, leaving a bad scar. In *The Precious McKenzie Story* he recounted how he and Gloria were tied up, beaten severely, and then left out in the garden overnight. Precious, who had never been so scared, eventually escaped with Gloria when neighbours called the police. Back in the care of welfare officers, they were taken to a doctor who struggled to cut their clothes away from suppurating wounds. He said the children would be scarred for life, and that their growth had been stunted by heavy lifting. Precious and Gloria, who are still scarred, both stand 4ft 10in, whereas Laurence and Leslie grew a foot taller.

At another foster home, where they stayed for 10 months, they found themselves next to a riding school. They would sit on a fence to look into another world where the privileged visitors, children of all ages and sizes but only one colour, would ride around on horses and ponies. Precious remembered them as 'those lucky, lucky children whom God had made white'.

The unlucky ones, whom 'God had made coloured', were moved on again, this time to live with the Mkizes, the religious couple who introduced them to baptisms and exorcisms, and denied them their chance to see the royal visit. 'We were treated like slaves,' Precious recalled. Life became unbearable, yet again, for young Precious and Gloria. After a severe beating for losing a two-shilling coin, they ran away to stay with an aunt, before being reunited with their mother, who had moved in with an elderly white man. Because Christina was still drinking heavily the authorities took decisive action, sending the children far away from her to a remote mission. Christina's attempt to fight the decision was doomed when she arrived drunk at the welfare office. A mix-up over their destination meant they first travelled more than 1000 miles to a Voortrekker settlement near the border with Namibia. They were taken in for a few months by a Protestant church home where they learned Afrikaans, before being driven on a sheep lorry for nearly 200 miles to Vanrhynsdorp Catholic Mission. They arrived in January 1949, here to remain 'until old enough to look after themselves', which became five years for Precious and seven for Gloria. Although there were no beds and little food, here there was stability: respected teachers, strict but not brutal discipline and, perhaps most important of all for Precious, horizontal bars and climbing ropes on which he could improve his gymnastic skill and strength, tutored by one of the priests. Precious learned to read and write. He was the proudest boy at Vanrhynsdorp when his mother wrote to tell him that Leslie had been 'discovered' by a boxing promoter and was a welterweight champion. Precious, determined to excel himself physically, dreamed of being a circus acrobat.

In his teenage years Precious, hard-working and strong, was given many demanding tasks, one of which took him close to a death that would, he believes, have been even worse than his father's. He teamed up with other boys to pull a cart nearly two miles to the cesspits, where they would shovel out dried sewage for use as fertiliser at the mission. 'I used to hunt birds, with a sling, and one time I was taking aim by the cesspits,' he said. 'I stepped backwards and fell in. The pit was six feet deep and four feet wide, and I sank to my stomach in fresh human faeces. I was being sucked down, and when it was up to my chest I thought I was going to die. What a death that would have been! Can you possibly imagine anything worse? I was saved by a strong tuft of grass at the edge of the pit. I grabbed hold of that and shouted for the other boys, and they pulled me out.' After washing in the nearby river he still 'smelled diabolical' and the nuns, who scrubbed him clean with a strong disinfectant, could not bear to go near him. 'The worst thing was cleaning my fingernails properly. That took ages.'

Precious grew ever stronger when he started an after-school job at a local farm. Here he would sit and wonder, as he had all those years ago at the riding school, about the differences between blacks and whites. At 15 he could not understand why even terrible drunkards had to be called 'Baas' if they were white, while hard-working, reliable, trustworthy blacks were looked down upon.

At the age of 17 Precious asked the Catholic fathers for permission to leave. Early in 1954 he was away and free, able to return to Pietermaritzburg. He watched Leslie lose narrowly in a big fight in the boxing ring, moved in with his mother and found a job in a shoe factory. Although his mother took most of his wages to spend on drink he decided to pay half a crown a week to become a member of Steve's Gym in Church Street, Pietermaritzburg. It was a decision that would change Precious McKenzie's life in ways he could never have imagined.

Precious started with boxing, which was not for him. Desperate to realise his ambition of becoming a circus acrobat and performer, he made training the most important part of his life, improving his lifting, balancing on bars, walking on his toes and somersaulting. Ready to join the circus, he went to ask for an audition in Durban, where the German manager threw down his cheroot and told him to get lost. His skin was the wrong colour: Precious was an outcast.

Back at the gym he heard a trainer talking to two brothers about weightlifting. He decided to try that, as well as his circus acts and, having watched others for tips on technique, he lifted far more than his own bodyweight at his first attempt. He trained hard on his own until one day he showed trainer Kevin Stent what he was capable of: he lifted 200lbs. 'Extraordinary,' Stent told him. 'You have the makings of a world champion.' That made up Precious's mind – forget the circus, he was now a weightlifter.

Life was good. Gloria returned from Vanrhynsdorp in late 1956; Precious treated himself to a piano and a motorbike after a big pay-rise the following summer; and when he won a bodybuilding contest he started to feature in local newspapers, who named him 'iron man'. He won the Natal bantamweight title in weightlifting and, although eligible to enter the national championship, he decided to train hard for another year to give himself a better chance of victory. To counter all the good news, there was a hint of trouble ahead when those two brothers in his gym, the Webbers, had to leave because they were training on the same premises as coloured athletes.

In 1958, a Commonwealth Games year, Precious retained his Natal title, and then won the national championship in East London with a total of 590lbs from the three styles of lift – snatch, clean and jerk, and press. He was billed to give a demonstration of his prowess at the 'European' championships before a big crowd in Pietermaritzburg, only to be told, by telegram, that he could not lift on the same platform as whites. He felt humiliated; worse was to follow. He was lifting more than Reg Gaffley, the best white lifter in the minimum-weight category, and should have been in the team for the Cardiff Commonwealth Games, said the newspapers. He was not selected: Gaffley was, and won gold.

In the 1959 nationals Precious finished first, with Gaffley 10lbs behind. Even the white press said he was 'a sure prospect' for the Rome Olympics in 1960. Reg Honey, president of the national Olympic committee, said 'any non-European sportsman in South Africa worthy of competing at the Games will receive the opportunity to do so'.

Cape Town was the first stop for Precious on his planned route to Rome. He moved to train under Ron Eland, a coloured South African who had lifted for Britain in the 1948 Olympics before returning to teach PE. When Eland teamed up with Precious it made front-page news in Cape Town. Despite Reg Honey's promise, Precious was not invited to the official Olympic trials, at which Reg Gaffley failed to make a total (that is to say he failed to make at least one legal lift in each category). In the separate trials for non-whites, Precious was in record-breaking form. Gaffley went to Rome; a disbelieving Precious stayed at home.

It was not all heartbreak in that Olympic year. Precious met and fell in love with Elizabeth, a lodger at Eland's home. When they were married in December, Precious pledged that their children, when they arrived, would not suffer the instability that had blighted his own childhood. He won his third straight national title in 1961, shortly before the birth of his first child, Sandra – but there was no way through the apartheid barrier. In 1963, the year when Elizabeth gave birth to another daughter, Vanessa, Precious decided the only option was to do what Eland had done: move to Britain. Unlike his coach, he had no intention of returning. How could he, after what had happened when he was selected for the 1963 World Championships in Stockholm? Precious was told that he was a second-class citizen who could not fly out with his white teammates, one of whom was his good friend Chris de Broglio, a great campaigner against sporting apartheid. He would have to wear a different blazer badge to everybody else. He must resign from the Western Province Weightlifting Federation and affiliate to a different body for non-white weightlifters. He had been humiliated enough times before and refused to compete under those terms. It was a huge story that would have serious repercussions for South African sport.

John Harris, chairman of the anti-apartheid sports body SANROC (South African Non Racial Olympic Committee) wrote to commend Precious. 'Your magnificent gesture in the interests of the highest principles in sport … will place the name Precious McKenzie in a very special and unchallenged position in South African sport for all time … What you have done will become a famous part of our country's sporting history.'

Ahead of the trials for the 1964 Tokyo Olympics, the *Cape Town Post* reported, 'The eyes of the sporting world are focused on a mighty Cape Town midget called Precious McKenzie.' If he was selected for Tokyo and travelled as a representative of a non-racial team his country may remain within the Olympic movement. If he refused, South Africa, already departed from the Commonwealth, would surely be kicked out because of their apartheid policies in sport.

In that excellent 1975 biography, author Connock wrote, 'Precious knew in his heart that the white body [who governed weightlifting] would remain obdurate. They were not going to give in and neither was he.' He would never represent South Africa, at the Olympics or the World Championships, on their terms. South Africa would not compete in the Olympics for more than 30 years.

A director of the shoe company where Precious worked arranged his transfer to England. The South Africans questioned him for hours about his politics before finally giving him a passport, just in time for him to leave his tearful family, who would join him later, at the dockside, as he boarded his boat for Southampton. If the white South African passengers ignored him on the journey 'as expected', on arrival in England in 1964 Precious was astonished. As he took his seat on the train to London, a white couple said, 'Good morning.' Precious immediately felt welcome.

He was soon joined by his wife and daughters – there would later be a son, too, born in England. After a difficult search for rented accommodation they settled in Northampton. Precious and Elizabeth worked in the same shoe factory, although they had very little spare money because of childcare costs and gym fees. For nearly two years Precious fretted over his status, thwarted in his attempt to gain a British passport. He even considered moving to Canada.

Precious believed that the delays in processing his paperwork were caused by Oscar State, Britain's Olympic weightlifting coach in 1948, who was now a respected secretary of the International Weightlifting Federation. 'State was a close friend of a South African official who wanted to stop my progress,' said Precious, who never warmed to State. He got along far better with Wally Holland, secretary of the British Amateur Weightlifting Association and a legendary figure within the sport in the UK.

Eventually a solicitor suggested Precious ask the British Amateur Weightlifting Association (BAWLA) to approach the sports minister, Denis Howell, on his behalf. Almost immediately, Howell went to work: in the first week of January 1966, Precious had his passport. It helped him to take a better job, raise his income and take out a mortgage on a family home (with the help of a loan from Chris de Broglio, who had fled South Africa to become a hotelier in London, as well as a leading figure in SANROC). He trained hard, broke the British bantamweight record twice, and after a nervy victory in the trials he was soon being measured for his first international team uniform: he had been selected by England for the Commonwealth Games in Jamaica.

While others enjoyed the relaxed, friendly atmosphere at the athletes' village at the University of the West Indies, Precious was tense and edgy until his competition was done with. He was unable to go to the opening ceremony because his was the first medal event of the Games on Saturday 6 August. Wally Holland was on hand to try to calm Precious, who had never felt so nervous in his life. He had not slept, so fearful was he of letting down those who had helped him to this point. He regarded rivals from Singapore and Guyana – gold and bronze medallists at the previous Games – as the favourites. The Singaporean Chua Phung Kim did not register a total after failing with all his lifts in the press, while Martin Dias, whose victory in the 1963 Pan American Championship led to his appearance on a Guyanese postage stamp, was well beaten. Precious won easily, on 705lbs, with Dias in second place, 27lbs behind. Holland hugged him, others lifted him off his feet, the flag was raised and 'Land of Hope and Glory' sung. Precious was in tears when he realised that this was all for him. He told Connock:

It hit me all of a sudden. I was standing in front of all those people as a representative of the country, like an ambassador, and I was so proud! It was a great, great honour. But then I thought how come? A little while ago you were in Africa. You were born in Africa. How come you aren't winning the medal for your own country? And I was sad. But I told myself 'you are British now' and I was proud to belong to a country where my colour didn't count, only my ability.

He was not the only English gold medallist. Louis Martin, perhaps Britain's best-ever weightlifter, was one of the biggest stars of the Kingston Games. He was a local hero, having emigrated from Jamaica in the 1950s – so popular that the competition schedule was changed, enabling Martin to finish off proceedings by winning gold. Martin switched from bodybuilding to weightlifting with astonishing success when he settled in Derby, becoming Britain's first world champion by defeating the Russian favourite in the middle-heavyweight division in Warsaw in 1959. So determined were the Soviets to avoid a repeat performance that that they put two lifters in against Martin in the same weight category at the Rome Olympics the following year. 'How's that for credibility?' said Martin, who finished a highly respectable third, improving to take Olympic silver in Tokyo in 1964. He also won three more world titles, in 1962, 1963 and 1965, earning an MBE in the process, set two world records and won Commonwealth gold for England in three successive Games from 1962 to 1970. He stood as a Conservative candidate in the local elections in Derby in 1971. Although he lost that vote he was later elected president of the British Weightlifting Association. In Kingston he carried the flag for England at the opening ceremony.

Precious had something of a reality check in his next overseas appearance at the world championships in East Berlin two months after the Commonwealth Games. Neither he nor Louis Martin performed well as lifters from Iran and the Soviet Bloc dominated, just as they would at the Olympic Games throughout Precious's career. He finished a creditable ninth in both the 1968 and 1972 Olympics as a bantamweight, and thirteenth in 1976 as a flyweight. After Louis Martin's successes, 'Commonwealth lifters never stood a chance at world and Olympic level,' said Precious, who envied the lifestyle of those state-supported lifters who could train all day. They were not bound by the rules of amateurism that restricted athletes elsewhere, and showed no respect for other rules: many of them were boosted by performance-enhancing drugs. So badly was the sport's credibility damaged by doping in the 1970s and 1980s, when world records were repeatedly broken by state-supported athletes, that in 1993 the International Weightlifting Federation introduced new weight categories, scrapped all existing world records and started again in the hope that theirs would now be a 'clean' sport.

Back in Britain Precious moved to a better job in another shoe factory in Bristol, where he befriended another great Commonwealth Games hero and multiple champion, the bowls player David Bryant. He became ever more popular as time went by, appearing on television and in newspapers. After the 1968 Olympics the postman delivered a card to his home that Precious still cherishes. It read: 'The Master of the Household has received Her Majesty's command to invite Mr Precious McKenzie to a luncheon to be given at Buckingham Palace by The Queen and the Duke of Edinburgh on Thursday, 5th December, 1968, at 1pm.' He could not contain his excitement. The invitation made headlines back in Cape Town. Two years later Elizabeth felt equally proud when she was invited to join Precious at a reception at the Palace of Holyroodhouse at the Commonwealth Games in Edinburgh. As in Kingston, Precious had prepared well for the 1970 Games, taking unpaid leave from work as well as a well-timed two-week holiday. Once more he won England's first gold of the Games, finishing well clear of Anthony Phillips from Barbados, who had been fourth in Kingston four years earlier.

After the Munich Olympics in 1972 Precious went to the United States to win a powerlifting world title. He qualified as a fitness instructor but could not find work away from the shoe factory. He set himself the target of winning Commonwealth gold for a third time in 1974, in Christchurch. After that, he told Elizabeth, he would quit sport and make the family his first and only priority. His amazing success, fame and popularity in New Zealand made him change his mind and, soon after, his nationality.

The Christchurch Games were held early in the year, in the New Zealand summer. The make-up of England's team was changing, leading to a comment in the news pages of *The Times* on the number of black and mixed-race team members, most notably in athletics and boxing. When Precious won his third straight gold medal he was showered with congratulatory messages and telegrams from, among others, the sports minister and the inmates of Leicester Prison.

Christchurch was famously friendly, the Games a huge success. Precious had won the hearts of the host city and the rest of New Zealand with his 'naive appeal', according to Connock, who wrote, 'He was written about, interviewed on television and feted to an extent that had him surprised, delighted and convinced that the New Zealanders were the friendliest, most hospitable people in the world.' He threw flowers to the crowd at the end-of-Games parade and did not get back to his bed until 4am. Instead of sleeping he started thinking about his life. He would be 42 by the time of the 1978 Games but, having been told by Wally Holland that he could win again, he reconsidered his decision to stop. Nobody in any sport had ever won medals in four successive Games. If he could only find a more rewarding job, one in which he could use his skills as an athlete and gymnast, he could improve further. He was convinced that he had still not reached his peak: this was no time to give up.

Precious would need money to fund his dream of setting that four-gold Commonwealth record. An amateur could not earn directly or indirectly from his sport. All fees from television appearances, as well as the money he was paid for his authorised biography, had to be passed on to BAWLA, British weightlifting's administrative body. The *Evening Post* in Bristol raised money for amateur sport through an appeal, in partnership with Bristol City Football Club, and they arranged through BAWLA for Precious to be compensated for loss of earnings while he competed at international level. This allowed Precious to accept an invitation to return to New Zealand in June for an international series sponsored by John Player & Sons, the cigarette manufacturer (now part of the Imperial Tobacco Group). The series coincided with the announcement on 15 June that Precious had been awarded an MBE, which meant that on his next visit to Buckingham Palace he could take Elizabeth with him. Precious was so popular during the John Player series in Nelson and Christchurch that organiser Frank Baldwin called him 'the news media's dream'. He won two gold medals at featherweight and, as a 'thank you' gesture from the sponsors, a flight home via South Africa. For the first time in more than 10 years he could visit Gloria and the other relatives he had left behind.

At first he sensed a change. When he landed at Johannesburg at dawn, a loudspeaker announcement for Mr Precious McKenzie to make himself known at the information desk was greeted by loud cheers. He was welcomed by friends and family, feted by the non-white weightlifting community who arranged a reception and dinner for him and 100 guests, and was given free tickets for air travel within South Africa. Some things had not changed at all though: Ernest Clark, the man who had helped Precious with his transfer to England, wanted to attend the dinner with the Australian consul and his wife. All three were refused permits to attend a 'coloured function'. When Precious wanted to see the graves of his mother and stepfather, who had died within two years of each other after Precious's emigration, he had to visit separate cemeteries for blacks and whites.

An emotional Gloria was delighted to see Precious. While it was good to see his relatives there was no freedom here and Precious never had any thought of returning to live in South Africa, although he returned for Gloria's seventieth birthday a few years ago. He liked the idea of moving, but the destination for Precious, Elizabeth and their three children would be New Zealand. Why? 'It's the people, the New Zealand public. They are so welcoming.'

There were more highlights to come in 1974, a momentous year for Precious – 'the year when everything happened to me'. There was his third gold medal, his decision to go for a fourth, his MBE and the date at Buckingham Palace, his reuniting with Gloria in South Africa, where he spent many hours looking at official records of his childhood placements, his decision to emigrate to New Zealand and, in December, a famous gala dinner when he lifted Muhammad Ali above his head. At the time Ali was arguably the most famous man in the world, having regained his heavyweight world title from George Foreman a few weeks earlier in 'The Rumble in the Jungle' in Zaire, one of the most celebrated title fights in history. 'I was invited to a charity dinner as a special guest – me, Henry Cooper and Muhammad Ali. Can you believe that? It was fantastic for me and for weightlifting, which was just a minority sport.' When the three met before the dinner, a fundraiser for disabled children, Precious hoisted Ali, who weighed nearly twice as much as him, for the photographers.

Precious was offered work in the shoe business in New Zealand. If he moved fairly soon he would be able to claim New Zealand citizenship in time for the Commonwealth Games in 1978. With a good deal of help from Roy Williams, a New Zealand sports journalist and former athlete who had won the decathlon gold medal in the 1966 Games, he was able to make the arrangements quickly. There was a surprise along the way. During an interview in London at the New Zealand High Commission he was told, 'We don't accept black people for emigration. But you are a special case.' 'That shocked me,' he said. 'Thankfully, that policy was soon abolished.'

Before emigrating he made a 'farewell' appearance on the children's TV show *Blue Peter*, attempting a world record squat lift in front of the live cameras. He had three attempts and three failures. Determined not to leave in defeat, he asked the director for one more try: this time he made the lift. A few days later there was a surprise in the post – an invitation to Precious and Elizabeth to Buckingham Palace, where the Queen sent them on their way with her best wishes. Precious learned that Prince Andrew and Prince Edward, then 15 and 11, had watched the world record attempt on *Blue Peter*. 'When they told the Queen that we were leaving, she sent us the invitation. We had been before as a couple, for my investiture as an MBE in 1974, and on both occasions we had never felt so proud,' he said. 'The Queen told me that if I ever decided to move back again, I'd be very welcome back in England.' He has visited many times, working as a back injury prevention consultant, but has never for a minute regretted moving to New Zealand, where he and Elizabeth happily raised their three children. They have seven grandchildren.

To put the importance of that special day at the Palace in 1975 into context, it is necessary to go back to 1947, when Precious was 11 years old and being cared for, with Gloria, by foster parents in Pietermaritzburg. King George VI's visit, with his wife and the Princesses Elizabeth and Margaret, was the first by a reigning monarch to South Africa, a 'thank you' gesture for the nation's efforts in the Second World War. Precious and Gloria should have been there with all the other flag-wavers: instead they endured what came to be known as 'The day we didn't see the Queen'.

Pietermaritzburg was intent on looking the part. New roads were built, the best hotel in town refurbished and a new park opened. Schoolchildren had learned the words to 'God Save the King' and 'Rule, Britannia!'. After the royal party's overnight stay, locals made a carnival atmosphere for the parade. The Mkizes, the strict couple fostering Precious and Gloria, had arranged to host a church group in the evening of the great day. They wanted their home spotless, and would not allow Precious and Gloria out of the house. They were ordered to stay at home to freshen the floor with cow dung, a traditional skill they had been taught two years earlier. Never in their short lives had they been so distraught. Nearly three decades later Precious was able to relay this story to the Queen Mother.

'She thought it was tragic,' he said, a lifetime later. 'But what an honour and a privilege it was to be able to tell her. I never dreamed that one day I would be in England, that I would meet the Queen, that I would be able to tell my story to the Queen Mother at Buckingham Palace.' His next meeting with the Queen would be in Canada at the Edmonton Commonwealth Games in 1978. Accompanied by the Duke of Edinburgh, the Queen timed her arrival at the weightlifting to perfection. After watching for 20 minutes as Precious attempted to win a record-breaking fourth successive title, the Duke stood up to leave. The Queen would have none of it and said she would stay to the end. The royals were there for more than an hour.

Precious takes up the story: 'I had to delay my second attempt until the Queen and the Duke were settled. When I came out I missed the lift. I had cramp. For the third attempt I was pleased to see that she was still there, and I told myself "This is it, this is for the Queen. It's do or die." I locked it beautifully. The cramp just wasn't there – I had done it. I stood with four fingers raised, for the four in a row. Nobody had done that before. It was the highlight of my life – the only thing comparable was the visits to Buckingham Palace.

'The next day the Queen held a garden party in Edmonton for invited guests. She looked at the list and saw I wasn't there and wanted to know why. After all, I had made Commonwealth Games history. She said I should be there, and the Canadians called in the police to help, because nobody knew where I was. While this was going on I was just watching the weightlifting. I went out for a break at the interval and a policeman spotted me, walked over and said, "You're under arrest!" – I was genuinely worried. I thought they suspected me of shoplifting or something, I had no idea. The policeman could see I was in a bit of a state and said "No, we're only joking, the Queen commands that you attend her garden party."

'I was in the back of a police car, siren wailing, we even drove the wrong way round a roundabout to gain a few seconds. We got there just in time. I was taken straight to the Queen and she said "Where have *you* been?" I said I hadn't been invited, and she said, "Well, you are now." I asked her if I could have a photo taken with her and she said of course. I asked a professional photographer to take it with my own camera. I was worried it might not be a great shot because he hurried it, but it was perfect. Later on I sent the photo to Buckingham Palace and asked if the Queen would autograph it for me, and she did. It is one of my proudest possessions.'

The first time Precious met a member of the royal family was in 1966, when he asked Princess Anne for a dance. He was at his first Commonwealth Games in Kingston, Jamaica, which were attended by the Duke of Edinburgh, Prince Charles and Princess Anne, who was then 15. 'At the end-of-Games party they were playing calypso music, which I liked. I walked between all the legs – everyone was taller than me. There was Princess Anne at the centre of the floor, about the same height as me back then. Being forward, I cut in on a good-looking young athlete and asked her for a dance. She smiled and said yes, and we started doing the twist. All the other athletes gathered round, cheering and clapping, and it became such a crowd that the security guys had to come and break us up. I told her I was a big fan of hers, and she was happy to talk to me.'

If Precious remembered that occasion with some fondness, so too did the Princess. More than 20 years later Precious was invited to a VIP sports sponsorship dinner in Auckland, at which Princess Anne was the guest of honour. He sat with Elizabeth on a table of 'bigshots who didn't want to talk to us, a bunch of chief executives who thought we were nincompoops'. At the end of proceedings, Princess Anne, having spotted a familiar face, broke away from her entourage and came to speak to Precious, whom she had encountered variously at a reception in 1968, at the 1972 Olympics, and at the 1974 Commonwealth Games in Christchurch. 'She came over to ask me how I liked living in New Zealand. I introduced her to Elizabeth, and told her, "It's the best thing I've ever done. You should move here yourself, you'd love it." She said, "I remember when I was level with you," from back in Kingston in 1966, and said she could never forget our dance.' The bigshots were dumbfounded.

In 1990, when the Commonwealth Games returned to his home city of Auckland, Precious worked as a volunteer, helping with arrangements for the athletes' entertainment and sightseeing. The volunteers were arrayed in a semicircle to be presented to the Queen. 'She shook my hand and wouldn't let go, talked about my move, and spoke for a long time. I told her, as I had told Princess Anne, that moving to New Zealand was the best thing I had ever done. All the other volunteers couldn't believe it.'

In July, 2006, Precious was on business in Christchurch, where he happened to be staying at the same hotel as the New Zealand All Blacks, who were due to play Australia. 'I wandered down to the bar and met the team's manager, who was pleased to see me because he said he had a message for me.' The previous November, the All Blacks had been invited to a Buckingham Palace reception in the week of their Test match against England at Twickenham. 'You'll never believe this,' the manager told Precious, 'but when we were there the Queen asked "How is Precious McKenzie?" and asked us to pass on her regards when we saw you.' He could believe it.

While Precious's four-in-a-row effort will forever remain in the record books, another weightlifter came along after his retirement to match it and, in bizarre circumstances, win gold at a fifth Games – 20 years after his first. That man was Dave Morgan who, when he celebrates his birthday on 30 September 2014, can feasibly claim to be the fittest 50-year-old in the world. He beats global strength and fitness records time after time.

Although Morgan was born and raised in Cambridge he lifted for Wales, the land of his father. He started his career as a teenaged lightweight in 1982 and ended as a 37-year old middleweight in 2002. After winning at least one gold medal in four successive Games he travelled to Kuala Lumpur in 1998 expecting to go one better than Precious. 'I got overconfident, didn't train enough, wasn't properly prepared,' he said. He came back with a silver medal and 'after that I didn't want to know, I quit weightlifting'. He returned, however, for a sixth crack at the Commonwealth Games in Manchester. He thought he had a chance in the snatch, nothing more. 'I lifted 145 kilos and thought it might be enough, but Damian Brown lifted 147 and that was that.' Brown was Australia's flag-bearer at the opening ceremony and one of their main medal hopes. 'I lifted 160 in the clean and jerk and thought that would get me a bronze in the combined, and went off for a shower. When I came back I learned that Damian had failed with all three of his lifts in the clean and jerk. An Indian had won [Satheesha Rai], but a silver to finish my career was pretty good. Damian was very upset but we went for a beer later and he said, "Knowing your luck, the

Indian's going to fail a drugs test." Three weeks later I got a text message, and it had happened!' Rai was disqualified. Three months after the Games ended Morgan was in Cardiff for a much-delayed medal ceremony. It was his ninth gold overall, making him the only athlete, male or female, in any sport to have won gold at five Games.

Precious is not the only weightlifter to have suffered discrimination. Doug Hepburn, the Commonwealth's first heavyweight world champion in 1953, may have been a white Canadian but he was treated so badly by national selectors that he considered taking American citizenship.

Hepburn, born with a severe squint and a club foot, was called 'gimp', 'hopalong' and 'crosseyes' by cruel classmates in Vancouver. He took up weightlifting as a teenager, trained relentlessly and became a celebrity in the far west of Canada and the United States. He could bend parking meters to the ground, and he consistently broke weightlifting records. But his efforts were ignored by the body that selected international athletes, the Canadian Amateur Athletic Union (CAAU), more than 2000 miles away in French-speaking Montreal. The aloof easterners did not believe he could be that good, and would not go to see for themselves.

The CAAU refused to send any weightlifters to the 1953 World Weightlifting Championships in Stockholm so Hepburn paid his own way, raising the airfare from a series of public demonstrations of his great strength. He won by 25lbs – the only Commonwealth lifter ever to have held the world heavyweight title. A year later the Empire and Commonwealth Games were being hosted in his home town. The Mayor of Vancouver, fearful that Hepburn may move to the US, paid him to be a bodyguard even though there was no real work, just plenty of time to train full-time. According to the *Guardian* in England, Hepburn was 'a 20-stone lumberjack'. In reality he was, for a while, a full-time athlete. He cemented his status as a national hero when he won gold with ease.

Throughout the 1950s Hepburn was billed as the world's strongest man, the first to bench-press 400lbs, then 500lbs. He custom built gym equipment and was 'the grandfather of modern powerlifting'. He had a short career as a professional wrestler, wrote poetry, bred dogs, was a nightclub singer, and went broke several times. There is more to his story: in 1962, aged 36, he checked into a hospital for addicts, suffering from alcoholism and depression, to undergo a radical course of lysergic acid diethylamide (LSD) treatment. The hospital may have been the setting for *One Flew Over the Cuckoo's Nest*. While some patients were strapped down in bare cells, others ran around the corridors shouting 'I can fly!' Hepburn, a voluntary inmate, was given a room and meals, a shed to use as a gym and a course of LSD treatment to counter his addiction in exchange for working as an orderly to calm the rowdier patients. Some of them were desperate beyond words. One patient strangled himself with a lamp cord; another made a spear from a mattress spring and plunged it through his own heart. A woman choked herself to death by swallowing her underwear. An alcoholic stockbroker befriended Hepburn and asked to read newspaper cuttings of his weightlifting achievements. He killed himself by crumpling up the newspaper reports and forcing them down his throat.

It took a monumental effort for Hepburn to walk out into the real world after his treatment nine months later, cheered by the other patients. Hepburn would never drink again. 'At last I was free to pursue my life as I chose,' he said. And free many years later to sit and tell his good friend Tom Thurston the story of his amazing life, recounted in an excellent book, *Strongman: The Doug Hepburn Story*, published in 2004, four years after Hepburn's death.

Remarkably, Precious McKenzie has a rival for the best name in Commonwealth weightlifting. The Nigerian bronze medallist in 1982, Ironbar Bassey, is surely a contender for that award. The makers of the *Mad Max* films, starring Mel Gibson, must have thought so: one of the henchmen in the third film of the trilogy (*Mad Max beyond Thunderdome*) released in 1985 was named after him.

There was talk, in 2008, of a film being made of Precious McKenzie's life. The idea has been around for a while, and a script has been written, but nothing has come of it so far. What a pity for, as Denis Howell said 40 years ago, 'The story of Precious McKenzie is one of the most incredible in the history of sport.' It could be a bigger blockbuster than *Mad Max*.

3

Jump!

Dorothy and Debbie raise the bar
as teenagers and mothers

One was a pre-war British champion who said 'be in bed by eight until you're married', the other was a free spirited child of the 60s from Canada. But record-breaking high-jump mums Dorothy Tyler and Debbie Brill, despite competing decades apart, had a great deal in common.

Dorothy Tyler and Debbie Brill both did something quite remarkable – they both won a gold medal in their teenage years at the Commonwealth Games, and returned as mothers 12 years later to win again. If their sport had been one of those that did not require the very highest level of physical fitness, such as shooting or bowls, this would have been impressive enough. But they were high jumpers, among the best of their time. Tyler and Brill were both world record holders.

They were clearly good enough to follow their first triumph with a repeat four years later. The reasons why they did not could hardly be more different. When Tyler was on her way to Sydney in 1938 for her Empire Games debut, Adolf Hitler took command of the German Army. There was no fun and Games in 1942: she was driving lorries at an RAF base. Debbie Brill, the 1970 champion, was living a hippie lifestyle in the woods in 1974, grieving her dead brother and, after a depressing first taste of the Olympic Games, totally disillusioned with sport. She did not watch a single minute of the Christchurch Commonwealth Games on television. 'I wasn't even sure if I would ever compete again,' she said.

Dorothy Tyler loved the Olympics; Debbie Brill hated them. Tyler was a staunch nationalist; Brill was anything but. Tyler once advised aspiring young athletes: 'Go to bed at eight o'clock until you are married'; Tyler took recreational drugs and loved a party. Both have vivid memories of royal occasions. In 2001, at the age of 81, Dorothy Tyler was invited to

Buckingham Palace to receive an MBE for services to athletics. Prince Charles casually remarked, 'You have been a long time coming.' She replied, 'Well, Your Highness, you have been a long time asking!' At the Queen's reception at Holyroodhouse in Edinburgh in 1970 Debbie Brill was so drunk she could not stand up. Looking back on a wonderful stay in Scotland, she said, 'It was incredibly easy to drink too much, and I did. I didn't make a spectacle of myself, though.'

Britain built up the biggest empire in history during the late nineteenth century and the early twentieth. During Dorothy Tyler's athletic career she saw that Empire disintegrate, and the Cold War follow the World War. Her gold medals in 1938 and 1950 were both in the British Empire Games, her silver in 1954 in the newly named British Empire and Commonwealth Games. During her many years in sport women began to gain acceptance – Tyler was the first female to hold the qualifications necessary for coaching men – but change was slow. Athletics was strictly amateur from the start to the finish of her involvement.

Debbie Brill won golds in the Games under the two most recent titles: British Commonwealth (1970) and Commonwealth (1982). She said farewell in Edinburgh, the scene of her first victory, finishing fifth when the Games returned to Scotland in 1986. She carried on jumping just to be able to compete one more time at the Commonwealth Games – but in the 16 years since her first appearance, sport had gone through a defining change.

'In 1970 the Commonwealth Games were a well-grounded event, had high standing, and it was a big deal to be there,' she said. 'By 1986 that was not so much the case. It was not as carefree, not as lively, it was a time when track and field was moving from an amateur sport to becoming a lot more about money. When money is involved, people are so much more willing to abide by the rules. There was an innocence in 1970 that was not there in 1986.'

They have never met, the two best female high jumpers who ever competed in the Commonwealth Games, who between them competed in seven finals. But they are both well aware of each other, as Tyler made clear in a famous outburst against modern jumpers in 2008. She denounced all those who followed the over-the-bar-backwards style introduced by Brill and the American, Dick Fosbury, in the 1960s as 'cheats'. Brill's response, was, 'She sounds very funny. Straight-laced, maybe, but she has some interesting qualities. From what I've heard, I admire her.'

There are no two interconnected athletes who better define half a century of Commonwealth Games history, and the great sporting and social changes of the twentieth century, than Dorothy Tyler and Debbie

Brill. They have both led fascinating lives that tell a story of the times they lived through.

Her parents were about to separate but, without their financial support Dorothy Odam, as she would be until her marriage in 1940, would not have been able to compete at the third British Empire Games in Sydney in 1938. She gave up her office job and, with a few pounds to live on from her parents, she set sail with the rest of the team from Tilbury, on the east coast of England, on the SS *Ormonde* in the final weeks of 1937. The athletes were away for about four months, during which time Tyler celebrated her eighteenth birthday. The team spent Christmas Day in the searing heat of Colombo, at a stopover en route.

'It took six weeks to get to Australia and we got five shillings to spend when we got there,' said Cyril Holmes, the Lancastrian sprinter who was England's star performer on the track. 'We had to train on the deck to keep some kind of fitness.' To reduce their loss of earnings two of England's oarsmen, Basil Beazley and Jan Sturrock, worked their passage as ship's engineers. It must have done them good: they won gold.

Sydney was buzzing as never before throughout the early part of the year. An estimated one million people flooded the city, many of them sleeping on the streets because all hotel rooms were taken, for celebrations to mark the 150th anniversary of the British settlement of Australia. There were parades, pageants and exhibitions, countered by a 'Day of Mourning' protest by the aboriginal people, who were outcasts from society and would remain so for many years to come. The grand opening of the Empire Games, at the Sydney Cricket Ground, came on 5 February, 10 days after Australia Day.

Cyril Holmes won the 100-yard and 220-yard sprint double for England with some ease, and was so popular that, at a boisterous closing ceremony at the cycle track, he was carried around on the shoulders of the Australian team. His running achievements were curtailed by the War, and he later focused on rugby union, winning three caps for England. For years he would bulk up to 15 stone for rugby in the winter, and cut down to 11 stone for sprinting in the summer.

If Holmes was the outstanding male performer, he could not match the astonishing performances of 'Dashing Dess', the first superstar of the Empire Games. Decima Norman was ineligible for national selection for most of her life because there was no women's athletics club in Western Australia, where she lived. She finally got her chance, and took it, in the national championships in Melbourne in 1937. At the Empire Games, Australia won six athletics golds, and 'Dashing Dess' had five of them: 100 yards, 220 yards, long jump and two sprint medley relays. She was 'given the sort of ovation normally reserved for Don Bradman,' said the papers, which were at the time full of stories about the exploits of the world's most famous cricketer. When she moved to Sydney in 1939, the year when she ran 11.0 seconds to equal the world record for 100 yards at the age of 29, 'Dashing Dess' was feted and photographed wherever she went, and given a newspaper column and a regular slot on radio.

Dorothy Tyler had time to watch the exploits of Holmes and Norman, as she was not called into action until the final day of competition. Watched by a crowd of 30,000, she won with a clearance of 5ft 3in (1.60m) from teammate Dora Gardner: this was England's only gold in women's athletics. It had been 'the most wonderful trip, and wherever we went we were treated like celebrities,' she said. The *Sydney Morning Herald* said the Games had been 'an international gathering which has never been equalled in Australia' and that the athletes had 'thrilled the crowds all week with their magnificent deeds'.

Tyler knew all about the difficulties that 'Dashing Dess' had faced. Women's athletics in the 1930s was restricted to very few events by the men who ran amateur sport and who believed a lot of nonsense about how women were too frail to run further than half a lap or otherwise exert themselves. 'They didn't like us to do the long jump back then, because they said it would damage our abdominal muscles,' she said.

Sydney was much friendlier and more relaxed than Tyler's previous overseas contest, the 'Hitler Olympics' in Berlin in 1936. Tyler had finished second in the national indoor championships in 1935, as a 15-year-old, and in the same event a year later, at Wembley, she drew favourable comments from the most famous name in the press box, the former Olympic sprint champion Harold Abrahams. She was selected for Berlin, but first came her international debut, aged 16, for England against Scotland, Sweden, France and Holland in Blackpool in June. She jumped 5ft 3in and finished well clear of Fanny Blankers-Koen, the Dutchwoman who would be the star of the 1948 Olympics.

Britain sent 12 female athletes to Berlin, with three chaperones – they were still part of the team in Brill's day – who accompanied Tyler and her teammates to a drinks reception given by Adolf Hitler and Joseph Goebbels. Tyler, who described Hitler as 'a small man in a large uniform' and Goebbels as 'a bit of a womaniser', made her own shorts and vest, and responded to soldiers' 'Heil Hitler!' salutes by shouting 'Heil King George!' During the Games one of the Danish high jumpers took a fancy to this bright 16-year-old English girl and asked her out. The chaperones reported back to team management, and Tyler was told that she could accept the invitation – provided the rest of the team came along, too.

In Berlin's Olympic Stadium Tyler was first to clear 1.60m, and nobody went higher in an enthralling three-hour contest watched by 80,000. She lost, however, in a jump-off against the Hungarian, Ibolya Csák: under today's rules she would have won, having been first to clear the height. She had 'certainly excelled herself and with a little luck might have been our first woman champion in the athletic section,' said the official report of the British Olympic Association. Not the first in Berlin, that is, but the first at any Olympics.

Many years later a future chairman of the BOA, Arthur Gold, became Tyler's coach. 'He was the only one willing to take me on,' said Tyler, who switched, with Gold's help, from scissors to Western roll style. The scissors technique, which had been around for decades, required a diagonal approach to the bar before the jumper threw the inside leg up and over, followed swiftly by the other leg in a scissoring motion. By the time of the Berlin Olympics the Western roll was becoming more popular – using the inside leg for lift-off with the other leg thrusting up to take the body over the bar sideways. The straddle – before Debbie Brill and Dick Fosbury changed everything in the 1960s – became the 'must-have' style in the 1950s. It was similar to the Western roll, except that the athlete turned over in the air, clearing the bar belly first.

Gold had been an international high jumper. Their work together helped Tyler to extend her career at the highest level and to further develop the coaching skills she had picked up during the war. She always regrets not having mastered the straddle: she was put off by the fear of landing hard in a shallow sandpit. 'If I had learned to straddle I could have gone higher,' she said.

By the time Gold took her on, Tyler was 29 years old, had set a world record, still to be ratified many years later; driven lorries at RAF Scampton in Lincolnshire, base for the 'Dambusters' squadron; married and given birth to two sons, David and Barry; won a second Olympic silver, in London in 1948; and was preparing to go 'Down Under' again to compete in the 1950 Empire Games in Auckland, where she won gold a second time. She married Dick Tyler, a fellow local athlete, in 1940 and did not see him for five years, when he fought on five continents and, for a while, went missing in Burma. In the RAF she played sport whenever she could, while she trained to be a PE teacher. As soon as the War was over she resumed her training, and in 1948 she again came agonisingly close to Olympic glory. The rules had changed since 1936, and the victor in London, the American Alice Coachman, won because she did what Tyler had done 12 years earlier: she cleared the winning height before her rivals. Coachman became the first black woman to win Olympic gold, and

Britain's long wait for a female champion went on. It would not end until 1964, when Mary Rand won the long jump in Tokyo. But for the Empire and Commonwealth Games, British women would never have known what it was like, before then, to win a gold medal on another continent.

For the 1950 Empire Games in Auckland, Tyler was named captain of England's women. It was another long journey, with many more weeks away, and it was difficult to stay fit because training time on board ship was restricted. But for the offer of childcare support from her mother she would not have been able to travel. On Tuesday 7 February, Tyler triumphed again and, as in Sydney, she was the only woman to win athletics gold for England. 'The St George's cross was sent fluttering to the masthead,' reported *The Times*, 'as, very late in the day, Mrs D. Tyler (Mitcham A. C.) retained the high jump title which she won in Sydney in 1938. She cleared 5ft 3in to equal her own Games record, which she shares with Miss M. Clark, of South Africa. Three of the last four left in the jump were English girls.' Tyler was also best of the English in the long jump, in which she finished eighth behind Yvette Williams, the New Zealander who was one of the world's great all-round performers before the pentathlon became established. Tyler may have been a useful pentathlete herself, for she also came fourth in the javelin in Auckland, and ran in the hurdles. There was no mention in *The Times* of the fact that Tyler's victory had been achieved a week short of 12 years after her first Empire Games success. Over time, however, the newspaper would come to regard her as 'the remarkable Mrs Tyler', as she stretched her jumping career beyond 20 years.

At the Helsinki Olympics in 1952, Tyler was below her best because of injury, finishing eighth. Another British jumper, Sheila Lerwill, who was then Tyler's great rival, took the silver medal. Lerwill respected Tyler but was not close to her. Team officials put the two of them in the same room at the European Championships in Brussels in the summer of 1950. 'It was a silly thing to do with two competitors,' said Lerwill, who beat Tyler into second place. 'My coach wrote to the AAA and said it must not happen again. Our paths were always close together but I do not know Dorothy Tyler as a person, one to one. I have tremendous admiration for her – there's nobody quite like her – but I do not think she was a team player.'

Others clearly disagreed, because Dorothy Tyler was made team captain again for the 1954 British Empire and Commonwealth Games in Vancouver, where Lerwill finished fourth and Tyler second. This time the team travelled by air. There were 23 countries competing, among them newcomers Nigeria, Kenya, Uganda and Pakistan, compared to only a dozen back in 1938. While Roger Bannister hogged most of the headlines,

Tyler cleared 1.60m, or 5ft 3in, for the third Games in succession to finish one place behind Thelma Hopkins, the first athlete to win gold for Northern Ireland. Britain had never had such an array of jumping talent: Hopkins, Lerwill and Tyler were all world record holders at some point in the 1950s, even though Tyler's achievement was retrospective and highly unusual.

Her final appearance at the Olympics was in 1956. In 1957, when Tyler finally retired from top-level athletics, *The Times* reported that her jump of 1.66m at Brentwood a few months after the Sydney Empire Games back in 1938 was being recognised as a record by the governing body of world athletics 18 years late. A German, Dora Ratjen, who competed against Tyler in the Berlin Olympics, had won the European title with a world best of 1.67m in 1938, and later the same year was credited with a remarkable 1.70m. Even more remarkable, Dora Ratjen was a man. 'My parents brought me up as a girl,' said Ratjen in 1938, a few weeks after setting the world record. He later went under the names of Hermann and Heinrich. 'I therefore wore girl's clothes all my childhood. But from the age of 10 or 11 I started to realise I was male.' The Nazis were said to have been aware of Ratjen's sexuality but they wanted him to be a her to provide an excuse for not selecting their top contender for the Olympics, Gretel Bergmann, who was Jewish. Another 1930s' high jumper, the Czech champion Zdenka Koubkowa, competed in women's athletics despite being a man. As Zdenek Koubek, he later moved to the United States to become a cabaret artist.

The Germans withdrew Ratjen's record claim in 1939. But, explained the secretary of the International Amateur Athletics Federation (IAFF) to *The Times*, when the IAAF gathered all their paperwork at their London headquarters in 1946, Ratjen's record 'inadvertently was not deleted'. The mistake was not officially corrected until 1957. This record, added to all Dorothy Tyler's achievements since the mid-1930s, prompted the athletics' statisticians union, in 1959, to vote her Britain's greatest ever female athlete.

All this with so little support from the men in her family. Her father left home when she was 18 and she never saw him again – 'that's probably why I went full-out on athletics'. Her brothers 'got very cross at being called Dorothy Odam's brothers', and not once in her entire life, she said, did either of her parents, or her brothers, see her compete. Her 'very supportive' mother was a great help, however, in looking after the children to allow Dorothy to compete. Dorothy took up athletics as a girl 'as a means of escape' from home, and after winning a schools contest, for which the prize was a membership at Mitcham Athletics Club, she got better and better by 'doing my own thing'. She had no coach for her first

15 years in competitive sport. For her first two Commonwealth victories, she did not even have a measured run-up.

'But, back then, if you were good at something, as I was with the high jump, you just stuck with it and that was your event.' On one occasion she tried something else, and finished second in the national girls' hurdles championship. 'The father of the champion came and told me to stick to my own event. Not that I ever could run very fast.

'I didn't ever think being good at the high jump was of any great importance. But while I could run, jump and hurdle, while I could travel the world for nothing, I wasn't going to give it up. What would life have been like without sport? I don't know what I would have done. I would have been very bored. As long as I was competing or officiating, I was happy.'

Tyler was an innovative coach. Her mother had been a dancer, and Tyler and Gold asked two of the greatest ballet dancers to help with their coaching at Bisham Abbey, where elite young athletes would gather. Margot Fonteyn and Michael Somes were pleased to turn up every week. 'Ballet gets to your very fingertips, to every muscle in your body. I had a big session at an RAF camp one time, and the men dropped their weights and came to my ballet sessions. They couldn't move the next morning.'

Besides being a coach and selector, Tyler taught PE at her old school. In her forties she took up golf, at which she became a very capable player. In her eighties, she won national age-group golf titles. She had a stroke in 2006, but it did not keep her off the golf course. 'Since then I only play three times a week,' she said later. She was the official starter of the London Marathon in 2012, aged 92.

Tyler's most controversial public appearance was in 2008 when, with Princess Anne, Dick Fosbury and others, she was a special guest of the Sports Journalists Association at an awards lunch in London. Fosbury was the American who, with Brill, changed high jumping forever. As a teenager, Brill introduced the 'Brill Bend', and, at the age of 16, was the first North American woman to clear six feet. Fosbury won Olympic gold in 1968 with the 'Fosbury Flop': both went over the bar head-first, on their back, with their legs coming last. This was revolutionary and, Tyler announced to an audience of hundreds, everybody who did it was cheating. 'You can't go over the bar head first,' she said. She was wrong: as Brill and Fosbury had shown so successfully 40 years earlier, it was both legal and highly successful.

The 'Brill Bend' was ideal for headline writers, with its nice touch of alliteration. What would her radical new style have been called, however, if her father had not changed his surname? She should really have been Debbie Verigan.

There were dark tales in the Verigan family history. Debbie's paternal grandmother, from a family of strictly religious Russian immigrants, had led an unhappy life and felt persecuted by her relatives in Alberta. She had a breakdown, killed her baby daughter, and was lobotomised: she spent the rest of her life in an institution. Her son Gene – Debbie's father – read widely about psychology, and changed his name to that of the pioneering psychoanalyst, Abraham Brill. Debbie's mother, Ruth, also had an interesting background: her Mormon great-grandfather had nine wives and 54 children. When she suffered a crushed pelvis in a car crash she was told she would never walk or give birth again, but she proved the doctors wrong and gave her son Karl four siblings, Debbie, Connie, Neil and Stan.

Life was hard but rewarding for the young Brills. Gene, who could not bear to live in a city and work in an office, joined the forestry service before designing furniture and building prefab homes. The children could all cook and milk cows. They were brought up to love animals, said Debbie. 'When you asked my little brother Stan what he wanted to be when he grew up he would say, "A cow." There were no boundaries to our adventures. Connie liked dolls, and I liked to climb trees and beat up boys.' With no running water in their first family home the children grew strong fetching it from a well. In their teenage years all five Brill children were, according to their father, capable of building their own home.

Brill showed promise as an athlete when very young. In her excellent 1986 biography, *Jump*, also written by James Lawton, she recalled her father building a high-jump pit with fishing nets and foam rubber. She made her first formal high jump aged nine, at junior school. She approached the sport in her own unique style. 'I worked on instinct. My instinct told me to run straight at the bar and just fly up into the air.' It was not long before she was 'discovered' by Pete Swensson, a Swedish immigrant who was a useful javelin thrower and local athletics organiser. Even at that stage Swensson could see international potential, so he raised money to take Debbie to competitions. For her first senior contest Brill had to take a 6am flight and wait all day in Kelowna, 250 miles from home, before clearing 4ft 11in (1.50m) and winning. She would become accustomed to waiting, just like Tyler: the women's high jump has traditionally been one of the final events at a major Games.

For three years she used the scissors style but 'quite naturally and without any theoretical input' her jumping technique evolved into the backward style, which Swensson christened the 'Brill Bend'. She approached the bar more directly than her American contemporary, Dick Fosbury. 'Seeing the way Fosbury performed at a meet in Vancouver in 1967 gave me tremendous relief and encouragement,' she told James Lawton. 'People came running over to me and said "Hey it's amazing, there's someone else who jumps like you!" When he came up to me I couldn't speak. I sort of felt Gosh! Wow!' Others were less exuberant: a report by Associated Press, the main news agency in the United States, in 1968 revealed that 'a noted orthopaedic surgeon has warned high school jumpers that the backward style of high jumping could lead to broken necks and quadriplegia'.

Brill scoffed then, and laughs at that now, as she does at later advice from 'experts' that too much high jumping could prevent her being able to give birth. It was not funny, however, when she first competed for Canada, as a 15-year-old on a tour of Scandinavia and Britain. Nobody in Europe had seen the backward style of jumping, and the crowd in Stockholm laughed at her. It was humiliating. She lost confidence, performed well below her best, and was in tears. 'It was terrifying. It made me withdraw into myself.'

She started to gain a reputation for being shy and needy but persevered with her jumping. The innate talent of Brill and Fosbury helped them to overcome the doubters. In *Jump* she explained:

> We were both talented, not held by rigid scientific coaching, and that talent helped. If we had been less good the failure would have been seen as one of technique. What Dick Fosbury and I did, it would have happened anyway eventually, but it could never have come from somebody who had lots of coaching. Neither of us had a coach right at the start – it was just natural. Coached jumpers would have been taught the 'right' way to do it. Had I been from back east I probably wouldn't have done it. I couldn't have been creative. It would have been coached out of me.

The reference to 'back east' is frequently heard in the far west of Canada. Doug Hepburn, the world and Commonwealth champion weightlifter from Vancouver, suffered discrimination in the 1950s when eastern officials, who selected national teams, simply ignored him (*see* p. 30). 'The west–east thing is still there in Canada,' said Brill. 'People tend to think of Canada only in terms of Toronto, Ottawa and Montreal. There's a bias in the newspapers, too.' How had the Vancouver area produced so many great athletes: Olympic, world and Commonwealth champions such as the sprinters Percy Williams and Harry Jerome, strongman Hepburn, and Brill? 'It's just such a different place. You can train year-round outdoors, which you can't do elsewhere in Canada. I feel enormously privileged to live here.'

In 1969 Brill won the national championship and her first gold medal, in the Pacific Conference Games in Japan, and took on a new coach.

Lionel Pugh, a Welshman who had been the top coach in British athletics, moved to the University of British Columbia and headed Canada's Olympic team. He was something of a character himself, a gifted, authoritative coach who also wrote short stories for radio, commentated on the 1964 Olympics for British television, and once met the Beatles. He was happy with the Brill Bend, and worked with Debbie two hours a week, as well as giving her a strict programme of training. Brill watched hours of film of jumping, trained hard and improved enough to set a landmark in Toronto early in 1970, becoming the first North American woman to clear six feet. This bettered by a centimetre the winning height in the 1968 Olympics, and was rated in the all-time top three athletics achievements in Canada, after Harry Jerome's best efforts at sprinting.

Brill felt 'a wonderful rush of confidence' that made her feel unbeatable as she prepared for the Commonwealth gold in Edinburgh in July. She just knew she would win. A gold medal would not be enough, however. She was going to come out of her shell and have a good time, too.

Not long before, Debbie, her sister Connie and a high-school friend had discovered drugs. They were on a school basketball trip that included an overnight stay. They bought LSD 'from the school dealer' and took it in the motel after the game. They felt they were 'entering a bizarre, wonderful world' and drugs became a part of Brill's life. 'Not a dominating part, though,' she said. 'And never for performance.' She turned to drugs as 'a change of pace, rather like a weekend away, and by the time of the Commonwealth Games it is probably true that they had changed my attitude to track and field'.

Brill changed her attitude to life, too: she was determined to shed her image as 'a little mouse' and to overcome her shyness. 'I was going to do whatever I wanted.' This included chopping up the official team uniform, getting drunk at the Queen's reception and repeatedly breaking curfew at the athletes' village. There were several good athletes from the Vancouver area in the team, and they all had a great time. Brill's best friend among them was the sprinter Patty Loverock. 'We were all into rock n' roll, short skirts, that sort of thing. We had been issued with a team uniform that our group didn't like and we decided to shorten the skirts. I took a pair of shears to mine and so did a friend, and the skirt now came only to the same depth as our jackets. It looked at the parade as though we were taking part with jackets on and no skirts, and that caused a bit of a sensation.'

Myrtle Cook, the women's team chaperone, was constantly on the lookout for misbehaviour and at night could be found 'prowling the corridors of the dorms in search of decadence'. Cook had been a gold medallist for Canada when women's athletics first featured in the Olympics, in 1928, and Brill never once saw her wearing anything but the official uniform – 'even her pyjamas, white with red maples on'. Cook's patrols made it difficult to get out, but Brill and Loverock were undeterred. 'Edinburgh was small enough that you could wander around the city, and one night I sneaked out with Patty and we walked up to the top of Arthur's Seat in the middle of the night. When we came back Myrtle was there, and she said we'd have to go and see the head coach and chef de mission, and have a serious discussion about this inappropriate behaviour. But the head coach was Lionel Pugh, my own coach, and although I said "I won't do it again," I was thinking "Inappropriate? This is exactly what we're supposed to do!" I knew they wouldn't send me back, because I was going to win a gold medal. I was too good to be sent home. And despite any telling off, I could tell that they liked me.

'There was a general feeling that the rules were meant to be challenged, especially some of the straight-laced rules. We didn't feel bound by the curfews and regulations.' This was the summer of the Isle of Wight rock festival, the biggest ever staged, and the year when British teenagers were given the vote. 'It was ebullient, 1970 was full of a sense of the world opening up.' Brill herself was opening up, too. She met her first boyfriend, Bob Casting, a Canadian swimmer, and enjoyed 'great drinking parties in the dorms', as well as the Holyrood House incident at the Queen's reception. 'I remember it was the first time I had too much to drink. It was wonderful. Drinking wasn't considered so terrible for an athlete back then, nothing like nowadays.' There followed a lecture from Myrtle Cook.

Those 1970 Games were the last time when Brill really felt she was competing for the sheer joy of it 'and interacting with people from all parts of the world'. Her confidence and self-belief were strong. 'After that it all became much tighter, there was less chance for personal expression. I didn't respond well to that.'

The following year Brill won the Pan-American title in Santiago de Cali, Colombia, and her home town of Haney held a 'Debbie Brill Day'. She sat in a truck 'waving to all those people I didn't know. I felt such a goof!' She came to think she was 'too much of a jock, not enough of a person' and sank into depression. She was sent to London to train for the Munich Olympics and, while she enjoyed meeting Lynn Davies, David Hemery and other British athletes at Crystal Palace, she felt that she was no longer jumping for joy.

The Olympics were a nightmare, and not just because of the Munich Massacre, the terrorist attack on the Israeli team that claimed 17 lives. Brill hated the Olympics, 'the intensity, the absurdness of top-level sport where all there is is the will to win. I found it all distressing.' On the day of the closing ceremony Brill and some of her teammates went up to the roof of their building in the athletes' village, smoked pot and walked out without telling officials that they had gone. They took the train to Italy, drank Chianti and went to the beach. On her return to Canada, Brill hitchhiked from Vancouver to her home in Maple Ridge, and went to live in the woods for a year with a family friend. There was no high jumping for two years. She met Greg Ray, who would later become the father of her son, Neil, named after the brother she lost in a road accident. It took her 'at least a year' to come to terms with her grief over her brother, but she had 'very happy memories of living penniless with Greg'. While the 1974 Commonwealth Games took place in New Zealand she was undecided about a return to sport.

In 1975, Brill made up her mind: she would compete again, but on her own terms. She trained hard in California for the 1976 Olympics, hosted by her own country in Montreal, but failed to make any of her first three jumps at only 5ft 8in (1.72m). She did not give up. Brill moved to California to join the Pacific Coast Club, which provided elite athletes for meetings. She formed a strong friendship with Kate Schmidt, the American who set a javelin world record in 1977. Schmidt said she had heard plenty about Brill. 'Most of the comments were negative – she was wild, undisciplined, a pure rebel. In the context of track and field, I saw these descriptions in a positive light.'

They 'competed hard and played hard, and did it because we loved it,' said Brill. She did not see it as a contradiction if they abused their bodies because their punishing programme of training and competition was 'a form of abuse anyway'. In good form and good heart, Brill turned up in Edmonton, at the 1978 Commonwealth Games, expecting to win. Instead she got 'a slap in the face' when she was beaten into second place by Katrina Gibbs, an Australian. She realised that her jumping was 'stuck', and that she may have reached her limit, of about 1.90 metres.

So she trained harder, with Lionel Pugh's input, and she did improve. Pugh's motto was: 'It's never over until it's perfect, so it's never over.' In 1979 Brill beat the world's best to win the World Cup in Montreal, the scene of her great Olympic failure. The Moscow Olympics were off limits because Canada joined the boycott against the Soviets after their invasion of Afghanistan, and when she discovered she was pregnant in December, 1980, she took a year off, and gave birth to Neil. On 24 January 1982, not long after her return to training, 'something strange and marvellous happened' in Edmonton. Brill jumped 1.99 metres and broke the indoor world record, only four and a half months after the first of her three children was born. 'In its way, it was the most incredible moment of my career.'

By the spring of that year she was struggling with injuries to her ankles, knees and hips and said in *Jump*, 'Physically I was living off credit built up over the years. Before the end of 82, there was no doubt that every account was exhausted.' Would she be able to make it to the Commonwealth Games in Brisbane late in the year? The answer was yes, and just as Tyler had done all those decades ago, she won a second gold 12 years after the first.

She thought long and hard before boarding the plane, having decided that even though she was feeling the strain, she was still capable of winning. 'If I dwelt on the negatives I knew I'd be destroyed before my first warm-up.' There was the lack of serious training over the past two years, the demands of childbirth and motherhood, the injuries and 'the general fear that I was facing the final phase of my career'. Her main rival was the Australian Chris Stanton, who had home support, but Brill felt she was the best jumper in the field. She won, felt 'triumphant but wrecked', and, amazingly, was back for more, in Edinburgh again, four years later at the age of 33. She came fifth in the Los Angeles Olympics in 1984, on 1.94 metres, and finished in the same position on her return to Scotland, when her 1.88 metres was two centimetres short of the medal positions. She retired in 1988 when she realised that her body would not withstand two successive days of jumping at the Seoul Olympics.

Had she taken the shears to her uniform in Edinburgh a second time 'there would have been no leeway, it would have been a serious matter and we would have had new uniforms made'. Sport had changed, and even the Commonwealth Games had 'tightened up', said Brill. The Commonwealth itself was creaking, too: more than half its countries boycotted these Games for political reasons. Meanwhile Britain was widening its horizons, with the official announcement of plans to build the Channel Tunnel, and the first visit by a British monarch to China.

Brill always preferred the Commonwealth Games to the Olympics. 'They are generally not so much about rampant nationalism as the Olympics, and that makes a big difference. There's a sense of all-inclusiveness that's so different to other Games. There's a much friendlier sense about it. Take out the money and the nationalism, and it becomes much more about the athletes and the competition itself, not about commercialism. People are more willing to loosen up. There's a really horrible feel, or was for me, in the Olympic village – thousands of people all really uptight.' Her comments bring to mind the words of the Canadians who brought the Games into existence in 1930: 'The event will be designed on an Olympic model, but these Games will be very different. They should be merrier and less stern, and will substitute the stimulus of a novel adventure for the pressure of international rivalry.'

'I love being Canadian and I am very privileged to live somewhere as nice as Vancouver,' said Brill, 'but I would not say I am a strong nationalist.

The Olympics was never really for me, so much nationalism, so intense. I don't quite get what it's all about. In my sport, I am on a whole other personal journey.'

Not quite what Dorothy Tyler would have said, as a proud captain of Britain's women at the Olympics. Their outlooks on life are a world apart, these two great athletes from different eras. Between them, however, Dorothy and Debbie have enriched and enlivened the story of the Commonwealth Games.

4

Friends and enemies

Friendship and tragedy for
'the Coe and Ovett of the pool'

Adrian Moorhouse and Victor Davis, 'the Coe and Ovett of the swimming pool', barely spoke to each other during years of animosity – then became great friends before Davis's tragic early death.

Victor Davis and Adrian Moorhouse dominated breaststroke swimming so spectacularly throughout the 1980s that their feats made the front pages of the newspapers. The Canadian and the Englishman set world records, won Olympic and Commonwealth titles, eclipsed the Americans and raced against each other many times all over the globe. As soon as the rivalry became established they were far from friendly. 'We first met in 1982,' said Moorhouse. 'Our first conversation was in 1986.'

Outwardly, they could not have been more different. Victor Davis was a brash, expressive Canadian with a maple leaf tattoo on his chest, whose motto was 'Go big or go home.' Adrian Moorhouse was a thoughtful Englishman who always had a deep interest in sports psychology. Davis was 'a very aggressive person who likes to go around hitting walls before he swims,' Moorhouse once said. 'I prefer just to sit and think about all the hard work I've put in. There was a lot of chanting from Davis and his cohorts. That doesn't do anything for me. I can motivate myself.'

'I like to intimidate my opponents, let them know I'm there,' said Davis, who marked out his territory before a race, like an animal leaving its scent. Davis was 'an aggressive and intimidating personality' in the words of his close friend Dave Stubbs, a Canadian swimming team official who now writes for the *Montreal Gazette*. 'Before a race, he looked like a caged animal, snarling and pacing.' While his competitors may splash their faces, Davis lay down at the poolside to duck his head underwater, and would emerge 'hissing water'. If it were a big race, he would spray a mouthful into his rival's lane. Moorhouse was not impressed.

Victor's father, Mel, said there was 'a bit of rough and tumble' in the relationship between his son and Moorhouse. Davis was often dismissive of his rivals and hated nothing more than 'losing to someone I know I can beat'. His problem with Moorhouse, for those first four years of swimming against him, was that he 'knew' he could beat him. He was wrong, and it took him a long time to realise it. In 1985, when Moorhouse took Davis's 100m breaststroke short-course world record, he looked ahead to their next race, in Canada, and said, 'I don't know whether he is looking forward to meeting me, but now I have taken his record I can smile and say hello to him.' Moorhouse won easily: the following year, in Edinburgh, Davis retaliated by defeating Moorhouse, who was favourite, to take the 100m breaststroke Commonwealth gold.

'He really annoyed me in the interview afterwards,' said Moorhouse. 'He said something like "I knew it must have been slow down the second half because Moorhouse was still with me," when I was sitting next to him.' Moorhouse redoubled his efforts and, amazingly, won the 200m, in which Davis, Olympic champion and world record holder, had never been beaten. 'Victor was really angry about it, you could see his annoyance on his face, which I was really pleased with at the time. I did resist the temptation at the press conference to say something like "I knew it was slow because Victor was still with me at the end". I guess he knew then that I was quite competitive.'

Davis got the message; he changed his opinion of Moorhouse. Here was a rival who deserved respect. Over the next few months the two became drinking buddies and, eventually, very close friends. Davis had had a tough upbringing and was an easy target for the Canadian press, who were never slow to criticise when he showed his emotions in public. 'I think I came to understand him,' said Moorhouse. 'He had amazing self-belief, bordering on arrogance. My own self-belief was very strong, too. It's a matter of how it comes out, either you keep it to yourself or you alienate people. A few of the Canadian swimmers were quite edgy.' Moorhouse and Davis would drink and talk, and became so close that, at the next Commonwealth Games, in Auckland in 1990 Moorhouse was one of the nine people who accompanied Davis on his final journey, when his ashes were scattered in the sea.

In July, 1989, Victor Davis announced his retirement from competitive swimming and started to plan for the future. He began the process of setting up his own business, and was asked by a television company to discuss possible work in broadcasting. It never happened.

On Saturday 11 November 1989 Davis went for a night out in Montreal with his girlfriend, Donna Clavel, and her friend Jennifer Watts. When they left a bar, Davis crossed the road to buy a soft drink, a bottle of Orangina. A group of three men who had been drinking in the same bar shouted at Clavel and Watts, and Davis, standing in the road, had a brief argument with them, according to Clavel. He threw his bottle at their car, a black Honda. The car was driven into Davis at speed, throwing his body 30ft into the air. He suffered horrendous injuries to his skull and spine, never regained consciousness, and was declared dead two days later. The driver, Glen Crossley, was called a 'callous coward' by a judge who later jailed him for 10 months.

The grief of Davis's parents, his brother Greg and Clavel (who shared a home with Davis), was there for all to see in the acclaimed 2007 television film of Davis's life story, *Victor*. Davis was 25, with a lifetime of achievement ahead of him. 'I wrote Victor Davis's obituary, and I wept,' said Dave Stubbs, who read a eulogy at Davis's funeral. 'I described him as a man with a passion for life who fearlessly set lofty goals for himself and, more often than not, achieved them. He made everyone around him happy to be alive.'

When Moorhouse heard the news he was devastated. It affected him so badly that he nearly failed to make the team for the 1990 Commonwealth Games. He asked permission to attend Davis's funeral in Canada, to which he had been invited, but officials at the Amateur Swimming Association insisted that the world record holder must stay to compete in the national championships in Leeds, which doubled as the Commonwealth trials. 'That really rocked me,' said Moorhouse. 'I kept thinking "This is trivial" and "What's the point?" My head wasn't right and I almost didn't make the team.'

Moorhouse was the 100m Olympic champion, and in August 1989, the month after Davis quit, he had broken the world record set by Steve Lundquist, of the United States, more than five years earlier. Here he was racing against English swimmers, most of whom were simply not in his class, and he scraped into the trials final in eighth place, a shockingly poor performance. 'I found Victor's death really hard to deal with and was struggling to motivate myself. Much as I knew how to, I couldn't box it away.' He sat down thinking 'the race is only 60 seconds, all you have to do is block it out for one minute, then deal with it'. It worked: Moorhouse won the final and was in the team. In Auckland he not only won the 100m, he equalled his own world record in doing so.

He won a relay silver, too, but the really important event was not in the pool. The day after the swimming finished, Moorhouse rose at 5am and joined eight others, Stubbs among them, on a boat that crossed Auckland Harbour to cast Davis's ashes into the sea near Rangitoto Island. 'That ceremony on the boat gave me some closure,' said Moorhouse. 'The last time I had seen Victor was at the Seoul Olympics in 1988. We were both walking up the tribune to talk to the press of our respective countries after the 100m final and I remember him saying "I'm not sure it's worth carrying on." He was feeling low because he had just finished fourth and I had won the gold, a reversal of the placings in the 1984 Olympics. I said to him, "It's all about the journey, not just this one race." On that boat in Auckland, I remembered that conversation. Victor had one heck of a journey.'

It started in earnest when Davis was still at junior school. He was labelled 'a hyperactive kid from a broken home', and said himself that he was 'kind of a derelict as a kid', brought up in a tough district by his father, with whom he always had a very strong relationship. Mel started to take Victor to the local pool in Guelph, Ontario, less than 30 miles from the Commonwealth Games' birthplace in Hamilton, when he was eight. He was clearly talented, and phenomenally strong. His grandfather had been a boxer who coached Canada's 1924 Olympic team, and Davis had a sportsman's physique. As a teenager he grew to 6ft 2in and 185lbs and, said Stubbs, his strength was legendary. 'More than one swimmer was hoisted above his head and tossed over two lanes into a pool.' He was also extremely agile, and would 'scale hotel balconies to terrorise unsuspecting victims, and shinny up flagpoles to take flags he liked'.

His times improved and by the age of 15 he was clearly a star in the making. He trained for five hours a day through his teenage years, and once said, 'You wish you had the social life of your friends, but swimming is too hard for that. The alarm goes off at 5am, you can hear the snow outside … no one wants to go and jump in the water.' He did it, however, and international success came on a trip to Australia and New Zealand in 1981, when he was 16. He won his first major title in Auckland, in the Pan Pacifics, and immediately fell in love with the place. The following year his big targets were the world championships in Guayaquil, Ecuador in July and August, and the Commonwealth Games in Brisbane two months later. The results were the same in both events: 200m gold, and 100m silver.

In Ecuador, Davis saw Lundquist – another opponent he never spoke to – as his main rival and his British target was not Moorhouse, but David Wilkie. As a boy, Davis would write on his bedroom wall the names of swimmers whose performances he wanted to better: one of them was Wilkie, who set the 200m world record at the 1976 Olympics, becoming Britain's first male gold medallist in the pool since 1908. Moorhouse led at halfway in the 200m in Guayaquil but could finish only seventh, while

Davis raced home to smash Wilkie's record. In the 100m, which would become Moorhouse's speciality, Davis was beaten by a fraction of a section, by Lundquist, and Moorhouse was a creditable fourth.

At that time a strong swimming rivalry was building up between Canada and Australia. Both countries failed dismally at the 1976 Olympics: Canada became the first host nation to end the Games without a gold medal in any sport, and Australia brought home one silver and four bronzes, one of which came in swimming. They improved their coaching and management programmes, and the results at the 1978 Commonwealth Games in Edmonton were spectacular. Graham Smith won six golds for Canada, and between them the two nations won 25 of the 29 events. 'It was intense, and there were tough contests between the two countries in 79, 80, 81 and 82, though it was always a healthy rivalry,' said Alex Baumann, Davis's friend, training partner and fellow gold medallist. Davis travelled to Brisbane full of confidence, aiming to show the Australians what he could do, and expecting to win three golds. He eventually came home with only one and, as far as the Canadian media were concerned, in disgrace. This was the scene of the infamous 'chair incident'.

In the 200m, the invincible Davis won, with Moorhouse third. Over the shorter distance Moorhouse turned a 0.33 second deficit in Ecuador into a 0.25 second margin of victory, a significant improvement in such a short time. If that was a setback for Davis, he exploded soon afterwards when Canada's medley relay team, having finished first, were controversially disqualified for a changeover infringement. 'He just went mad,' said Moorhouse. 'He kicked the timekeeper's chair, stormed off to the changing rooms and trashed a bathroom. It was quite funny at the time because the Queen was there to see it.' Much later, at a reception, the Queen mentioned the incident to the British Olympic and Commonwealth champion Anita Lonsbrough, and, said Lonsbrough, 'She thought Victor Davis was more embarrassed about it than she was.' Angry, yes, and Davis was accused by the Canadian media of insulting the Queen. But embarrassed? Probably not, at least not at the time.

One who would know is Alex Baumann, one of the world's best all-round swimmers in the 1980s who was in that disqualified team with Davis. Baumann, suffering from a bad shoulder injury, was forced to miss the world championships, and Brisbane was a make-or-break return to racing for him. His event was the individual medley: he wanted not just gold in the 400m and 200m, but records, too. He won both golds, with a world record in the 200m. Davis swam in that race, finishing fourth, and was first to congratulate Baumann, leaping across two lanes to hug him. 'It was great to have him there,' said Baumann, who has held senior roles in elite sport performance in Australia, Canada and, most recently, New Zealand, where he now lives. He won two Olympic golds in Los Angeles in 1984, where Davis, having recovered from a serious bout of glandular fever the year before, won a gold and two silvers. They were two of the great heroes of Canadian sport at the time: Canada had not won a swimming gold in the Olympics since 1912.

Baumann's verdict on Davis's 'disgrace' of 1982 is that it was overblown by the media, that the chair skidded across the poolside for only a few yards, and that far from showing Davis in a bad light, it showed how much he cared. 'One of the reasons we both excelled was that we both had an uncompromising approach,' he said. 'Our relationship helped both of us; we were very good training partners.' Baumann would swim in Davis's best event, the 200m breaststroke, to help improve his medley performances. There was 'a kind of tension' between them, because Davis got all the media criticism and Baumann got all the sponsorship deals. 'Victor felt hard done by,' said Baumann. 'We had an interesting relationship, we respected and pushed each other to new limits. Victor inspired me.'

Baumann and Davis partnered up early in their careers, travelling together on that 1981 Pan Pacifics trip. After the Brisbane Games they enjoyed a break in Australia, 'downtime after a very tough year for both of us', said Baumann. Davis had an aunt in Australia, so they stayed for a month of sailing, surfing and socialising. Victor, who loved sailing, had a great time. Baumann met his future wife, an Australian. Their son and daughter are now international swimmers for Canada.

That 1982 chair incident, coming so soon after defeat by Moorhouse, was the start of the animosity between Davis and his great English rival, said Baumann. 'There was certainly a rivalry between them, and I'm not sure how often they spoke to each other.' All the time, however, they were not so different after all. Moorhouse, like Davis, had a sense of adventure and he, too, stayed on in Australia after the Brisbane Games.

'I was only 18 at the time, the Commonwealth Games was my first major meet, and it was an important stage in my life,' said Moorhouse. 'In that 100m final I remember feeling very strong and almost moving into a higher gear. I had been tying up at the end of races, but I was shouting at myself in my head, all that positive reinforcement stuff, "Keep going! You can win this!" When I looked at the clock I got pretty excited. The Queen was watching, and she presented the medals. It was a significant moment for me because, in beating Victor Davis, I started to know that I was getting myself into the frame of being world class.'

After the Games Moorhouse phoned home to tell his mother he was going on a trip to the Barrier Reef and down the coast to Melbourne. He travelled with three other swimmers and an Australian diver, Steve Foley, who later became an elite performance director in Australia, Britain and the United States, and who did so much to develop the career of Britain's Tom Dalcy. 'It got a bit hair-raising at times but it was a great experience.'

While Davis and Moorhouse were separately enjoying their stay, Davis had become the bad boy of Canadian sport. His father, Mel, had been in Britain at the time of the Games, and after the chair incident he bought all the papers to see how serious it was. 'There was nothing,' he said. 'Only a brief mention that Canada had been upset at being disqualified. But when we got back to Canada, boy, they really laid into him.' Davis's behaviour was a disgrace, the commentators said. It would have come as no surprise to Davis, who held a lifelong dislike of reporters, Stubbs apart. 'Before Ben Johnson, he was probably the most vilified athlete going,' said Mark Lutz, the actor who played Davis in the film. 'From all the research I did, I really believe that Vic got the shaft, and I want to unshaft him a little bit.'

By the time of the next Commonwealth Games, Davis and Moorhouse had experienced extreme highs and lows. Davis was out of action for months with his illness in 1983, and then had the high of winning Olympic gold in 1984, with Baumann. For Moorhouse, the lows came in Los Angeles in 1984. He was built up by the press to such an extent that his fear of failure overwhelmed him: he could not sleep for more than four or five hours a night. He never really convinced himself he could win, and finished fourth in the 100m, with Lundquist and Davis filling the top two places, and ninth in the 200m, which Davis won in world-record time. Some writers said he should retire, aged 20, and his self-belief hit an all-time low. 'For the next four months my swimming results just got worse. My motivation to train was almost non-existent.' He sat and talked with his coach, Terry Denison, who told him to take the positives from his performance: he had been the top European finisher, and had 'achieved a lot'. That helped, Moorhouse rebuilt his short-term goals, and this period of recovery would become hugely important to him in the business world later in life. 'I was developing a lot of the skills associated with mental toughness,' he said.

By 1986 he was the world number one at 100m, and ahead of the Commonwealth Games the press labelled Moorhouse and Davis 'the Coe and Ovett of the pool', which was prescient, given what happened in Edinburgh. Sebastian Coe and Steve Ovett, the great middle-distance rivals on the athletics track in the 1970s and 80s, both won gold in the Moscow Olympics in the 'wrong' races. Ovett upset the odds by defeating Coe in the 800m, only to suffer his first 1500m defeat in 46 races when Coe beat him.

'Trouble had been brewing between us,' said Moorhouse. 'We hadn't really spoken for four years and avoided each other quite a lot.' Moorhouse's favoured distance, the 100m, was first up: he lost, and then had to listen to Davis's 'I knew it was slow' comment. 'He had the gold medal in the event I thought I was going to win.' Three days later Moorhouse had regained his confidence and felt positive about inflicting defeat on Davis, the world record holder, world champion and Olympic champion at 200m. 'It was probably the most painful race of my life but I held him off and won by about half a second.' Two weeks later, in the world championships in Madrid, Moorhouse touched ahead of Davis in the 100m only to be disqualified for an illegal turn. Davis told Moorhouse he would put that medal 'at the back of the cupboard'.

Edinburgh was the turning point, according to Baumann. 'In that 200m, Victor just couldn't believe he had been beaten.' Baumann finished fourth and expected the worst. Davis punched the water and threw his cap away, but nothing more. 'Victor always showed his emotion and right after that race I thought he might explode. But he didn't, because he was truly shocked that he had lost, particularly in the event in which he held the world record.' After that, said Baumann, Davis saw Moorhouse in a different light. Stubbs, too, noticed a difference. This was, according to reports in Canada, 'the most crushing loss of his career' but Davis was gracious in defeat in the press interviews. 'We worked together for many hours on his etiquette with the media, and on occasion I would interview him on videotape so he could see how he was coming across. I saw results in Scotland. As we sat together in a quiet medical room, he motioned to the warm-up pool where the media were awaiting him and said, "Well, let's get it over with." For the next 90 minutes, he sat answering questions, offering no excuses, congratulating the winner. A once poor loser had matured.' The frostiness between Davis and Moorhouse was gone.

Even the Queen may have noticed the change. Canadian medallists were presented with a Frisbee, an 'official toy' of the team, and, Mel Davis explained, 'Victor somehow – and I still don't know how he did it – got through the security and got close enough to the Queen to try to hand her the Frisbee. She didn't take it herself but one of her party did, maybe Prince Andrew. Victor said to her "Hello, Your Majesty, and all my friends say hello to you, too." You never knew what Victor was going to be up to. He was quite a character.'

In 1987 Moorhouse became the first man to swim the 100m breaststroke inside a minute and was on the front page of *The Times*. In 1988 he won Olympic gold, in 1989 he broke the world record and in 1990 he equalled it in winning yet another Commonwealth gold. In Auckland, the night before the 100m, one of the Canadian swimmers, Tom Ponting, invited Moorhouse on that boat trip to scatter Davis's ashes. 'He told me, "We're going to go and scatter them in a boat on Auckland Harbour the day after the swimming finishes because it was one of Victor's wishes, and he really liked it down here. Do you want to come?" It took me right back to that emotional state from the trials, and it shook me a bit, but fortunately I managed to put it to one side until the race was over. It was the first time I'd raced in a Commonwealth Games without Victor, but he still had an impact on my time there.'

Moorhouse had 14 years of top-level swimming before his retirement following the 1992 Olympics, after which he worked for the British Olympic Association, and in broadcasting. In 1995, at a pre-Olympic preparation camp in America, Moorhouse met Graham Jones, a sports psychologist. They soon started their own company, Lane4. Moorhouse had long had an interest in talent development, and, guided by their belief that 'mental toughness is the key to everything', he and Jones developed Lane4 into a hugely successful consultancy that has worked with some of the biggest names in business, among them Honda, Microsoft and Lloyds Bank, to improve the management skills of their executives, and to advise on recruitment. This was where his sporting experiences, and his recoveries from disappointment, were so valuable. 'I have been amazed by the number of businessmen who have trouble regaining confidence after a knock. Sometimes we find ourselves at companies explaining simple concepts such as self-belief.' Moorhouse and Jones wrote a book in 2007 titled, *Developing Mental Toughness: Gold Medal Strategies for Transforming Your Business Performance*. He has been hugely successful in business.

Moorhouse, born in Yorkshire and a talented swimmer from the age of nine, was keen throughout his sporting career to take an interest in other subjects. 'I would encourage athletes to be aware of the benefits of being rounded individuals. Not to make excuses so you don't do other things. Aim to organise time to be social and productive elsewhere. It can be tough, but say: "I could probably do that if I tried." There's more to life than just sport.'

Victor Davis was aware of that, too. He had once said he wanted to be a policeman, but was thinking more of business and broadcasting, like Moorhouse, when he was killed. Davis was wanted as a television analyst for the 1992 Olympics, and had a meeting scheduled with executives of the Canadian Broadcasting Corporation. In the immediate future he was about to set up a company that specialised in pool safety and a placement service for lifeguards. His coach, Clifford Barry, likened Davis to Johnny Weissmuller, the great swimmer who played Tarzan and became a

Hollywood star. Barry thought Davis – 'bigger than life, he always lived up to his billing as a great guy' – would also go into acting, and make a success of it.

A swimming pool is named after Davis in his home town of Guelph, Ontario, and a Victor Davis Memorial Fund, founded by Barry and others in 1990, provides grants for up-and-coming swimmers. Mel Davis is a director of the fund, and is proud that an annual memorial swim meet is staged in Victor's name in his home town. It features relays for teams of three, 'with the idea that the fourth leg is swum by Victor', he said. Mel was pleased when Stubbs suggested taking Victor's ashes to Auckland, and spoke fondly of his son's final journey. 'Dave Stubbs got upgraded on the plane over there, and he said "Well I'll leave Victor up in first class and I'll go to the back of the plane," so Victor's ashes travelled in style. Victor would have liked that.'

On the way to New Zealand, Stubbs called in at the Olympic pool in Los Angeles, scene of Davis's great record-breaking triumph in 1984, and scooped some water from his lane, lane four. He took it on the boat in Auckland to help the passengers to wash Victor's ashes into the sea. One of Victor's friends on board the boat was a photographer, who sent a selection of pictures of the ceremony to Mel. 'You can see one thing very clearly from those photos,' said Mel, 'and that's that Adrian Moorhouse was very upset.' Moorhouse recalled, 'It was an emotional moment, and it was strange in that it tied together all of my Commonwealth Games experiences, which always had this common thread of Victor, and our rivalry, running through them.'

Remarkably, for one so young, Davis had already intimated to his father that he wanted to be an organ donor if he died. So five Canadians benefited when Davis's heart, corneas, liver and kidneys were transplanted. His heart went to an ailing 51-year-old Quebec printer, Claude Jacques: within months, Jacques was skiing and swimming. Davis had even asked Stubbs to write his obituary 'if you're still around'. Here is an abridged version of what Stubbs wrote for the *Montreal Gazette* after the ceremony in Auckland:

RANGITOTO ISLAND, N.Z. – The leaden sky seemed to scrape the top of the volcanic giant pushing up through the Pacific Ocean, and the clouds were thick and threatening. As the waves slapped against the side of our chartered boat, Chancellor, a fine salt-water mist sprinkled our shoes and dampened our hair.

We were nine in all today – four swimmers and a diver, champions all; an aunt who came also as a godmother; a Roman Catholic priest; a trusted photographer whose pictures adorn the family's walls; and myself, who was proud to call him my friend and was privileged to deliver the eulogy at his funeral six weeks ago.

The spirit of Victor Davis, the Olympic and world champion swimmer who died on Nov. 13, was laid to rest the day he left this earth. Today, we scattered his cremated remains on the medium that made him a great athlete, in a part of the world he loved as a second home.

We brought with us the thoughts and prayers of his immediate family who could not attend the service – his father, Mel, mother, Leona, and brother Greg – and we shared the broken heart of his girlfriend, Donna. Mel Davis and Leona Heyens, Victor's parents, entrusted me to have their son's ashes placed off the coast of the country where he won his first international gold medal, nine years ago to the week.

It was shortly after 6 a.m. in Auckland, 12 noon the day before in eastern Canada. In 30 minutes, Victor's family and friends back home would pause for a moment of silent reflection, knowing we would be paying an intimate tribute to him on open water at that hour.

Someone noticed a tiny hole in the clouds that let one glorious ray of sunshine bathe Rangitoto Island in light … on the bow of the boat, each of us held the package containing Victor's ashes and said what was in our hearts.

We spoke to a common theme – we missed his friendship and his laughter and his love of life. He is at peace, we assured ourselves, and we hoped when we returned to shore we would be able to say the same for ourselves.

As the boat turned and began its return to Auckland, the hole in the sky closed and the sunshine disappeared.

5

Marathon man

The remarkable Ron Hill just keeps on running

Ron Hill – who has run more than 150,000 miles and is still going at the age of 74 – thought, ate and ran his way to a glorious victory in the 1970 marathon. At a time when Commonwealth runners reigned supreme, he helped to nurture the global boom in marathon running.

Ron Hill could empathise with Basil Fawlty when the angry Torquay hotelier, played by John Cleese, famously started thrashing his broken-down car with a tree branch. In that 1975 scene from the comedy *Fawlty Towers*, voted Britain's number one motoring moment in a survey by a car insurance company a quarter of a century later, the victim was an Austin 1100.

It was the same model of car that clapped out when Hill drove from his Lancashire home to Edinburgh, where he ran one of the Commonwealth Games' greatest races in winning the marathon in 1970. 'It was falling to bits,' said Hill. 'I'd had it a while, and it had done its job. I remember having it resprayed with a matt black roof and a mustard yellow body, but bits started dropping off and it was knackered by the time we got to Edinburgh.' When Hill took the Austin to a garage, a mechanic fitted a new brake disc for £4.50, which was not a lot less than the vehicle's value. 'He told me my car was worth £10,' said Hill.

Unlike Fawlty's car, the Austin managed one last valiant effort. Hill drove home, with his wife May and young sons Steven and Graham, before the vehicle was scrapped. How many miles were on the clock? Hill cannot remember, but according to the Austin 1100 owners' club a typical engine would have lasted between 100,000 and 120,000 miles. Considerably less, then, than Ron Hill himself.

Britain's most dedicated, innovative and remarkable long-distance runner has covered a lot more than 120,000 miles without ever breaking down or having bits fall off. He has never been in for a service other than in 1993, when he had a minor operation on a bunion, and treatment to a broken sternum after a car crash. In the week when the baton relay started for the Glasgow 2014 Commonwealth Games, Hill had gone past 158,000 lifetime miles. He has been for a run every day of his life since December 1964. Hill, born in 1938, could keep going for a while yet: illness and injury have never stopped him. He kept going after the car crash – 'luckily I'd already been for a run that morning, and I was released the next day' – and ran a mile a day in a plaster cast, in an adapted shoe, after the bunion surgery.

To Chris Brasher, Olympic champion and co-founder of the London Marathon, Hill was 'the greatest marathon runner ever to wear the British or English vest'; to the *Guardian* he was 'the best marathon runner in the world' in the 1970s. His PhD in textile chemistry helped him to design clothing for athletes that is still popular 45 years after its launch; he had a worldwide influence on elite runners' diet and training in the 1970s; he has raced in 100 countries, often barefoot; he once broke the Boston Marathon record by more than three minutes; he held world records at 10 miles, 15 miles and 25 kilometres; and he was awarded an MBE for services to athletics in 1971. There is one achievement missing, however, at least as far as the International Association of Athletics Federations (IAAF) is concerned: the marathon world record.

Hill's most famous victory came in the week when his Austin 1100 broke down. The field in Edinburgh in 1970 could not have been stronger: it featured the four fastest marathon runners in the world, one of whom was Hill. He ran the race of his life to win by two and a half minutes. His time of 2 hours 09 minutes 28 seconds was recognised by the Association of Road Running Statisticians as a world record – but not by the sport's governing body, the IAAF.

Hill was slower than the 'record' set the previous year by one of the men he beat in Edinburgh, Derek Clayton. The Australian – who emigrated after being born and raised within a two-hour journey of Hill's home in the north-west of England – had taken the world record in 1967 when he became the first man to beat 2 hours 10 minutes. In May 1969 he bettered his own mark by more than a minute in Antwerp, but that 'record' has always been disputed. The course was never adequately measured, was never used again and was said to have been anything up to a kilometre short. The Belgian Amateur Athletic Association refused to respond to queries; they never properly checked that the course was the correct distance. They managed to have Clayton's record ratified regardless. It meant that when Hill crossed the line in 1970, quicker than Clayton's 1967 time but slower than the disputed 1969 run, there was no great clamour for a world record. Only twice has an athletics world record been set at the Commonwealth Games since they went metric – Marilyn Neufville's 400m for Jamaica on the same day as Hill's Edinburgh marathon and Filbert Bayi's sensational 1500m in Christchurch in 1974. Hill believes that his effort should have been recognised, too. The fact that it was not still rankles.

'It was a world record as far as I'm concerned,' said Hill. 'The length of the course in Antwerp was measured by officials in cars, which is not acceptable. The Americans would not recognise it, nor would others but the only ones who did were the IAAF. It was weird. The Belgians never answered any questions about the course, never sent any maps or anything.'

If the IAAF had refused to ratify Derek Clayton's Antwerp run – it would not have stood the test of current measurement rules – Hill would have held the world record for four years. A world record by a British runner in a British Games would have been quite something. In different circumstances in Edinburgh in 1970 it may have happened twice on the same day. Marilyn Neufville's run could have been for England rather than Jamaica. Her father was Jamaican but she was born and raised in South London and had run for Britain. When she was asked to switch allegiance for the 1970 Games to a country she had never even visited she said 'Yes'. Neufville, 17 at the time, was heavily criticised by the British media – so much so that, after her record-breaking 400m victory in 51.0 seconds she did not say a single word at the post-race press conference. 'The media had a very nationalistic point of view and it turned so nasty that I even had death threats,' said Neufville, an ordained minister in London. 'I was much more practical about it. I had trips to Jamaica and a pre-Games team tour of Europe, and the Jamaican government helped me to get a scholarship to a university in California.'

Derek Clayton's disputed Antwerp time was finally beaten in 1981 by Australia's Rob de Castella, who won Commonwealth Games gold in Brisbane in 1982 and Edinburgh in 1986. Commonwealth Games runners held the official world record in the marathon from 1967 to 1985. So strong was the event in the 1970s and 1980s that the three fastest marathon times ever run in the Games are those by Ian Thompson, the 1974 champion, de Castella and Hill in those two decades.

Commonwealth runners also played their part in the worldwide boom in marathon running, both commercially and as a recreational sport, at the time. By the mid-1980s marathon running was enjoying a mass-participation boom all over the world, with hundreds of thousands taking to the streets of some of the world's biggest cities. Annual races, watched by huge television audiences, attracted fortunes in sponsorship. Nowadays, in the United States alone, more than half a million people finish a marathon every year. The women's marathon was also established in the 1980s, when it became an Olympic and Commonwealth event. A new force arrived in the men's race: African runners have won every Commonwealth title since 1998, as well as four of the last five Olympic golds. Going into the year of the Glasgow Games, no man from outside Africa has held the marathon world record in the twenty-first century.

When Hill was at his peak in the 1960s and 70s there was no such thing as the London Marathon. Invitations from prestigious races were rare, even to elite runners. The big-city boom first started in the United States in the 1970s, partly as a result of the growing popularity of jogging, but also because of Frank Shorter's celebrated Olympic marathon victory in 1972 in Munich, and the tireless efforts of long-distance running enthusiasts in promoting races. The London Marathon was born in 1981, thanks largely to Chris Brasher. More than 20,000 people applied to enter, although there was room for only about one-third of them. More than 6000 crossed the finish line. Could Hill see any of this coming?

'Absolutely not. Marathons had small fields when I started, and nobody could foresee the massive increase in numbers. When I went to Boston for their marathon in 1970 I didn't go because I was invited, I went because the Road Runners Club had a whip-round and paid for my fare, and helped me to find a family who put me up. I won the race, broke the course record by three minutes, and that was that. They didn't invite me back the next year. It just didn't happen back then. There were a thousand runners in that race in Boston. To people back here that was amazing: nobody else in Britain had run in a field of that size. They'd ask what was it like, but it didn't make any difference how many were behind you if you were at the front.'

As for the Africans, Hill and his fellow Britons knew they were good because of the Olympic results in the 1960s: Abebe Bikila (twice) and Mamo Wolde won the marathon for Ethopia in Rome in 1960, Tokyo in 1964 and Mexico City in 1968. 'We had our encounters in the 1960s and could see they were excellent runners, but what was a surprise was how many of them were waiting in the wings. They did have a definite advantage training at altitude.'

Gaining an advantage was always in Hill's mind. He would study and experiment with clothing, footwear, training methods and diet in his search for an edge over his rivals. When he had his 'eureka' moment for the marathon he could not resist telling his friend Chris Brasher. The former runner was sports editor of the *Observer*, in whose pages he wrote at length about the dietary 'secret' of Hill's great success in winning the

European Championship race from Marathon to Athens in 1969. By the time of the Commonwealth Games the following year, everybody knew about it, and others were trying it. Looking back 45 years later, Hill wishes he had kept his mouth shut.

Alf Tupper would have been proud of Hill, who spent his childhood in a two-up, two-down stone terraced house in Dale Street, Accrington, Lancashire. Tupper was 'The Tough of the Track', a character in the boys' comics *Rover* and *Victor* who fired Hill's imagination. 'It's not difficult to see why I would identify with someone like him,' said Hill.

Tupper was from a tough northern town, where he worked as a welder in a workshop underneath the railway arches. He slept on a mattress on the floor next to his workbench. 'His training places were all familiar to me – darkly lit streets, railway tracks, canal banks, around gasometers. Here was a lad who was always up against it: no proper home, always a challenge to overcome. We lived in a terraced house with a toilet in the back yard. Alf was slightly worse off because he didn't know who his parents were and lived under the arches. He would go down on the train to White City in London, hop over the railings and beat the people from Oxford and Cambridge. University boys hated him, so did foreigners. Greystones, the town where he lived, could quite easily have been Accrington.' Tupper's running career lasted nearly as long as Hill's. He first appeared in *Rover* in 1949, moved in the 1960s to *Victor*, and even trained for the Barcelona Olympics in Scotland's *Sunday Post* in 1992, his farewell appearance in British newspapers. In a 1970 storyline in *Victor*, Alf won the race that crowned Hill's career, the Commonwealth Games marathon. He made a comeback in 2012 when he was used in a cartoon strip to promote the Great North Run, for which his training partner was the great Ethiopian runner Haile Gebrselassie.

'Alf genuinely was my hero, more than any living athlete,' said Hill. 'There was much of him in me. His life was bloody hard and he was a working-class warrior always suspicious of the 'toffs' – the sort of people who ran British athletics when I started. Alf never gave up: I never gave up. There was so much to admire in Alf.' A fact-file about Alf published in *Victor* listed his age as 'younger than he looks', another similarity with Hill.

Hill started running a few years after Alf Tupper. In his two-part autobiography, *The Long Hard Road*, written in 1981 and 1982, he summed up his career thus: 'After training twice a day from 1957 onwards, unguided and with a multitude of experimentation, I slowly improved from moderate schoolboy ability, through university to county and eventually, in 1962, to international standard.'

He ran his first marathon in 1961. 'I was looking for a race one weekend and there was nothing except the Liverpool Marathon. There were 50 entrants, the race started at St George's Hall, went around the outskirts of the city and finished at Anfield.' The home of Liverpool FC was packed for a match. The runners arrived at the stadium for a finishing lap around the pitch before kick-off. 'The next day I was knackered, my legs hurt, and I wasn't going to run another marathon. But the race got a lot of publicity, so I thought I'd stick with it. Even so, I was never serious about marathons as a means of fulfilling long-term ambitions in running. I dearly wanted to be a great track runner. The ultimate symbol of success I wanted was a gold medal at the Olympics, or failing that at either of the two other major Games, European or Commonwealth.'

The British selectors saw the marathon as Hill's best event in 1962, when he made his international debut in the European Championships in Belgrade. He failed to finish. By the time of the 1964 Olympics, Hill was the second fastest marathon man in the world behind fellow Englishman Basil Heatley, who had broken the world record a few weeks before the Games. Heatley took silver in Tokyo but lost his record to the winner, Bikila. Hill again ran disappointingly, finishing nineteenth. He also ran the 10,000m, in which he was lapped.

Hill's first appearance at the Commonwealth Games was in 1966 when he travelled to Kingston, Jamaica and suffered yet more disappointment. His plan was to run the six miles in Kingston – the Commonwealth version of the 10,000m – and the marathon in the European Championships in Budapest soon after. He was well beaten in both races, after which he made a lifestyle change: he gave up smoking. Remarkably, until 1966 Hill smoked cigarettes and cigars.

The plane carrying the England athletes and officials to Jamaica arrived in the middle of the night, having diverted to Prestwick in South Ayrshire to pick up the Scotland and Northern Ireland teams. The opening ceremony, in sweltering heat, was 'more moving to me than the Olympics,' said Hill. While he was training in a solo session that mixed explosive bursts of running with more measured laps, his every move was watched closely by a Kenyan. 'I think his coach had told him to study me because I knew what I was doing. I'd never met him and we had a chat afterwards.' The Kenyan, who had finished 30 places behind Hill in the 1964 Olympic marathon, was taking him on again in the six miles, for which the favourite was the world record holder, the great Australian Ron Clarke. He told Hill his best time to date was 'about 30 minutes'. His name was Naftali Temu: he won the six miles in 27 minutes 14.6 seconds, beating Clarke by nearly half a minute, with Hill fifth. He also won the Olympic 10,000m in 1968.

The six miles was scheduled for a 10.25pm start but was not underway until after 11pm. Hill ran in bare feet, stayed at the back of the field and wilted in the heat and humidity. He was lapped. 'I was dejected, broken, completely shattered, covered in sweat, couldn't breathe.' Close to tears, he could not speak to anybody after the race. He kept pestering the team's travel officer for an early flight home. 'They could stuff the trip to Montego Bay when the Games were over. I was in no holiday mood.' He flew home five days later, on the day of the marathon. He was able to watch it before his departure, as he recounted in *The Long Hard Road*.

> Roused at 4.30a.m., I went down to the stadium with the Northern Ireland captain, Stan Vennard, who was competing in the marathon. I had a two-mile run in the dark round the stadium then entered the completely empty stands to watch 17 brave, rugged men, with an assortment of caps, hats, knotted handerchiefs and wetted scarfs, toe the line as the sun began to creep over the rim of the arena, for the 5.30 a.m. start to the marathon. There was Jim Alder, in the navy blue vest of Scotland, carrying a sponge, white handkerchief round his neck, and Bill Adcocks, England's runner, similarly kerchiefed and with another knotted hanky on his head, pattering side by side, sweating, running their own pace. The drivers of the thin horse-drawn carts on their way to market in Kingston must have wondered what kind of crazy people were flogging themselves along the road at that time of the morning.

Ron Clarke was, like Alder, running the marathon after his exertions in the six miles. He had a good lead at halfway but Alder and Adcocks reeled him in and then dropped him. 'He called it a day at 17 miles as Alder and Adcocks disappeared up the road,' recalled Hill. Over the last five miles, all uphill, Alder built a lead of 80 yards – and then lost it in the most remarkable circumstances. The Duke of Edinburgh, Prince Charles and Princess Anne had arrived at the stadium to watch the finish. Race marshals deserted their posts to see the royals, leaving the runners with no guidance on which route to take into the stadium. Alder went one way, Adcocks another: when they emerged on to the track, Adcocks was in front. Seeing nobody ahead of him, he thought Alder had finished. Suddenly Alder went past him to regain the lead, still full of running: he crossed the line five seconds clear, shouting 'Geronimo!'

'It was Bill who went the wrong way, not me,' said Alder, a bricklayer from England's north-east who was eligible to run for Scotland. 'Technically he could have been disqualified. But it was my day. Sometimes no matter what goes wrong you overcome it.' Adcocks agreed. 'It was a notorious race,' he said. The problem was that the organisers had predicted a

relatively slow winning time of 2 hours 30 minutes because of the heat.
The royals' arrival was timed accordingly, but Alder and Adcocks had run
much faster, even though it was close to 90 degrees by 8 a.m. 'My main
concern was whether they'd take my silver medal off me,' said Adcocks,
who was very happy with his performance.

Alder had been given strict instructions by Scotland's team officials to
win a medal. 'It was 90 per cent humidity in Kingston and some runners
couldn't handle it,' said Alder. 'The Scottish team management decided it
was too much for me and said I couldn't run the six miles, just the marathon.
I was in tears.' Menzies Campbell, later a prominent politician who was
knighted for services to Parliament, was Scotland's athletics captain. 'He
went and made my case, told them I could cope with two races. Just before
the six miles they gave me a number and I was in – and I got a bronze.
Because of that they said "Don't fail in the marathon". I didn't.'

Alder said of Hill, 'He had a bad big-games record at that time, but he
really clicked in 1969, when he proved he was a world force. When he
was spot-on Ron Hill was number one, he was fantastic. We won only
when he wasn't at his best and we were.' As for his thirst for competition
and his daily runs, Alder, who last raced competitively aged 61, said,
'Ron's being silly. Still racing aged 75 – what is the point? He's a brilliant
runner, brilliant man, but give it up. I guarantee that if there was a race on
the moon, the first entry would be Ron Hill.

'He's a great man, though, very funny when he's had a few drinks. We
used to be great rivals, and now we're good friends. He was a pioneer.
Ron was an analytical scientist who was ahead of his time. We went to
train in Puerto Rico once and because he was so keen to learn he spent all
his time looking round clothing factories. He pioneered the thermal vest,
string vest, tracksters [short training bottoms], and of course the diet. He
never really got the recognition he deserved.'

That point was emphasised in 2002, when the Commonwealth Games
came to Manchester. Hill could see the stadium from his home yet he was
not invited to appear, or even offered any tickets. 'If they had made any
effort they could have had four English Commonwealth Games marathon
champions there to do a lap of honour,' said Hill. They would have been
Ian Thompson, Brian Kilby (the 1962 winner), Jack Holden (who ran the
last 10 miles barefoot when he won in Auckland in 1950) and Hill himself.
'It beggars belief that they did nothing,' said Hill. 'Watch an England
football match and they'll always have players from the past there, like
Nobby Stiles. In athletics it's a different story.'

After Kingston, Hill flopped again in the European title race in Budapest.
In the 1968 Olympics he was seventh behind Temu in the 10,000m,

beaten by 26 seconds – a very good effort given that the race was run at altitude in Mexico City. 'That gave me hope that I was on the right lines with my finely developed training technique,' said Hill. He was about to enter what he called his 'purple patch'. Gold medals were on the way.

Hill had studied science at grammar school. He gained a scholarship to university in Manchester where, to his surprise after all those years of following Alf Tupper in *Rover* and *Victor*, he found his fellow cross-country runners were 'just normal blokes'. He gained a doctorate in textile chemistry. During his runs to and from work he 'came to realise that a lot of things were not right with the equipment for runners'. He designed vests, shorts, training bottoms, long-sleeve tops, high-visibility gear for safety and much more besides. He would have liked to run bare-chested, but that was not allowed, so he minimised the material used, which was always white. 'Black garments can be many degrees higher in temperature than white in sunlight,' he explained. 'I always maintained it was suicide for New Zealand marathon runners to run in their traditional black vests, whatever the weather.' He gained an edge by making shorts from elastomeric fibre that would stretch with the legs rather than be pushed aside by their motion. He started his own company in the 1960s and still sells to runners more than 50 years later.

Hill also experimented with footwear, running barefoot where practical and seeking ever lighter shoes where not. 'The lighter the weights on the feet, the less work has to be done in lifting and carrying them, therefore the more energy is available for driving the body over the ground. You might not think a couple of ounces would make much difference but the number of strides taken in a marathon is very high and it can add up to a hell of a lot of work in the end.' He developed track shoes without spikes – Bikila wore them when he won Olympic gold in 1964 – and tried silver shoes to reflect the heat. He even ran cross-country races barefoot, with two toes taped together on each foot. 'I was planning to run the 1972 Olympic marathon barefoot, but the Germans relaid the roads and the chippings would have shredded my feet,' he said. All these ideas were his own: he never had a coach.

His innovative approach to running paid dividends in the 1969-71 period, when he started to think about diet, and fuel for the body. Alf Tupper always lived off fish and chips: Hill was more scientific. Early in 1968 he received a letter from Martin Hyman, who had run long-distance events for England at the 1958 and 1962 Commonwealth Games. Hyman was passing on information about Swedish scientists' experiments with trained athletes, mostly skiers. The Swedes measured glycogen content – the storage form of glucose in the body – after the athletes pedalled on an ergometer for hours, often to the point of exhaustion. When the athletes were fed a high-protein diet for a set period in the days before their exertions, followed by a high-carbohydrate diet, they were able to cycle for far longer. A carefully planned change in diet, allied to rigorous training at the right times, could effectively increase the storage of energy in the muscles by huge amounts. The experiments were not thought to be of any great significance to marathon running because the duration of a race was less than the time the Swedes spent on their bikes. But Hill made some calculations and thought it could be adapted.

Runners had always hit 'the wall' at around 18-20 miles, or about two hours into a race. Hill realised that 'the wall' was the point at which the muscles had run out of glycogen. As he explained in *The Long Hard Road*: 'The muscles got stiff and tired, the pace dropped, and that was because the body was having to metabolise fats and maybe even protein, the muscle tissue itself, to get energy, and very inefficiently at that. Now, if that point could be delayed from two hours up to two and a quarter hours...'

The simplified formula for the diet was four and a half days of fish and meat, followed by two and a half days of pasta and potatoes. It became known as the glycogen depletion diet, or the carb-loading diet: its official title, according to Chris Brasher, was the Saltin–Hermansson diet, named after the Swedish scientists who invented it. Hill tried it, testing it to the full in Manchester in the Maxol Marathon in July 1969. The race, started by the Manchester United manager Sir Matt Busby, was the trial for the European Championships. World record holder Clayton was there, as was Bill Adcocks. In his ultra-light shoes, string vest and brief shorts, Hill won easily with Clayton nearly two minutes behind in second place. Many years later, Clayton looked back on Manchester as the toughest marathon he ever ran. Hill, conversely, had run without hitting 'the wall'. He was going to Greece to represent Britain, and the diet was going with him.

'It was very hot in Athens, and I didn't take any drink during the race. But the diet worked again and I took the lead with about a kilometre to go,' said Hill, who won his first major championship in great style from the Belgian Gaston Roelants, with Alder third. In the immediate post-race excitement he just had to tell somebody how he had done it. 'I explained what I had done to Chris Brasher, stupidly, and he put it in the *Observer*. That's how everybody else found out about the diet. I just couldn't wait to tell somebody about it, but I should have kept my mouth shut.'

There was another consequence of that talk with Brasher. The journalist was still a keen runner: he tried Hill's diet himself and flooded the kitchen. Shirley Brasher wrote about it for her husband's newspaper. 'When Chris was back from reporting the European Games I could hardly fail to detect that the most fascinating aspect of Athens was that the glycogen diet assisted Ron Hill to win his gold medal in the marathon. Chris had entered a two-day, 50-mile race in the Lakes and was going to try the diet.

'At first it was not too bad, though I was irritated when I wanted to go play tennis and Chris refused his boiled eggs – instead he wanted fried eggs and bacon. Lunch was high protein but I had to fry a potato that had already been baked and the children complained of the smell of fat.' Brasher had an afternoon run 'to the point of exhaustion' followed by rashers of bacon and fat pork chops for dinner. He was so tired he fell asleep before finishing it. 'Sunday was bacon and eggs for breakfast, a snooze in the deckchair, and another enormous fried meal for lunch. He was too lethargic to train. In the evening there was an ominous flood coming from the drain that connects to the kitchen sink.' Mrs Brasher found that the drain was blocked by solidified fat. 'Avoid these up-to-date ideas,' she warned readers. 'You cannot win, even if he does.'

Hill followed his Athens triumph with his record-breaking win in Boston, and a second-place finish in the prestigious Fukuoka Marathon in Japan before preparations began for Edinburgh. 'That was a purple patch for me – Manchester, Athens, Fukuoka, Boston, then the Commonwealth Games. I was learning all the time, getting faster and faster.'

Which brings us to the Edinburgh Commonwealth Games in 1970. When the Austin 1100 spluttered into the Scottish capital Hill left his family at a guesthouse and headed for his single room at the university campus that became the athletes' village. He was happy with his accommodation and even happier with the food – 'the best I have ever experienced at any Games throughout the world'. The race was 'virtually a world championship', said Hill, with the four fastest runners all there. The other three besides Hill were Jerome Drayton from Canada, Bill Adcocks and Derek Clayton. The defending champion from the 1966 Commonwealth Games, Jim Alder, was also there. 'It was my fifth marathon in a year and Jim told me I was due a bad one,' said Hill. 'I remember seeing Jim reading detailed sheets of what he should be doing with the diet – Chris Brasher had helped him – and I couldn't believe it when I saw him eating a plate of chips at the wrong time. I don't think he completely understood it. Still, he finished second so good for him.'

His meticulously kept diary itemises Hill's breakfast on race day, Thursday 23 July: porridge with lots of sugar, poached egg, bacon, brown bread with jam, sweet coffee, multivitamin tablet, iron tablet, vitamin C tablet, vitamin E capsule. For lunch he had two slices of brown bread and marmalade, a glass of orange juice with a teaspoon of salt, and another glass with sugar. He read a book about bullfighting, listened to the Beatles on his cassette player, travelled to the stadium, realised he had forgotten his shoes, returned to the athletes' village to fetch them, and went out to run the race of his life.

Clayton had said before the race, 'I love this course. I'm going to go off like hell from the gun and I reckon it could be the greatest marathon ever. Ron Hill and Bill [Adcocks] are gutsy boys. They'll be in there too.' Clayton, who never once beat Hill in a marathon, could only watch as it was Hill who went off like hell. Neither Clayton nor Drayton finished; Adcocks was sixth, nearly six minutes behind Hill. Alder recalled, 'I could hear the ropes on the flagpoles thwacking, hear the flags – it was a very strong wind. Derek Clayton was pacing up and down, you could see by his body language that he was gone, too tense. He was world record holder and he said beforehand that the Brits were only ever any good in bad weather, that I didn't have it. He derided us. And after eight miles, one each side, we took him. It was a great feeling. That was the fastest first half of a marathon ever run. To his great credit Clayton went on BBC after the race and apologised, said he was wrong, and he came and said the same to me later, apologised man to man. I shook his hand. It took a lot of courage to do that.'

The following day *The Times* reported:

Hill began to pull away between seven and 10 miles, and built up an inexorable lead until he was six seconds clear at 10 miles. He reached that stage in the remarkable time of 47min. 44sec. and the first 15 runners were all under five minutes a mile. But no one had the strength and mental resilience of the 31-year-old Hill. At the turn he was half a minute up on the Canadian Jerome Drayton, who had been thought one of his chief rivals, and by 20 miles Hill had nothing to fear from his only pursuer, the defending champion, Jim Alder, of Scotland. He destroyed any real challenge from a field of great talent.

Hill said later that he had 'almost got an ulcer in the last six miles from the worry of whether I could keep going or not. I lost once before by easing off, so I just kept pushing.' After the race, during which the leaders all lost about 8lbs in weight, he had a few drinks. The *Guardian*'s John Samuel reported the following day, 'As Hill said, swigging beer after beer, "Doesn't really put it back, this stuff. You either chose the physiological drink or the psychological. I think I'll get stoned."'

Was it his best run ever? There was, he said, one to match it. In 1968, trying to prove to the national selectors that he could run a marathon, Hill entered the Pembroke 20, a road race of four five-mile circuits. He ran the first five miles in 24 minutes and could not believe it, shouting at the timekeeper that he must have got it wrong. He covered 10 miles in less than 49 minutes, the whole race in 1 hour 36 minutes 20 seconds. He would still have had a 'wall' to hit then, as he had not tried the new diet, but had Hill been able to continue at the same pace for the full marathon distance he would have broken the world record by four minutes. 'I don't think the selectors even noticed,' he said.

Sadly, Hill was unable to repeat his effort in the 1972 Olympics in Munich, when he felt he could have won. He covered too many miles in training, up to 160 a week, and 'made mistakes with the glycogen-depletion diet – I had a bad one'. There was another 'bad one' in New Zealand in 1974 when Ian Thompson emerged from nowhere to win Commonwealth gold in Christchurch. 'I had a troublesome left foot injury for weeks and it went bad in the race,' said Hill who, as in Kingston, was homesick after the race. 'I finished way behind the leaders, my ankle swelled up like a balloon and I was really struggling. It was agony even to jog, which I did for my daily run.' When he received touching notes and letters from his wife and sons, then aged eight and ten, he just wanted to go home.

The man who took his title was Thompson, a student teacher from Luton who, until a few months before, had never run a marathon in his life. He won the first five marathons he ran: the Games trial in Harlow in October 1973, the Christchurch race, another in Greece and the European Championship all in 1974, and a fifth in Finland in 1975. 'I probably overtrained that year, got a series of illnesses and infections, and was unwell for the trials for the 1976 Olympics. I think I'd have won if I'd been there.' He went to the Moscow Olympics in 1980 but overtrained again and failed to finish. 'I was running 140 miles a week when I didn't need to. I should have focused on speed work.' Like Hill, his glory days were confined to a relatively short 'purple patch'.

Although Hill and Thompson both ran in the trial late in 1973 they did not meet properly until they were in Bahrain, where the jumbo jet carrying the athletes to New Zealand had stopped for refuelling. 'He daren't miss a day's training, so we both got off the plane to run around Bahrain airport,' said Thompson. On the day of the race his parents back in Britain were fretting. 'There had been news reports saying it was so hot we were all going to die and my mum and dad were a bit worried. We started at 5pm in very nice conditions – it was warm, but not as hot as it had been the day before.' The streets were well lined for most of the race, with spectators offering plenty of support for the leaders, among whom was the New Zealander Jack Foster. As he neared the 20-mile point Thompson realised he was running a lot faster than world-record pace. 'I thought "I don't need to go this fast", took it easy and cruised home. I sprinted the final lap, and the Games record still stands.' He was not as bothered as Hill about Clayton's disputed time, which denied him a world record. 'I was more interested in winning races,' he said. Foster finished second in Christchurch and Richard Mabuza of Swaziland took the bronze. It was the first Commonwealth marathon medal for a black African runner. Back in twentieth place, eight minutes behind Hill on 2 hours 38 minutes, was a Kenyan, Johnson Kiptanui Sirma, who was only 15 years old.

Thompson viewed Hill much as Alder did – as a pioneer. 'He was both thoughtful and thought-provoking about running. Slightly off the wall maybe, but he pushed our understanding and knowledge of running to new levels. I ran that 1974 marathon in shoes he designed, and I still have them. I can't believe I actually ran a race in them. They were basically track shoes with no spikes – no support, no padding. They only lasted one race.

'Back then I couldn't foresee the boom in marathon running, the numbers who took part in New York and London and so on – especially when so many are not suited by it. Back then fields were very small but elite, very good quality. There was just really the Commonwealth Games, the Europeans and the Olympics for big international championships. Ron Hill and some of the others created a buzz around the marathon, and that helped when Chris Brasher got involved with the London race.'

Mabuza was back for more at the Commonwealth Games in Edmonton in 1978, when he only managed to finish seventh. There was an African winner, though – Gidamis Shahanga, from Tanzania, who had finished 11 minutes behind Mabuza in the African Games in Algeria a couple of weeks earlier. The 10,000m gold medallist, Brendan Foster, went out on the press truck, from where he encouraged Shahanga in the closing stages to 'run like Filbert'. Foster had finished seventh behind Filbert Bayi in the Tanzanian's world-record 1500m in 1974. Shahanga responded to Foster's urgings, making up nearly a minute and a half on the leaders in the last eight miles to win from Jerome Drayton.

Another Tanzanian, Juma Ikangaa, looked a certain winner in Brisbane in 1982 only to be overtaken by the home favourite Rob de Castella, who won in 2 hours 09 minutes 18 seconds. The world-record holding Australian won another high-quality race because of a sensationally strong finish – thanks largely to being on Hill's glycogen-depletion diet. De Castella triumphed again in Edinburgh in 1986, when his fellow Australian Lisa Martin won the first women's marathon, running the fifth fastest time ever.

There was an interesting footnote to the 1982 race. Recreational runners had started to take up the marathon in large numbers, and the last-placed finisher in Brisbane was closer to their ranks than the elite. 'A provincial runner, not an international,' was how he described himself.

His time was 3 hours 02 minutes 33 seconds, 20 minutes behind the man in front of him: by the time he reached the finish line it was being dismantled, along with the stands. He was representing the Cayman Islands despite having been there for only 10 days in his life. He was a desperately keen runner named Nick Akers, better known as Nick Vladivar.

Akers was from Britain, where he trained with Steve Ovett in his youth. He moved to New Zealand, then Canada, holding passports for all three countries. He was never good enough to represent any of them internationally so he wrote to Guernsey, Jersey and Fiji instead. No luck. Then he discovered he could represent the Cayman Islands, with the help of Joel Bonn. A Canadian, Bonn had gone to the Caribbean islands to teach speed reading, and stayed. He created an Olympic association and raised a team for the Commonwealth Games in Edmonton in 1978. He was an engaging character who, when asked where the Cayman Islands were, replied 'in between Juantorena and Don Quarrie'. It was his way of saying they were equidistant from Cuba, home of the double Olympic champion Alberto Juantorena, and Jamaica, from where the sprint champion Don Quarrie hailed. Budd persuaded Ian Wooldridge, the eminent *Daily Mail* journalist, to march with the Cayman team at the Edmonton opening ceremony: Wooldridge was deemed an impostor by officials and it nearly led to the team's expulsion.

Nick Akers was told he could join the team provided he signed a deal: he must change his name to that of a popular brand of vodka. Vladivar's sponsorship money would go to the Cayman sports bodies, Akers would be given the paperwork and a chance to run in the Commonwealth Games. He got a Cayman driving licence but not a passport: somehow it was enough. He ran last in the 5000 metres – heats, of course, not the final – in which he was slow, but not as slow as fellow Caymanian Godfrey Bevan, whose time in the other heat was four minutes worse. In the 10,000m he was a respectable eighteenth, and in the 1500m he was 35 seconds slower than gold medallist Dave Moorcroft but 35 seconds faster than the slowest man from the Turks and Caicos Islands. He still holds the Caymanian record for the 10,000m.

Injury, and a row over his amateur status because of the vodka affiliation, kept him out of the Moscow Olympics but he was back for the 1982 Commonwealth Games in Brisbane. 'Vladivar' was two minutes slower than in 1978 but still faster of the two Cayman runners in the 10,000m. Then came the marathon. At the end of the race he 'was wandering around alone, not knowing anybody, and staggered into a pub'. It was free drinks all round for him. 'I would say I represented the true amateur racers,' said Akers, who changed his name back again after he became a father. 'Vladivar paid £10,000 but it went to the Commonwealth Games Association of the Cayman Islands. Whatever changed hands was between them and Joel Bonn – I was never paid a dollar. I ran in the true spirit of being an athlete. I wanted people to get into running.'

What of Ron Hill: why does he do it?

'I ran to be the best that I could at running. I ran to win races and, if possible, to break world records. I ran to get into Commonwealth, European and Olympic Games teams and win medals. Now I race for the excitement of the event and to see where my performances or capabilities are. My daily runs are a mindset, more mental than physical. They are also a barometer as to my health and an aid to keeping my mind and body healthy. I feel alive and well, therefore I run. I run, therefore I feel alive and well. I love the fresh air. I weigh the same today as I did 50 years ago. I look back and I have no regrets. The more you run, the better you'll be.

'I did everything I could to be the best in the world. I couldn't train full-time, couldn't train at altitude, couldn't afford back-up support – I only ever had two massages in my life – and when I was injured I just had to run through it. I never made any money at it. But you can't take away the gold medals.'

Hill is not the only dedicated long-distance runner in his senior years. Until his death aged 88 in 2007 there was the American Ted Corbitt, a grandson of slaves who was, according to the *New York Times*, 'the father of long-distance running'. Corbitt, an Olympian in 1952, once ran 300 miles in a week. His method of accurately measuring the distance of road races is still used today – although there was never an opportunity to use his method in that disputed Antwerp marathon. Also from the United States is Mike Fremont, who was told he had three months to live when he was diagnosed with cancer in 1991. More than 20 years later he was setting a world record at the age of 91 for the half-marathon, for runners aged 90–94. 'There's not much competition in my age group,' said Fremont, who attributed his longevity and success in running to his strict vegan diet. Another vegan, the British-Indian Fauja Singh, became the first centenarian to finish a marathon in 2011, and was still running aged 101 in 2013. He once appeared in a sportswear advertisement alongside David Beckham and Muhammad Ali. The Canadian Ed Whitlock, another multiple world record holder who was born in England a few years before Hill, is the only man aged over 70 to have run a marathon in less than three hours. He is still going strong in his eighties.

Perhaps most remarkable of all is the Greek-Australian Yiannis Kouros, a poet and Greek literature expert who is known as 'the running god'. For Kouros, a youngster born in 1956, a marathon is a sprint. He once won a

72-hour race in the United States by more than 60 miles; he started the Sydney–Melbourne race half a day after everybody else and still won easily. Among his tally of more than 150 world records is every single one for distances more than 100 miles. During his six-day run of 643 miles in 2005 his shoe size swelled from nine to 11. It takes a week after such a run for the feet to return to normal. He, too, is an expert on diet: he can take on 15,000 calories a day while running extreme distances, and has even put on weight during a race.

Ron Hill never did that. It is a source of great pride to him that he has not gained weight since his younger days. He describes his non-stop running as 'a mindset, more mental than physical' and always feels better after his daily run than he did before it. In this Commonwealth Games year he will celebrate 50 years of consecutive daily runs. How long does he intend to keep going? 'I can't answer that unless I can predict my own death,' he said. 'I'll keep going until I die.'

6

The forgotten

The sad, swift sporting decline
of a Scot and a South African

A car crash, apartheid and a cold-hearted headmaster effectively ended the sporting careers of two world-class gold medalists at the 1958 Games. Gert Potgieter and Ian Black might have achieved so much more.

Wrong time, wrong place. Just plain out of luck. Victims of a cruel fate. There are plenty more clichéd explanations of what befell two great sportsmen of the late 1950s, men who should have lit up the 1960s with their talent. The Scotsman Ian Black and the South African Gert Potgieter deserve to be lauded far beyond their own borders and yet, to most people younger than their own generation, they are not even famous within them. They both have cause to look back at their gold medals in the 1958 British Empire and Commonwealth Games and think of what might have been, of the further glory that would surely follow in future years. It never happened.

A car crash just before the Rome Olympics in 1960 nearly cost Potgieter his life. He was blinded in his left eye, lost a favourite's chance at an Olympic gold medal, and along with it any hope of continuing a winning streak in his event, the one-lap hurdles, that stood at 44 consecutive victories.

There is no saying how far Potgieter might have gone: although he had not competed against the top Americans in that Olympic year, his best time was markedly better than that in which Glenn Davis took the gold. Watching the American win in Rome from his hospital bed was 'the worst experience of my life' for Potgieter, who would have won a medal as a teenager in the 1956 Olympics, before his unbeaten run started, but for a stumble on landing after the last hurdle.

He had another handicap, one that he could never have overcome regardless of injury, and one that would have halted his run of victories soon enough. Potgieter was South African. Much as he hated apartheid, he could not argue against South Africa's banishment from world sport when they left the Commonwealth in 1961 and were kicked out of the Olympic movement in 1964. After Potgieter's second gold in Cardiff in 1958, in the 4 × 440 yard relay, no South African would win a Commonwealth Games track title until the next century.

Potgieter took risks and broke laws in working with black coaches and athletes during three decades of South Africa's sporting exile, and his efforts in trying to stop segregation in sport did bring him some recognition. In 1999 he was voted South Africa's athlete of the century.

Ian Black's is an altogether different story. He was a victim of his own success, of a quite astonishing lack of support from a school where he was made to feel 'a disgrace', and of a paucity of resources that made his achievements in swimming all the more remarkable. His many successes as a 16- and 17-year-old, including Commonwealth gold in Cardiff, made him Scotland's first winner of the BBC Sports Personality of the Year award in 1958, when he was also voted the world's best all-round swimmer.

Not everybody was impressed: Black's fame and glory as a schoolboy so irked his headmaster that the teenager was denied the chance to properly prepare for the 1960 Rome Olympics, and after finishing a highly creditable fourth when nowhere near fully fit, he gave up swimming. The reason cited by Black at the time was loss of motivation, but there was far more anguish in his decision, which, even half a century later, he is reluctant to discuss. Black, a fervent Christian, could not bear to be regarded as a 'whinger' and would not contemplate criticising David Collier, the headmaster who did so much to ruin his chances of winning many more gold medals.

In the view of one of his schoolmates and teammates, Black is 'the greatest swimmer Britain has ever produced'. That man is Athole Still, a multi-talented international swimmer, opera singer, and agent to the stars of sport and stage. He was a relay silver medallist with Black in Cardiff, swimming correspondent for *The Times*, and a television commentator on the sport. He co-wrote a book on swimming with the man more widely regarded as Britain's best, David Wilkie, the record-breaking Olympic, World and Commonwealth champion who – like Black – is a Scot. Still is best known within sport nowadays as an agent for, among others, Britain's greatest Olympian, Sir Steve Redgrave, and the former England football manager Sven-Göran Eriksson.

'It is a big regret for me that Ian Black has never had the kind of recognition he deserves,' said Still. 'People might say I am biased because I am close to him, but I know what I am talking about. Sport has been my life for 60 years, and I have watched swimming all over the world. In my view he was the best. He did things that I thought were impossible. For example, he had never in his life swum a 400 individual medley and in Cardiff, unpaced in a time trial in the new 55-yard pool, in the June after the Games, he broke the world record by more than four seconds. That was simply an incredible performance.'

Black was young and good-looking, and after his Commonwealth and European victories in 1958 he had a good chance of becoming Britain's first male gold medallist in Olympic swimming for more than 50 years. 'It's hard to imagine, but he had pop-star status at the time,' said Still. 'When he arrived in Cardiff for that record attempt he had to fight through the crowds. It was like being one of the Beatles. It's a pity that people only judge you on what you did in the Olympics. He was a god, he really was, and he came to earth in extremely unusual circumstances. There's a film in it, the story of Ian Black's life.'

Eighteen months before the Glasgow 2014 Games, Black took a telephone call from one of the administrators in Scottish sport who were calling former Commonwealth champions to check their availability for the baton relay and other events. Black asked the caller if she knew why his name was on their list. No. Did she even know what sport he had competed in? No. Black laughs about it now. He is loath to complain about the past, the disadvantages and lack of support that ruined his short but stunning sporting career. It is easy to imagine that it still hurts.

Ian Black was born in the far north of Scotland, where his father worked first as a local journalist, and then as a radio operator at airports in Inverness and Aberdeen. Black could always swim well and when, aged nine years and four months, he became the youngest competitor in the annual open-water race that followed the route of the Kessock ferry from Inverness to the Black Isle, people began to take notice. Athole Still, a pupil at Robert Gordon's College in Aberdeen and already an international swimmer, persuaded Black's parents to send Ian to the same school, as it had a pool, paid for by three former pupils who had clubbed together. Black enrolled in 1953 and came under the tutelage of Andy Robb, the college's pool manager who was also a very successful swimming instructor.

Within two years he had beaten Scotland's senior butterfly champion, and at 15 he was representing Britain. Swimming was televised live in the 1950s: Black soon became famous, as did his tartan dressing gown made from towels. He excelled academically and was, in the words of Still, 'very correct' in everything he did. 'He never swore or did the sort of things other lads might do. He looked down on people who misbehaved, but was never arrogant, quite the reverse. I remember walking down Union

Street in Aberdeen with him and he would walk on the inside, next to the shops, so people couldn't see him. He had a colossal shyness.'

All the while, Black's only training was in the school pool, 25 yards by 10, often with other boys splashing about in the water during their recreational swim. He had a key and could turn up, alone, at 6am. Black faced problems familiar to all of Britain's best swimmers at the time: poor facilities, lack of training time and little or no formal coaching. Talented teenaged swimmers elsewhere in the world, most notably in Australia and the United States, had countless advantages over Britain's best.

When Black was judged, controversially, to have finished fourth in the 400m Olympic final in Rome in 1960, the three men on the podium were those he considered his main rivals in freestyle: Murray Rose and John Konrads from Australia, and Tsuyoshi Yamanaka from Japan. 'I knew all about them, and the Aussies were well ahead of everybody else at the time,' said Black. 'Swimming was a very big sport in Australia, and the emphasis they placed on it made so much difference. Mostly it was the coaching, and the professional approach to conditioning. Everything here was run by well-intentioned amateurs.'

Tsuyoshi Yamanaka and Murray Rose were two years older than Ian Black, John Konrads a year younger. All three gained scholarships to the University of Southern California (USC), where elite swimmers had the very best of everything, and they competed against one another many times. Swimming was strictly amateur, but they had a professionally operated support system behind them. Later in life, when Black was teaching in Bahrain, he saw a film about the three of them. 'I just about wept,' he said.

Murray Rose, whose global fame was enhanced by the media's fascination with his strict vegetarian diet and especially his liking of seaweed, did not compete for Australia in the Commonwealth Games in Cardiff in 1958 but won four Olympic titles in 1956 and 1960, and three Commonwealth golds in Perth in 1962. Born in Birmingham, he moved to Australia as an infant when his family emigrated. His coach in his teenage years was Sam Herford, arguably the most influential figure in the swimming boom in Australia in the 1950s.

Herford led Australia's Olympians in 1956 and 1960, and the Commonwealth teams of 1958 and 1962, who between them won a small mountain of medals, 41 of them in Perth alone. When Herford stepped down from the Olympic team the man who took his place was Don Talbot, another of the world's greatest swimming coaches, and the first director of the famed Australian Institute of Sport (AIS). Talbot was John Konrads's coach. Konrads would have three hours of top-quality coached training before and after school every day.

Then there was the question of facilities. Melbourne had hosted the 1956 Olympics and the Australians excelled in the pool, topping the medals table, with Rose famously winning three freestyle golds as a 17-year-old. Throughout the 1950s, according to Australian Government records, Olympic pools were opening all over the country and 'local municipalities regarded an Olympic pool as a must-have, standard community facility'. There were dozens of them: by comparison, until the new Cardiff Empire Pool opened for the 1958 Games, Britain had only one. It was in Blackpool, hundreds of miles away from Black's home.

Making the best of what he had, and with the help of Robb, Ian Black nevertheless became a world-class swimmer by his middle teens, and was all but unbeatable (at least in Europe) at about the time of his seventeenth birthday in the summer of 1958. A list of highlights taken from British newspapers from April until September of that year features the following:

April: Black beats H. Weber of Germany, one of Europe's best butterfly swimmers, as a 16-year-old. This is 'the best long course swim ever achieved by a British swimmer'.

June: Black leads the Robert Gordon's College team to an easy victory in the national schools challenge cup.

July: At the Commonwealth Games Black swims 'close to world record time' in the last leg of the medley relay, taking Scotland from last place to fifth. He finishes behind Konrads twice, silver to the Australian's gold, in the 440 freestyle, and the 220 relay. When Black wins gold in the 220 yards butterfly, Andy Robb is thrown into the pool fully clothed, and almost the entire Australian team line up to congratulate Black. (On the same day Konrads wins the 1650 yards freestyle by more than half a minute in 'the finest example of distance swimming ever seen in Europe'.)

August: 'A near capacity crowd rose to its feet,' to cheer Black in the national championships in Blackpool, where his win by 20 seconds in the 440 yards freestyle is 'one of the greatest displays ever seen by a home swimmer'. Later, Black 'wrote a new page of swimming history' when he became the first man to win four national titles, two of them coming within half an hour of each other. He finished with five.

September: Black is in sensational form, setting records in the heats and taking three golds – 400m and 1500m freestyle and 200m butterfly – at the European Championships in Budapest, two of them within 20 minutes of each other. He is 'The Human Torpedo' and 'Golden Boy' in the headlines. Britain has never had a male swimmer in this class. On his return to Heathrow from Budapest 'loaded down with honours, gold medals and trophies', Black was a 'very shy teenager' who told the *Daily Express*, 'I just want to get off the train at Aberdeen in the morning and get quietly back to normal.'

Intriguingly, at the end of September 1958, Black was among 30 international swimmers who signed a letter addressed to 50 administrators of the Amateur Swimming Association, complaining about bad management, messed-up travel arrangements, poor facilities, lack of time for training, repeated changes in leadership and late amendments to competition schedules made to suit television broadcasters. 'We are tired of wondering,' they all said, 'what is going to go wrong next.' Meanwhile, in Australia, John Konrads, who had four Olympic-size pools within 10 miles of his home in the Sydney suburbs, would have put in another day's work with Don Talbot. In California, Murray Rose would be making use of the world-class facilities at the USC.

At the end of his *annus mirabilis*, there were more triumphs for Black. He was the Sports Writers' Association, now known as the Sports Journalists' Association sportsman of the year, voted by the country's top writers. He won the public's backing, too, in taking the prestigious annual award from the *Daily Express*, then the most respected mass-market newspaper for sport. The ceremony was televised and, according to the *Express*, was watched by 12 million. Finally, Black was interrupted in class at school to take a telephone call. It was the BBC on the line, telling him he had finished ahead of the England and Manchester United footballer Bobby Charlton, a survivor of the Munich air disaster that had claimed the lives of 23 people in February. As well as being the first Scot to take the honour, Black was the youngest ever winner of the BBC Sports Personality of the Year award.

These awards, looking back, perhaps contributed to Black's downfall. His photograph was often in the national press, he was always winning races on television, and even in 1959, when there were no major championships, he finished third in the BBC Personality voting. Headmaster Collier was not happy with his shy 'pop star'.

At a dinner for Robert Gordon's alumni, Collier said, 'While recognising the outstanding performances of this champion swimmer of ours, Ian Black, I cannot help deploring the fuss which has been made of him, while the solid achievements of pupils in the academic field and in services to the community receive relatively little recognition. It is a little trying to think of Gordon's College, with its more than 200 years of not undistinguished history, being known as Ian Black's school!'

Black was deeply hurt. The people of Aberdeen, and throughout Scotland, could barely believe it. Local newspapers criticised Collier, who had also written to Black's parents to say the school was there for education and nothing more. Collier responded to his critics by repeating and re-emphasising his comments at another dinner, this time in London. When he returned to college he sneaked up on Black, who had been training unscheduled at the pool, and demanded the return of his prefect's badge. Black walked out of Robert Gordon's, where he was no longer welcome, and sat his one remaining exam at the University of Aberdeen.

Black said, 'Yes, there was animosity between the headmaster and me. He never once gave me time off to go to an international meet. Far from being seen as somebody who brought great credit to the school I was made to feel a disgrace.'

Black attended the University of Aberdeen and continued to use the Robert Gordon's pool, under Robb's guidance, throughout 1959. But when it came to readying himself for the 1960 Olympics, and trying to catch Konrads, there was nowhere to train: the college had closed the pool for repairs. Black had swum a sensational time trial in February – faster than the time Murray Rose would register in winning the Olympic 400m gold – but now found himself 'at the mercy of Aberdeen council', who were asked for training time in the city's 25-yard municipal pool in Justice Mill Lane. They refused, and gave Black no priority whatsoever. The council offered half an hour during the changeover between public sessions. Otherwise, if Black wanted to use the pool for training, he would have to weave in and out of recreational swimmers. 'There might be 300 of them in the pool,' said Black, who pointed out that, when he won a medal or award of note, the council dignitaries were happy to invite him to lunch to mark the occasion.

So Black travelled to swim in an outdoor pool at Stonehaven. It was 18 miles each way and the unheated pool was heavily chlorinated, which, before the use of goggles, was a problem. 'The cold was impossible to bear,' said Still, and as a result Ian Black arrived at the Olympics three-quarters fit, at best. He had at least enjoyed one novelty: he had travelled to Hove in April, with Robb. In exchange for use of the pool for a week's training, Black would make an attempt to break the national record over 440 yards, which he duly did. That week, he said, was the only time in his life when he trained in a roped-off lane.

If Black had enjoyed great success in 1958, Konrads had done even better. He and his sister, Ilsa, were refugees from Latvia who became known to Australians as 'the Konrads kids'. Between them they set 16 world records in the first three months of 1958. John won three golds in

Cardiff, and Black was convinced he would be the man to beat in the 400m in Rome. Black knew he was well short of race fitness and withdrew from the butterfly, in which many thought he had a better chance of a medal. No British man had won a swimming gold since 1908 and Black went into the 400m freestyle more in hope than expectation. He stayed with Konrads all the way, but Rose went clear. Yamanaka was second, and then Konrads and Black touched together. There was no photo finish and, of the seven judges, three gave the verdict to Black, three to Konrads and one went for a dead heat. The officials arbitrarily decided Konrads had touched first and awarded him the bronze; Black got nothing. Konrads later won the 1500m gold.

There was a gold medal for Britain: Anita Lonsbrough won the 200m breaststroke. Lonsbrough had won two golds in Cardiff and would add three more, as well as a silver, in Perth in 1962 when she – like Black – was named BBC Sports Personality of the Year. Black was 'a dour character, very much Scottish rather than British,' she said. But he was right about the advantages the Australians had as the sport developed from the late 1950s. 'We would have liked to have been able to compete against them on an equal footing,' said Lonsbrough. 'It would have been good for our coaches to be paid, so we, like them, could have full-time coaches.'

Black's parents went to watch him compete in the Olympic Games in Rome. Robb had planned to be there, too, but headmaster Collier, true to form, would not allow him the time off, so his wife went instead. Black felt he had let down his family, his coach and his country. Never mind that he had been unable to train properly for months, or that the verdict of his race in *The Times* was, 'Keeping this sort of company for the first time, Black was far from disgraced.' He saw himself as a failure, and his swimming days were effectively over. Officially, he was concentrating on his studies until the following summer, but Black had had enough. He tried to return to competitive swimming for the 1962 Perth Commonwealth Games, but officially announced his retirement in June of that year, saying in a statement, 'The burning flame of ambition has dimmed and is practically non-existent.' He found it so difficult to talk about his 'shame' that, when he started working on a biography, he had to give up.

'All my life I've said nothing. For me personally … no, I'd better not say anything. There's no point in saying what might have happened. My father always said, "If you have to tell them, then you weren't really good enough." Never make excuses…' Eventually he began to explain. 'It was a frustration and a shame. I was so ashamed that I hadn't been able to produce the performance the Scottish people deserved. I didn't have any help at all. I knew why it had happened, why I had not won, but I just couldn't say it.

The Games' founding father, Melville Marks 'Bobby' Robinson. Without the efforts of the Canadian athletics coach and journalist, the first Empire Games in Hamilton, Ontario in 1930 would never have happened.

Precious McKenzie has friends in high places. The weightlifter, who won his first gold medal in 1966, bottom, is pictured with Princess Anne, top left, and the Queen in the 1970s, when he was at the height of his fame.

High jump heroine Dorothy Tyler, with Dick Fosbury at a Sports Journalists Association lunch in 2008, when she accused him and all who followed his style of being cheats.

Debbie Brill in action in 1985, top, and at the 1970 medal ceremony in Edinburgh, where the Queen had to disentangle the ribbon caught in her hair.

Victor Davis is unimpressed as Adrian Moorhouse, left, shows off his 100m breaststroke gold medal at the 1982 Games. Moorhouse and Davis did not speak to each other for years, then became close friends.

Ron Hill, having left a world-class field in his wake, finishes alone to win the 1970 marathon in Edinburgh and, below, shows off the gold medal in 2014. He still runs every day and intends to continue those daily runs 'until I die'.

Great champions of 1958. Gert Potgieter, hurdling to victory in Cardiff, and, bottom left, with his medals at home in South Africa in 2014; and Ian Black with his drenched coach Andy Robb, who was thrown in after Black's win in the butterfly.

Mike Bull and Mary Peters training in Belfast, bottom, before their double success at the 1974 Games in Christchurch; weightlifter George Newton, who like his teammate Precious McKenzie, emigrated to New Zealand after winning gold for England, and, top right, a Maori dance at the opening ceremony in the QEII Stadium.

'The best run I've ever seen' was Roger Bannister's verdict after Filbert Bayi, top, led all the way to break the 1500m world record in Christchurch; and Norm Scott Morrison, the Scottish 10,000m runner who was one of six British émigrés.

Emmanuel Ifeajuna, feted on his return from Vancouver, poses with a trophy awarded in Nigeria for his landmark success. The national hero was condemned to death by his 'friend' Emeka Ojukwu, leader of the short-lived Republic of Biafra.

Two of Australia's greatest sportswomen, who competed in different eras but became firm friends: Dawn Fraser with her coach, Harry Gallagher, in Cardiff in 1958; and Kathy Watt, top, after winning her second successive road race gold in 1994.

Marcus Stephen with President Obama and his wife, Michelle, in 2009 in New York. Stephen, pictured below with the great Oceania coach Paul Coffa, gave a speech to the United Nations during his presidency of Nauru.

The central characters of a dramatic afternoon in Vancouver in 1954: Roger Bannister after his famous mile victory; Jim Peters, in training for the marathon that was to be his last race; and Yvette Williams, who won two events at the same time.

Headline-makers of Edinburgh 1986: Liz Lynch (later McColgan), on her way to victory in the first women's 10,000m (right); and the larger-than-life Daily Mirror owner Robert Maxwell (above), with the eccentric Japanese billionaire Ryoishi Sasakawa.

The Friendly Games: Australian swimmers try on robes belonging to Ghanaian boxers in Cardiff at the 1958 Games, after which all athletes were invited, below, to an official reception hosted by London County Council.

Nobody wants to hear whinging and whining. I did start a comeback for Perth in 1962, but Andy Robb's wife had died and it destroyed him as a man, and I just gave up. How can you train with no coach, without facilities? It was impossible. Such a sad experience. All my career I was a boy, not a man. I was 17 in 1958 and it was all over when I was 19.

I do regret not having had the opportunity to do all that I might have done. Not for personal glory, but because I wanted to do it for Scotland. I have always been fiercely patriotic and I support Scotland in everything they do. I got a lot of support from ordinary people. For a spell I held the attention of the nation. That was important to me. People knew and recognised me, and the people of Scotland were proud of me. But I am very accepting of the situation I found myself in. I am a Christian, fervently so, and I just accept that things are working out as they should. I don't want to criticise Collier, the headmaster, he is dead now.'

After he won those awards, Black wanted to say 'thank you' to those who voted for him. Every fortnight from the start of 1959 he would travel with Robb all over Scotland. 'We went to every small place with a pool, even to people sitting on an upturned fish-box, to thank them for their votes. We went everywhere, giving demonstrations, meeting and greeting, and always to a full house. That was a great time.' Clearly, Black appreciated and thrived on support: and yet, from those in a position of influence who could do so much to help him, he had none.

He might have moved to warmer climes, to train with professional coaches. Immediately after his Cardiff gold medal there were reports of an offer from Australia, and a letter arrived from the United States. It would have been a wonderful opportunity to go to either country but, said Black, 'Why would I do it? I was only 17, just a boy and too young for university. Besides, there was nothing formal.' The letter was from John Henricks, a triple gold medallist for Australia in the 1954 Commonwealth Games, double champion in the 1956 Olympics and multiple freestyle record holder who was then at the University of Southern California, with Murray Rose. He wrote to tell Black that USC would love to have him. The Australian offer, according to the *Express*, was from an unnamed businessman who 'would sponsor Black through high school and university, guarantee his business career and see that he gets top coaching'. The real story, as reported by the *Aberdeen Press & Journal* (now called *The Press and Journal*), was that an offer had been made by Harry Gallagher, the man who had coached Henricks in Australia, and whose top swimmer at the 1958 Games was one of the greatest of all, Dawn Fraser. John Konrads would have welcomed him. 'We'd love to have him with us in Australia,' he said after Black's butterfly victory.

There was no money to be made from swimming and, as Black pointed out, Collier was right to put academic achievement first, even if he was wrong to make the point in such a belittling way. 'The priority was to study and get a university degree, to provide a life and help to bring up a family. The emphasis was on that.' He would stay in Aberdeen to study, and would train at the college. Until the pool was closed, at least.

If Ian Black was in the wrong place at the wrong time, the opposite was true of 'the Konrads kids'. John and Ilsa learned to swim while staying in a migrants' hostel soon after their arrival from Latvia, and were very good at it. When John started at Revesby Primary School in the Sydney suburbs, he asked classmates if there were ever any swimming races. No, they said, but why not go and see Mr Talbot in Class 4 – he coaches swimming. 'Mr Talbot' was Don Talbot, who later left teaching to become one of the world's leading coaches, and who took John and Ilsa under his wing in 1953–4.

Talbot was keen on interval training – swim at speed and then rest, and repeat – and was 'a stickler for technique', said Konrads. There would be a session on technique every week, usually on a Monday. 'The Americans were ahead of us, and they were swimming about three miles a day in training. We started swimming six miles a day, or more, and we got the jump on them in terms of sheer fitness. Right from the beginning I had the ability to push myself.'

Konrads could empathise with Black's dislike of training in a busy pool. It was the same at Bankstown Pool, where Talbot worked with another top coach, Frank Guthrie. 'The temperature would be over 100°F at times and the pool was very busy,' said Konrads. 'We would dive in at the middle and every time we came to a bobbing head we'd treat it like a water polo ball and duck it under. That way we soon cleared some space.'

Konrads was a teenage sensation. He was in the training squad for the 1956 Olympics in Melbourne and was selected, at the age of 14, as a reserve but, much to Talbot's annoyance, did not compete. On his arrival in Cardiff two years later, having set all those world records, he was 'on top of the world' and was not aware of Black. That changed when the Scot pushed him close in the 440 yards.

When, more than 50 years later, Konrads heard what had happened to Black, he was shocked. It was a 'cruel story', one that highlighted the academic snobbery that pervaded many private schools at the time. While Black had been made to feel 'a disgrace' by headmaster Collier, Konrads was the hero of his state school, Sydney Technical High School. 'The headmaster, Harry Brown, was so proud of the fact that one of his kids was a champion that he lobbied for me to be School Captain. It was quite the opposite of Ian's school.'

After the Rome Olympics Konrads went to the USC, but his performances flattened out rather than improved. 'I discovered Californian girls, and Budweiser beer,' he said. 'Suddenly I had a social life.' He still won plenty of races but his gold medal days were over.

In 2003, in his biography, Don Talbot wrote that John Konrads would have won an Olympic silver medal in Melbourne in 1956 had he been selected for the 1500m. 'That made sense,' said Konrads. Sixteen months after Rose's 1956 world record at that distance, Konrads smashed it by 31 seconds – 'nearly a whole lap'. What, in retrospect, might Black have won, with more support and better resources? Athole Still has a strong opinion. 'Had he been properly fit and properly prepared in Rome, to the same level as his rivals, he would have won the 400m freestyle, the 1500m freestyle, and maybe the 200m butterfly.'

Further confirmation of Black's ability came from Harry Gallagher, the world-renowned coach of Dawn Fraser and the Australian Olympic team, who recalled the 1958 Games. 'Ian Black came through the hard way in Scotland,' said Gallagher at his Brisbane home in 2013. 'He was an exceptional talent, world-class, and with better coaching here he would have made it right to the very top. Perhaps what he needed most was a new challenge, a new goal. He had outgrown his coach.'

Black was not interested in 'what ifs'. He quit competitive swimming, emigrated to Canada and took up teaching. He married, had four children and worked in Canada, Hong Kong and Bahrain before eventually settling back in the north of Scotland. He became head of a primary school in Elgin and in 1990 took on a new role as head of the Junior School at a place he knew well: Robert Gordon's College. Sadly, on the day Black took the job, welcomed back by the school that had effectively kicked him out all those years ago, Andy Robb collapsed and died.

Black took after-school swimming classes, just as Robb had done, and remembers spotting a young lad who 'was very good in primary school, when he was 10 years old'. Black advised the boy's parents that their son could go far, and he did. His name was David Carry, winner in 2006 of two gold medals in the Commonwealth Games, and now a director of Swimming Scotland. 'I didn't coach him, but I can claim to have discovered him,' said Black.

In 2003 Black retired. He does not even have any medals to remind him of his glory days. They were stolen – all of them – when his house was burgled in 1986, while he was working overseas. Konrads even had the edge over Black in this respect, too. He had his Olympic gold medal stolen from his Melbourne home in 1984. A quarter of a century later he got it back when a woman who had bought it at a bric-a-brac sale in Brisbane tried to sell it. Black has no medals, only memories. His final word on his remarkable life in and out of sport: 'I just accept that things are working out as they should.' ·

Two days before Ian Black's victory and Andy Robb's big splash in Cardiff in 1958, Gert Potgieter won the 440 yards hurdles on the athletics track. Four days later he was on top of the podium again, as part of the team that won the 4 x 440 relay. The wait for South Africa's next track gold medal at the Commonwealth Games was a lot longer: it was 44 years and three days, by which time the country had a black president, a new anthem, a multiracial team and a new outlook on life. The man who ended the wait was Mbulaeni Mulaudzi, an exceptional 800m runner who followed his Manchester 2002 gold medal with a string of achievements. At the World Championships he won bronze in 2003 and gold in 2009; he was flag bearer for South Africa at the 2004 Olympics, where he won a silver; and he became the first black South African athlete to be ranked number one in the world.

For most of those 44 years South African athletes were unable to compete internationally because of apartheid. Internal policies forbade the selection of non-white athletes, and the rest of the sporting world would have little or nothing to do with a country that was banished from the Olympics and Commonwealth Games for more than three decades.

Potgieter was an unlikely campaigner against apartheid, given his background. He was an Afrikaner policeman, and a sporting hero to the white establishment. At school he excelled in rugby, athletics, diving and gymnastics, representing his state in all four sports. He chose the police, which had a good reputation for athletics, over the military for his national service, and he took to hurdling astonishingly quickly. Within a year of his first race he was running in an Olympic final, in Melbourne in 1956. 'At the last hurdle I did get the feeling that I could be in for a medal but I approached it with the "wrong" leg and the result was disastrous. I hit the hurdle with my knee and fell. I got up and finished sixth.' Potgieter was encouraged rather than distraught. 'As a 19-year-old, the Olympics was a fantastic experience. Being in a good position at the last hurdle I felt encouraged, as I was still a youngster and had several years in front of me.'

He still had a rugby career ahead of him, too, but only for a few months. Potgieter played at centre for Northern Transvaal (now the Blue Bulls), and might have risen to international standard, but a serious neck injury in 1957 ended his days as a rugby player. From now on it was athletics all the way.

With the help of a German coach who lived in South Africa, Jos Sirakis, Potgieter changed his stride pattern. He would take one hurdle with his left leg, the next with his right, and after four months of intensive training, he started setting world records in 1957. 'The media said this 14-pace rhythm was only a flash in the pan, but today most of the hurdlers are applying this method,' said Potgieter, who ran a 440 hurdles world record in the Cardiff final, and won the 'best athlete' award at the first invitational World Athletics Championship in Helsinki in 1959. On his birthday, 16 April 1960, he again broke the 440 yards hurdles world record. A few months later he had run his last race.

South African, Greek and Japanese athletes had gathered at the German town of Edenkoben to train and compete in preparation for the Olympics in Rome. On Friday 10 August, three days after his last hurdles victory and two weeks before the Olympics, a journalist drove three athletes to a local concert in a Borgward Isabella, a stylish, sporty German sedan. One of the South African sprinters asked to drive the car home, with the journalist in the passenger seat and Potgieter in the back with his girlfriend and future wife, the German long jumper Renate Junker. The car skidded out of control on a bend, hit a tree, and Potgieter took the worst of the impact. The others escaped uninjured: he awoke in a Heidelberg hospital several hours later. He had lost an eye, his Olympic dream was over: his doctor told him he would never participate in sport again.

'Wow – what a disappointment when I realised I would not be able to compete in Rome! I had the best time in the world, I was in top condition, and as I watched Glenn Davis winning the gold in a slower time than my best, on television, so many things went through my mind. Why did this happen to me at this crucial time of my life? I really felt hopeless, useless, melancholy, negative, absolutely down in the dumps, with no self-confidence to tackle the struggles of future life. But, as the days went by and I came back to South Africa I studied the medical reports and realised that had it not been for the excellent physical condition I was in, I could have died. So I made up my mind to take up sport again, despite what the doctor said, and set my mind on the decathlon, as I had had this in mind before the accident.

'Well, it was hell – my balance was totally out, I was uncertain of my step and when a ball was thrown at me I was catching too quick or too late. My depth perception was all wrong. Gradually my balance improved and playing volleyball, mini-cricket, soccer, and touch rugby, which required quick reflexes and reactions, became a regular activity. Six years later, in 1966, I won the South African decathlon championship. I had reached my goal and decided to quit competitive sport. Even now, at 76 and blind in the left eye, my balance is good and I have no problem with hand–eye coordination. I still do regular exercises and play ball games, and it's wonderful to experience how the will to do something, and mastering of sporting skills, can positively influence self-confidence.'

The name Potgieter featured again in hurdling when his two daughters both won the national schools championship. His son was also a national champion, in the pole vault. Renate, a keen painter and pianist whom Potgieter met at an international meet in 1959, runs fitness classes for senior citizens, and one of their daughters is a physiotherapist, so Potgieter has every opportunity to stay in good shape. If his overcoming of those physical challenges showed Potgieter's dedication and fortitude, there has been a great deal more to his life than winning mental and physical battles. His biggest fight was for equality in South African sport.

'Through my international participation and experiences with black athletes abroad and locally since 1956, I strongly came under the impression that our apartheid system was inhuman,' he said. The United Nations agreed, although it would be many years later before they officially said so. 'Our thinking in the sporting world, from a human point of view, was far ahead of our politicians. The majority wish from the sporting fraternity in South Africa, by far, was that non-whites should absolutely have the same rights and opportunities as whites.'

Potgieter befriended black Africans in Cardiff, as he had done elsewhere, and in 1959 he was called in by the national police commissioner. Gert had been to Rhodesia (now Zimbabwe) to run against the American world record holder, Josh Culbreath, the Olympic bronze medallist in 1956 who had taken advantage of Potgieter's stumble. 'I beat Josh and, as often happens after a race, the participants posed for a photo. We would stand with our arms around each other's neck or shoulders. The photo with me and Josh hugging each other appeared on the front page of a South African magazine for the black population. I was called in by the Police Commissioner and although he treated me politely his request was that I should avoid being pictured socially with blacks. I told the Commissioner that this kind of behaviour was common in sport, that it showed respect and promoted friendship. The military, police, and politicians were handling me with kid gloves as I was at that time a "hero" and they were careful to avoid conflict with me, as it would receive media coverage.' Potgieter built up friendships with several black runners from the United States and a number of Commonwealth countries, among them Culbreath, Tom Robinson (Bahamas), Mike Agostini (Trinidad), Melville Spence and George Kerr (Jamaica) and Bartonjo Rotich (Kenya).

He had a further setback in 1961 when he represented South Africa at the inauguration of the International Olympic Academy in Olympia, which made him even more determined to end segregation in sport. On his return from Greece he attempted to set up a non-racial Olympic Academy, but was refused permission by Frank Waring, the sports minister, because the body's constitution called for equality and non-discrimination. Before the next Games, South Africa were booted out of the Olympic movement.

Potgieter studied physical education in Cologne in 1962, and left the police in 1963. Over a period of many years he would use his status to help victims of discrimination. In 1973 he broke the law when he appointed a black coach, James Mokoka, to a full-time senior post at the National Sports Foundation. Potgieter was director of the Foundation and because of his connections, Mokoka – an athletics specialist from Soweto – was allowed to work alongside white coaches. 'He was very bold in appointing me, it was a great surprise that a black man should be given such a job,' said Mokoka, who had first met Potgieter in 1964, the year when Nelson Mandela was sentenced to life imprisonment. 'Others might have wished to give sports jobs to black men, but none except Gert Potgieter was bold enough to do it.' Forty years later, James Mokoka is still helping out with coaching in the townships.

The appointment was illegal because of apartheid laws that, in the year of Mokoka's appointment, were described by the United Nations as a crime against humanity. 'Those were tough apartheid days, with strict laws, and I had James share offices with other white sport coaches in the middle of Pretoria, which was unheard of because of the Group Areas Act,' said Potgieter. 'He had the same privileges, such as motor car, travel allowances, and salary.' Potgieter turned to an old acquaintance, Pik Botha, an influential politician who would later become South Africa's foreign minister. 'He contacted the chairman of the Pretoria Municipality Board who then informed me to carry on but to keep it quiet. Sometimes it's who you know...'

It did not always work. In 1973, the same year as Mokoka's appointment, Potgieter was thrown out of a government minister's home when he went to discuss the setting up of a non-racial academy. He accused the minister, Piet Koornhof, of double standards, as Koornhof had stated in a recent radio interview that apartheid was dead. 'He reacted extremely negatively and said that the Springbok emblem and sports clubs should remain only for whites. I had a tape recording of his radio speech in my bag.'

Potgieter had many fruitless meetings with the ministers of education and sport, and became 'an embarrassment to our government by confronting them on human rights'. He founded the first non-racial

Committee on School Sport in 1980, and would take black and white athletes to Europe on different planes. 'Once we landed in Frankfurt, Vienna or Brussels, we mixed – the athletes always mixed spontaneously with absolutely no racial incidents.' He was invited to lecture on sport and education in Belgium, Austria and Italy, and as a result of international press coverage he was called in by the minister of education, Gerrit Viljoen, and told to disband his organisation and stop all school athletics activities.

For 20 years from 1978 Gert was director of sport and recreation at the University of Pretoria. In this role he introduced sport management and coaching courses in the townships through an outreach programme. In 1989 he was finally able to establish a non-racial Olympic Academy of South Africa, of which he was chair, and at their first conference in 1990 delegates arrived from all over the world to discuss such subjects as 'Sport and human rights' and 'Ethics and youth sport', which would have been unthinkable a few years earlier. He was president, for 20 years, of the Sport Council in Gauteng North, and organised the national youth sport programme to celebrate the inauguration of Nelson Mandela as president of South Africa in 1994. The following year he founded Altus Sport, a non-profit organisation whose aim is to use sport to provide a better lifestyle for disadvantaged young men and women, and to take coaches to primary schools and township communities.

In 2012 Gert Potgieter stepped down from his administrative duties to focus on Altus Sport, after 51 years in management, coaching, lecturing, writing sport publications and establishing structured sport in the townships. There is still much to be done. 'Our athletics administration is in a bad state, we only have a few qualified coaches, and our black athletes are not being introduced to the more technical events such as hurdling, shot-put, discus, pole vault and javelin. Our golf stars such as Gary Player, Louis Oosthuizen and Ernie Els do run academies for young black golfers but much more could be done in so many sports.'

He looks back with pride over half a century of hard work in sport, and going back to his days as a competitor he still has very fond and vivid memories of the 1958 Cardiff Commonwealth Games.

'I pulled a hamstring three weeks before leaving for Cardiff, and two days before our departure I had to take part in a fitness test by running a 440-yard flat race. I ran a bad time as I could not give maximum effort, but I was informed that I was finally selected. The local press wrote that I should go only as a member of the relay team as I was not fit for the hurdles.

'Meeting the Duke of Edinburgh was a wonderful occasion. I found him pleasant, friendly and he certainly knew sport. The general public were really great – most supportive, friendly and helpful. Their hospitality was outstanding. I knew about the Welsh singing talent and bought a long-play record which I still have today.'

There was an unusual incident before his golden moment. 'We were called to the start, and when the Canadian runner stripped he discovered he did not have his running shorts on. He had to stand there in his underpants while his manager went off to bring him a pair of shorts. While we were waiting for him, the discus throwers were called to the rostrum and our Stephanus du Plessis received the gold medal. Our anthem was played while our flag was hoisted. This was a real booster for me, and I forgot about my troublesome hamstring and my opponent in his underpants.

'I always loved to run in lane two or three and hoped that the best rivals would be in the outside lanes as there are physical and psychological advantages. Here I drew lane five and felt a little discouraged but only for a short while as I saw David Lean, of Australia, my biggest rival, walking to lane six. I wanted to pass David as soon as possible, which I did, and over the last hurdle I could hear the loud applause of the spectators. I did not expect a world record and it came as a very pleasant surprise. We also did not expect to win the 4 × 440y relay.

'It's so long ago, yet it's still fresh in the memory. The wonderful hospitality, warm applause and encouragement by the spectators, the condition of the track, my world record being the first one on the track, flattering and positive media coverage, great friends made, the outstanding atmosphere in and around the stadium, meeting Prince Philip, excellent all-round Games organisation, my personal best times, two gold medals… The Cardiff Games were the highlight of my athletic career, for sure!'

7

Exodus

'The Games were great – let's go and live in New Zealand!'

The Games in Christchurch provided such a welcome escape from the desperate gloom engulfing the United Kingdom in 1974 that six British competitors went back for more. They emigrated to New Zealand.

When a jumbo jet carrying members of seven British teams flew into Heathrow in the first week of February 1974, the many Commonwealth Games competitors on board might have thought that they were completing a journey from heaven to hell.

The athletes who represented England, Scotland, Northern Ireland, Wales, Jersey, Guernsey and the Isle of Man, had been away in the New Zealand summer for three weeks enjoying themselves at what, by common consensus, were the friendliest Games ever staged.

On the day the plane landed the Irish Republican Army (IRA) bombed a coach carrying off-duty soldiers and their relatives on the M62 motorway. Twelve people died, among them an entire family: Corporal Clifford Houghton of the Royal Regiment of Fusiliers, his wife Linda and their sons Lee, 5, and Robert, 2.

That was described as 'the worst IRA outrage on the British mainland' by newspapers who had several opportunities to revise their view in the remaining months of 1974. The IRA bombed the Houses of Parliament and the Tower of London in the summer, and pubs in Guildford, Woolwich and Birmingham in October and November. Twenty-one people died and 182 were injured in the Birmingham explosions.

There was more to worry about. Industrial action by miners left Britain so short of coal that the prime minister, Edward Heath, put the entire country on a three-day week starting on New Year's Day. It would last until early March, by which time Heath was out of office. He was ousted in the first of two general elections within eight months. The economy was in recession, unemployment steadily rose throughout the year and inflation was running at about 17 per cent.

Among the newspaper headlines the morning after that plane touched down were '420,000 could be laid off' and 'Call to abort babies'. The first was about the threat of further strikes in the energy industry. The second concerned a plea by a Labour councillor in Hull for compulsory abortions in a part of the city so deprived 'it is unfit for children to be born in'.

There was misery elsewhere in the world. Countless lives were still being lost in the Vietnam War, which would not end until the following year. Watergate was growing 'from a political scandal to a national tragedy' in the words of Richard Nixon who, in August, would become the first president of the United States to resign from office. Patty Hearst was kidnapped by urban guerrillas in California. Hundreds of Chileans were tortured and killed by the new regime of General Pinochet. In the tenth year of Nelson Mandela's imprisonment South Africans were told by their prime minister that 'one man, one vote' would never happen. In the week of the athletes' return West German police arrested 14 suspected terrorists who supported the Baader-Meinhof group. Seventeen months earlier the country had suffered its most infamous terrorist atrocity, the Munich Massacre, when Palestinian gunmen attacked the Israeli team in the athletes' village at the Olympic Games. Seventeen people died.

So, how did New Zealand compare? Security was not even a feature on the budget for the Christchurch Games when the first plans had been drawn up six years earlier. Now, because of Munich, there were strict checks and double-checks of credentials when athletes, officials and journalists arrived in New Zealand. For a while, that is, until Christchurch grew into the most relaxed, informal, friendly, welcoming Games ever staged. If Edinburgh 1970 was first to be known as 'The Friendly Games', Christchurch went a step further. Their masterstroke was the 'host families' idea. Local families of all ages and sizes volunteered to 'adopt' athletes for the duration of the Games. The competitors were given an address where they could pop in for a chat over a cup of tea or a beer, watch television, meet the neighbours and escape from the intensity of training and competition.

The friendliness was taken to another level at the farewell party, as the Christchurch organisers recorded in a very matter-of-fact style on page 331 of their official post-Games report. 'Competitors not accompanied by wives or fiancées were catered for by some 300 girls specially selected to act as hostesses.' This report also stated that the partygoers enjoyed one another's company. Just how far this enjoyment went is left open to the imagination. Perhaps wisely, journalists were not invited.

The English swimmer Steve Nash, a relay bronze medallist, was particularly struck by the number of women at that closing party. 'I defy any English or British team before or since to say they enjoyed themselves as much as we did,' he said. 'The party was attended by half the population of Christchurch.' Decades later, he said, he looked back and wondered 'was that three-week period just a great dream or what?'

According to the *NZ Listener*, Christchurch 1974 was 'Woodstock in tracksuits'. To the *Observer*, in London, it was 'The land where all is fun and games and happiness.' Sports editor Chris Brasher, the former international athlete, said Christchurch was 'a haven in a troubled world'. While the citizens of wintry Britain feared a fuel shortage and financial woe, visitors to Christchurch feasted in high summer on Canterbury lamb and fresh strawberries. Another journalist reminisced about going to the opera in his shorts.

The England athletics officials still managed to make an official complaint – about their 'noisy neighbours from the Jamaican women's team' who were having such a good time they kept the English athletes awake all night. William Young, the Australian team manager, was shouted down when he complained about over-boisterous behaviour in the presence of the royal family at the closing ceremony. The sight of athletes climbing on to the two Land Rovers carrying the Queen, the Duke of Edinburgh, Princess Anne and her husband, Captain Mark Phillips, was 'a disgrace to amateur sport' he said, but even the Queen effectively told him to shut up, saying there was no need for anyone to apologise for 'a spontaneous and honest expression of feeling'.

Everybody was won over, even those who had feared the worst when they first saw the venues for some of the sports. Wrestling was staged at the town hall, Woolston Working Men's Club hosted the bowls and Canterbury Court was home to the boxing. This was a sheep auction hall that was also used for needlework and food displays during the local agricultural fair. The venues drew praise for their 'wonderfully unpretentious charm', but British newspapermen were not impressed. Ian Wooldridge, in the *Daily Mail*, predicted 'an imminent disaster is at hand'.

Wooldridge soon changed his mind, and was asked afterwards to write for the organising committee's official report on the tenth Games. The only disaster, he said, had been his own prediction. 'Two weeks later almost every journalist, most officials, and a large majority of the competitors were declaring the Christchurch Games the friendliest, the most efficient and generally the best they had yet attended. They made half a worldful of friends.'

The Times described the Games hosts as 'the most generous, helpful, hospitable people in the world'. On the day after the closing ceremony their correspondent, Neil Allen, wrote, 'At least a dozen members of the United Kingdom teams, conscious of the grey land which awaits them on return, are seriously talking about emigrating here. I have never known sporting guests to pay such a compliment.' His information came from Sandy Duncan, honorary secretary of the Commonwealth Games Federation.

It was not just talk. Six of them had such a good time in Christchurch, and such a grim existence when they returned to all those British woes, that they later left for good. They took themselves and, if they had families of their own, their wives and children to live in New Zealand.

The man who best articulated why they did it is one of those 12, who – after a period of reflection – decided not to move. Dave Bedford was one of the biggest names at the Games, the 10,000m world record holder who arrived early to acclimatise and spent Christmas in New Zealand.

'Coming out of the gloom and despondency of that British winter, and being transported to what appeared to be paradise had a massive effect on people's feelings,' Bedford said. 'Most of us were in our early twenties, it was the first time we'd been to an event held on the other side of the world and, in the middle of our winter, the sun was shining. All the planets were aligned. You could leave the problems of the world behind and start again. I would think a lot more than 12 people talked about moving.'

His recollection was of a society where recreation was very important. 'One of the locals told me that if the sun's shining you've got to go sailing. You wouldn't call in sick, you'd tell the boss you were off sailing and you'd make up the time later. It was a wonderful attitude to life, taking advantage of the sea and the mountains.'

The athletes' village was 'an absolute riot, so lively, so fun,' and 'the social side of the Games was absolutely astonishing'. Bedford was lucky with his host family, too. 'The guy was a little older than me, nearly 30, and was a New Zealand All Black. He loaned me a motor scooter and we went off shooting and fishing one time, camped out for a long weekend, the sort of thing you could do so easily over there.

'The host families were a great idea by the organisers. They welcomed us, supported us, and it really made the locals feel they were a part of the Games as well as giving us an incredibly warm welcome.' Bedford made lasting friendships with New Zealand runners Dick Quax, Rod Dixon and John Walker. He had a troubled relationship with the British press at the time and felt 'at peace with myself' in New Zealand, which he described as 'the best country of them all'.

'When I got back I reappraised the situation,' he said. He feared that if he did move he would very quickly lose contact with his friends and family.

Even making a phone call was 'a very big deal down at the Post Office'. Eventually he decided to stay in Britain. Later, with Chris Brasher, he helped to develop the London Marathon into one of the world's great races.

Keenest of all to emigrate was Bedford's friend Keith Falla, a middle-distance runner from Guernsey who, tragically, was killed soon after moving. Falla, a popular athlete who represented England as a junior, ran the 800m and 1500m when Guernsey first competed in the Games in 1970. He flew to New Zealand late in 1973 to prepare for Christchurch, trained with Bedford and John Walker, fell in love with the country and emigrated with his wife, Caroline. In May 1975, jogging home after a training session in Waikato, he was run down on the road. He died 30 minutes later. 'He was just shy of his 27th birthday,' said his brother Stuart, an official in the Guernsey Commonwealth Games team who still organises a memorial run for Keith every Easter. 'He loved New Zealand, and sent letters saying how he really felt at home there.'

Another of the émigrés also died before his time in New Zealand. Morgan Moffat, a Scottish bowls player who won a fours bronze in Christchurch, moved with his wife and young family. He competed for New Zealand at two Commonwealth Games and won a triples world title for them in 1988. Kerry Clark, chief executive of New Zealand Bowls and a gold medallist in 1974, said, 'I rated him the best team player for New Zealand throughout the eighties. Sadly, he had a hereditary heart disease problem which had affected the male line of his family. His father and grandfather both passed away in their late 40s and he did the same.'

Weightlifter George Newton, three times a gold medallist for England and twice an Olympian at featherweight and lightweight, left Britain on New Year's Day 1975. 'I met a woman in Christchurch and fell in love,' he recalled nearly 40 years later. Newton married that woman, Sandra, and they raised three sons in Christchurch.

Newton, from Guyana, moved in his teens to London, where he qualified as an electrician and worked on the railways. He trained in Bethnal Green and Putney, and won golds at the Perth, Edinburgh and Christchurch Games in 1962, 1970 and 1974, with a silver in 1966 at Kingston. Despite his success he feels he was a victim of racial discrimination in Britain. 'I never got any recognition, never seemed to gain promotion,' said Newton. 'It was discrimination, definitely. New Zealand offered me much better opportunities.' Newton came fourth in the 1978 Games lifting for New Zealand at the age of 43 and was still lifting weights at home to keep in shape in his late seventies. He and Sandra have 15 grandchildren and a comfortable home. He has no regrets about his move.

Precious McKenzie (see Chapter 2), who also won his third Commonwealth title in Christchurch, was the best-known of the six émigrés. He was more than a popular weightlifter: the 4ft 10in flyweight was a celebrity 'strongman' who famously hoisted Muhammad Ali above his head at a dinner in London at the end of 1974. He set a record by winning a fourth gold, this time for New Zealand, in the 1978 Games in Edmonton, watched by the Queen and the Duke of Edinburgh.

Norman Scott-Morrison, who ran for Scotland, adopted the more antipodean 'Norm' after moving to New Zealand in 1975. Echoing Bedford's views, he said, 'Leaving your friends is not easy. You give up quite a lot when you emigrate.'

He need not have worried about leaving his family back in Britain: they followed him out to New Zealand. He met Pauline, his future wife, in Auckland and when they married in 1976 his sister visited, loved the country, and emigrated. His parents spent long months on visits, and when the grandchildren came along they, too, moved to New Zealand. 'They were in their late sixties, early seventies,' said Scott-Morrison, now a grandfather himself. 'My father played bowls for Scotland and I play a lot of bowls now.'

Scott-Morrison was a teacher. As a junior athlete he had been coached by Gordon Pirie, the great British runner who set five world records in the 1950s. Pirie had been to New Zealand and told Scott-Morrison that he intended to move there, which he later did. 'Maybe he first put the idea of New Zealand in my mind,' said Scott-Morrison, 'but when I was thinking about emigration in the early 1970s I was thinking of Australia or Canada. I just loved the Christchurch Games so I resigned from my job and came out here instead. The host families were so welcoming, it was so friendly. When I arrived it was known here as God's Own Country, the land of milk and honey.' The New Zealand economy was booming but, said Morrison, 'as soon as I moved it started going in the other direction'.

The price of petrol more than doubled in a year because of the global energy crisis, and New Zealand's post-war economic boom came to a halt. 'Financially, I probably would have done better in Britain or Australia, but in terms of lifestyle you can't beat New Zealand. People had more land, more space. It's a wonderful place to bring up a family.'

Scott-Morrison had no idea that so many British competitors had moved after Christchurch. 'It was a very personal individual decision. I only met Precious McKenzie by chance after his move.' He also bumped into Steve Hollings, an English steeplechaser who took on a senior job at the University of Auckland and held many posts in New Zealand athletics. Hollings, whose room-mate in Christchurch was Brendan Foster, returned to visit his host family several years later.

'They were lovely people, an elderly couple and their daughter. I'd just go round there and have a cup of tea and a chat during the Games, and I was made to feel like a celebrity. They put on a barbecue one day and invited the whole street along. You could genuinely feel part of a different culture.'

Hollings was lecturing in physical education at the University of Liverpool at the time of the Games and was looking for another position. Early in 1975 he spotted an advertisement for director of physical education in Auckland. While he was in Rouen, at a France v Britain international, he received a telegram inviting him to an interview in New Zealand. 'I went out for 24 hours and back again, got offered the job and emigrated with my wife and nine-month-old daughter in February 1976. If I hadn't been to Christchurch I wouldn't even have applied.'

He became heavily involved in Athletics New Zealand as director of coaching, high performance manager and statistician, travelling with teams all over the world. He also coached Samoa's athletics team at the 2008 Olympics in Beijing, and has recently finished a PhD on the transformation of elite junior talent into successful seniors.

What helped to persuade him to move was one memorable day trip on the Sunday before the Games started. He joined the 1970 and 1974 marathon champions, Ron Hill and Ian Thompson, and Hill's friend John Mills, a British athletics fan who had emigrated to New Zealand. Mills drove them in his Volkswagen Beetle from Christchurch to Mount Cook, five hours away, with lunch at the famous Hermitage Hotel.

'It was a beautiful clear day, cloudless skies all the way, and the views of Mount Cook and the Tasman Glacier were stunning. It stuck with me. I said to myself "One day I'm going to bring my wife here," and I did. The cleanness, the variety of the landscape – it was all so good.'

In Britain, on the Monday morning after Hollings's Mount Cook trip, the main headlines made grim reading. An Ulster Defence Regiment captain had been murdered by the IRA, there was a threat of further industrial action by the train drivers and an attempt by unions to bring an end to the three-day week. There was also a report from the New Zealand High Commission in London. In the first two weeks of 1974 inquiries about emigrating from Britain had risen by 250 per cent compared to the previous year. More than 9000 people had been in touch by phone, letter and in person, all with the same request: get me out of here.

Of the lucky six Commonwealth Games émigrés, none ever voiced any regrets. How about Dave Bedford: had he ever wondered what might have been? 'Yes, I have, and then I've swiftly moved on. When you're in your mid-60s you're just happy to be alive.'

David Bedford played a major part in the Games being such a huge success on the athletics track, even if it was at his own personal cost. He was a strong favourite to win the opening race of the Games, the 10,000m. While he was a great runner against the clock, he had failed in big races before. It happened in Christchurch and a New Zealander profited. The country went wild and the party mood took hold immediately.

The other main contenders besides Bedford, the world record holder, were David Black, also of England, Scotland's Ian Stewart, who had won the 5000m in 1970, and Richard Juma of Kenya. New Zealand's Dick Tayler, coached by the great Arthur Lydiard, was in good form but was rated even by one of his own teammates as a no-hoper. Tayler suffered from arthritis that rapidly worsened after the Games. Within a year his running career would be over. 'I felt helpless and got very low,' he said decades later. 'It took years for me to get my life back on to an even keel.' What a contrast to Friday 25 January 1974.

The race developed into one of the most famous in New Zealand athletics history. Bedford was jostled around by Juma and his two Kenyan teammates. After 'a catalogue of tactical errors', according to his press critics, he finished fourth. Tayler bided his time behind all the trouble, the excitement rising to such a pitch when he came through to lead that one spectator collapsed and died. Tayler's joyous celebration as he crossed the line ahead of Black and Juma was voted, in 1999, his country's favourite TV sport moment. It was the first major sporting event broadcast in colour in New Zealand: Tayler was suddenly a household name throughout the nation.

'It was a very rough race and Bedford obviously got upset,' said Tayler, who sat back 50 metres behind the trouble. While Bedford dropped away Tayler gained on the leaders and the crowd responded. 'They picked me up and carried me along,' he said. With half a lap to go Tayler took off and the gold medal was his. The Games had started spectacularly and there was much, much more to come, including a magnificent front-running world record in the 1500m.

Steve Hollings's steeplechase race, in which he finished seventh to the Kenyan Ben Jipcho, was one of the other highlights. The versatile Jipcho had broken the world record twice in 1973, when he also set a Commonwealth mile record and became the first African to be named athlete of the year by the American *Track and Field News* magazine. Christchurch was Jipcho's final meeting as an amateur. He signed up for the new professional circuit in the United States straight after the Games and famously said, 'Running for money doesn't make you run fast, it makes you run first.' He was true to those words 37 times in two years in the United States, where he never finished worse than second. Jipcho later became a wealthy farmer in Kenya. Brendan Foster, who held the 3000m flat world record at the time of the Games, said, 'He was a truly phenomenal athlete.'

Jipcho won the steeplechase and the 5000m, three days apart, both in very fast times. Four more days went by before Jipcho, in the form of his life, ran in one of the great races in athletics, the 1500m final. He matched the world record, set nearly seven years earlier by the American Jim Ryun, but it was good enough only for a bronze medal. Jipcho finished a full second behind the sensational Filbert Bayi, of Tanzania, who led all the way to beat the great New Zealander John Walker, the runner-up who would win Olympic gold two years later while Bayi stayed away because of a political boycott.

Filbert Bayi was announced to the crowd before the race as 'the most exciting athlete in the Commonwealth Games'. He had said beforehand that the newly laid track at the QEII Park was too hard for record-breaking. 'It has not had time to settle down … it may be difficult for anyone to make a new world record.' He said he was in 'maybe 75 to 80 per cent form now compared to last summer, but who can tell until you really race?'

That previous summer had been a glorious time for Bayi, an aircraft engineer who later set up an educational foundation in Tanzania and led his country's Olympic Committee. None of his many victories in 1973 could compare, however, to his amazing front-running triumph in Christchurch. Brendan Foster broke the UK record and yet he was beaten by five seconds. There have been some great runs by middle-distance men throughout Commonwealth Games history, by Roger Bannister, Herb Elliott, Peter Snell and Steve Cram. None came close to matching Bayi's peerless effort. Bannister, the first man to break the four-minute barrier in the mile, said, 'That was the greatest run I have ever seen.'

Pat Butcher, the writer and promoter who was himself a useful runner, put it in perspective in *The Perfect Distance*, his 2004 book – soon to be a film starring Daniel Radcliffe – about the rivalry between Coe and Ovett:

> When Bayi dared to run away from the field … he created a template for Sebastian Coe, for Steve Ovett and for any middle-distance runner who wants to be proud of having stamped his or her personality and authority on the events which have done so much to define international athletics throughout the century and a half of organised competition. Bayi opened with a lap of 54.9 seconds and just kept going. Almost a second off the world record and he had run every step of the way in front. What a man, what a hero!

'We knew from the way he was running the year before that he might do it,' said Brendan Foster. 'It was an amazing race, one of the greatest in history. In fact the entire athletics programme of those Games was sensational, unbelievable.' The Africans, more than anybody else, made it so. Besides the exploits of Bayi and Jipcho, Kenyans won the 400m, 800m, 110m hurdles and the 4 × 400m relay. A Ghanaian won the triple jump. Modupe Oshikoya, of Nigeria, became black Africa's first female gold medallist when she won the long jump. She almost denied Mary Peters the pentathlon gold, and would become one of Nigeria's most celebrated athletes.

Other heroes included the great sprinters Don Quarrie and Raelene Boyle, who were born a few months apart in 1951 in Jamaica and Australia respectively. Quarrie won twice for a 'double double' over 100m and 200m, having won both those events and the sprint relay in 1970. Boyle won both sprints and a relay gold, as she had done in Edinburgh, thereby securing a 'double treble'.

Both of them had other matters to deal with before their races. 'DQ' sat an exam for his business administration degree at the USC on the Tuesday, flew to New Zealand on Wednesday and won gold three days later. Raelene Boyle was involved in a big argument over her tracksuit. She worked for, and wore, Puma, a rival to the Australian team sponsor Adidas. 'The whole thing ballooned out of proportion and at one point it appeared I would be banned from running for my country,' she said. The dispute was resolved and Boyle, who had suffered severe damage to her Achilles tendon in 1973, was a very relieved winner. She would have quit had she lost: she was still winning gold eight years later.

The BBC's television coverage from Christchurch offered an uplifting alternative to all the grim news back in Britain. One of the highlights, which has since been viewed many thousands of times on the internet and featured in 'TV Blooper' programmes, was Alan Pascoe's victory, and more notably its aftermath in the 400m hurdles. Pascoe, who was then a teacher at Dulwich College in London, stretched away in the outside lane after clearing the final hurdle. Christchurch's famous hospitality was partly to blame for what happened next. Pascoe famously landed on his backside, twice, in trying to jump two hurdles from the wrong side.

'I took on the two extra hurdles because I wanted to go down the track and wave to my host family,' he explained. 'They had Games tickets for one day only and it happened to be the day of my final. I knew they were down at the start of the straight.

'My tumbles made a difference back home. People had a laugh, it cheered them up.' Pascoe's falls were so well received that he was called to speak on *Wogan*, one of Britain's most popular television shows, the following day. 'I had to be very careful with my words,' he said, 'because I had been out for a good few drinks to celebrate.'

Pascoe gave up teaching to become one of the most influential promoters in athletics, as well as vice-chairman of the London 2012 Olympic bid and an influential figure in two successful Commonwealth Games bids, Kuala Lumpur 1998 and Glasgow 2014. He was an international athlete for 11 years and rates Christchurch 'the best Games I competed in, very high quality'.

There was a remarkable achievement in the marathon. Ian Thompson – one of those teammates who had travelled to Mount Cook with Steve Hollings and Ron Hill – had never run a marathon until the last weekend of October, less than three months earlier. The Luton runner defeated Jim Alder and Hill, the 1966 and 1970 Commonwealth champions, in a very fast time to make the team for Christchurch, where he followed up with a stunning victory. He won by more than two minutes in 2 hours 9 minutes 12.2 seconds, which at the time was the second quickest marathon ever run. It is still the Commonwealth Games record. Thompson set such a strong pace, going clear after 10 miles, that Hill was beaten by 20 minutes and the world record holder, the British-born Australian Derek Clayton, failed to finish.

Thompson, whose medal was presented by the Queen, won the European title later in 1974. In less than a year he had gone from being a novice to one of the world's best. How did he explain that? 'For a marathon runner, I've got rather stubby legs, short levers which stand the pounding. Pain is anaesthetised by the euphoria of running. There's a part in every marathon where you lose a sense of identity in yourself. You become running itself.' He had never felt better in a race, he said, than when he went away from the field in Christchurch. Sadly he failed to make Britain's team for the 1976 Olympics, suffering from cramp in the trials.

Thompson helped England to finish top of the athletics medal table. They had 10 golds; Kenya won six, from an overall tally for Africa of nine, and yet the continent would not have been represented in Christchurch but for the cancellation of a rugby tour the previous year. In 1970, six days after Christchurch had won the vote to host the Commonwealth Games, the New Zealand Rugby Football Union, unperturbed by the exclusion of apartheid-era South Africa from other sports, invited the Springboks.

The African countries would take no part in the Games, and could count on the Caribbean and Asian teams to follow their lead if that 1973 tour were to take place. It was eventually cancelled by a New Zealand Government who feared widespread civil disorder by supporters and opponents of the tour. South Africa retaliated late in 1973: they banned the Games' anthem, Steve Allen's 'Join Together', from their charts because it featured 'unsuitable' words such as 'freedom', 'race', 'peace', 'black' and 'white'.

The Nigerians made another point in Christchurch. They suggested a change to the title of the Games, which was approved by the Duke of Edinburgh and voted through. The word 'British' was gone: from 1978 they would be known, as they are now, simply as the Commonwealth Games.

If Dick Tayler's victory meant so much to New Zealand then the gold medal double of Mary Peters and Mike Bull was also a welcome piece of good news back in trouble-torn Northern Ireland. For Peters and Bull it was glory not just for themselves but for the man who, until his tragic death 10 months earlier, had been their coach and inspiration.

Buster McShane, a bodybuilder, weightlifter and gym owner, was an innovative fitness expert whose work produced sensational results before his life was ended in a car crash in April 1973. Mary Peters, who started as a shot-putter before becoming a pentathlete, met him at the 1958 Empire and Commonwealth Games in Cardiff, after which she did weight-training at his gym. He became her coach and, after the Perth Commonwealth Games in 1962, her employer: she worked as a 'general factotum' and instructress at McShane's gym. When the business expanded McShane moved the gym to bigger premises. Soon afterwards the old building – that also housed a strip club on the ground floor – was bombed to the ground by the IRA.

Robert Terence 'Buster' McShane was a small man with a huge personality, 'the prototype seven-stone weakling and a champion of the underprivileged' in Peters's view. Raised by his grandparents, he left school to work at the Belfast shipyards aged 14, when he still wore short trousers. He was fascinated by bodybuilding and, unable to afford any equipment, fashioned his own weights from lumps of metal he stole from the yards. He read all he could about physical education and bodybuilding, became an international weightlifter and coach and gained worldwide respect in bodybuilding as a trainer and writer. McShane was staunchly atheist, as is Peters, and became a successful businessman, art collector and in Peters's words 'owner of an extremely cultivated mind who thought freely and packed his life with style. His motto seemed to be dedication with fun.'

Peters won the first Commonwealth pentathlon in 1970. When she followed up with Olympic gold two years later she became a national hero. Without McShane's coaching, and his support as employer, she could not have done it. After winning at the Munich Olympics in 1972 she was invited to lunch by the prime minister, Edward Heath. Peters asked that McShane come along, too. He was not allowed to attend because he was not part of the official Olympic party, so she said 'No thanks'.

Mary Peters and Mike Bull had jointly made a pledge. 'We both had to win gold,' said Peters, who had already decided to retire after Christchurch.

'Our legacy to Buster would be showing everyone that he had produced the best all-round athletes in the Commonwealth.' They trained in Northern Ireland, and then in the United States en route to Christchurch, where they arrived early. 'That extra preparation time gave us the edge we needed,' said Bull. Peters won the pentathlon in a tight finish, in dramatic style, just as she had done in Edinburgh. In 1970 it was victory in the final event, the 200m, that held off the challenge of Ann Wilson, of England. It was even closer in Christchurch, with Peters under threat from the Nigerian Modupe Oshikoya who, at 20, was 14 years younger than Peters. This time Peters had to finish within eight metres of Oshikoya in the 200m: she did it with a couple of metres to spare.

There was a memorable moment for Peters after that victory when she heard a group of spectators calling her name. They were all in wheelchairs, members of the Northern Ireland team who had competed at Dunedin, 225 miles south of Christchurch, in the paraplegic competition that preceded the Commonwealth Games. They had asked to be taken to Christchurch to cheer on Peters, despite the fact that it made their tortuous journey home even more complicated. Mary, delighted and moved, said, 'These were the gold medal winners of an altogether bigger game.' These were early days in organised sport for the disabled. Miners were making headlines back in Britain, and here in New Zealand a third of the England team, who won 102 medals in Dunedin, were former miners who had suffered severe spinal injuries at the pits.

Mike Bull was a pole vaulter. He held the British record, won Commonwealth silver in Kingston in 1966 and gold in Edinburgh in 1970, and competed at the 1968 and 1972 Olympics in Mexico City and Munich. Shortly after the Munich Games, when Bull was 26, Buster McShane approached him and said he should try something else. 'You could be the Olympic decathlon champion.' Bull, who made a record 69 international appearances for Britain between 1965 and 1977, was immediately sold on the idea. He put the pole vault in the background and worked hard on McShane's training programme. A few months later McShane was dead. 'We made a pact to complete the project and win Commonwealth gold in Christchurch,' said Bull. 'We were rudderless without a coach but we worked very hard.'

It started well in Christchurch. Bull was ahead after the first day in the decathlon. He cleared 5m in the pole vault to go a long way clear after eight events but, because he was out on his own, still vaulting long after the others had run out of attempts, he had too little time to warm up for the javelin. He then damaged his elbow while rushing his preparations.

'Sean Kyle, the national coach, came down and stuck a bag of ice to my arm with sticky tape, which made it very difficult to bend my arm,' said

Bull. 'My first attempt landed about 25ft away, so I took the tape off and the second throw was even worse. There was a searing pain and everybody thought that's it, he's out. Somehow I worked out a different throwing technique, had one last go, and it was fine. I scored enough points to be able to jog home in the 1500m.' That, for Bull, was 'The Buster Moment'.

Bull had been only 12 years old, and Peters an established international athlete, when they first met in Belfast in 1958, so they did not really get to know each other until much later. Their double triumph caused a stir: New Zealand television interviewers wanted to know how Northern Ireland, a country with a population of under three million had produced the best all-round athletes in the Commonwealth, male and female. 'That gave us a chance to tell all about Buster,' Bull said.

Bull went out and celebrated so hard it may well have cost him a second gold medal. 'I was out drinking all night, I was knackered, and I had to do the pole vault the next day,' he said. 'I got a silver, but if I hadn't gone out on the town I definitely would have won it.' When Mary Peters retired, Bull, without a coach, reverted to the pole vault. He ran a gym and became fitness coach to Ireland's rugby team.

Peters's first encounter with 'The Friendly Games' had been 16 years earlier, in the week of her 19th birthday, before she had even worn her Northern Ireland kit for the first time. 'I met some of the Australians who came to compete in Belfast before the 1958 Games in Cardiff,' said Peters. 'We're still good friends nearly 60 years later. I went to visit them when I was in Australia last year, and had a wonderful time.'

One of those friends, Marlene Mathews, won the 100 yards and 220 yards double in Cardiff: Peters finished unplaced in the shot and high jump and sixth in the sprint relay on her international debut. 'I was deliriously happy just to be there,' said Peters, who regarded the trip as 'a super, exciting holiday' and spent one of her evenings riding the dodgems and eating candyfloss with a group of boxers at nearby Barry Island. 'Every moment was a joy.'

By the time she made her fifth and final appearance at the Commonwealth Games in Christchurch Peters had become one of the all-time greats of British athletics, revered on both sides of the sectarian divide in Northern Ireland, and throughout the mainland. She was determined not just to win for herself and Buster, but, as ever, to enjoy herself, too.

'I have very warm memories of Christchurch,' she said. 'I'll always remember the end-of-Games athletes' parade. I persuaded the biggest man in the village, a Canadian shot-putter, to carry me round on his shoulders. And he curtsied when he passed the royal box.' That was quite a sight as the carrier, Bruce Pirnie, stood 6ft 7in tall and weighed 22 stone before he added Peters to the equation. 'I got sad after the closing ceremony and nearly cried. I will never forget the village, such a happy, friendly place.'

Peters's work in athletics and in the community during three decades of 'The Troubles' in Northern Ireland led to her being awarded an MBE and a CBE before she was made a Dame of the British Empire. A local athletics track is named after her, she was appointed Lord Lieutenant of Belfast and she played a leading role in the London 2012 opening ceremony.

Sadly the stadium in which all these exploits took place in Christchurch is no longer there. The QEII Park, described by the International Olympic Committee's 1974 bulletin as 'probably the most elaborate sports complex in the southern hemisphere', was irreparably damaged in the 2011 earthquake in Christchurch.

There were many more notable achievements away from the athletics track. David Bryant, of England, won a fourth bowls gold while Precious McKenzie was the star in weightlifting. Two swimmers set world records: Steve Holland of Australia and Wendy Cook of Canada. The Scottish swimmer David Wilkie won two titles ahead of his magnificent Olympic triumph in 1976. Wilkie had flown in from the University of Miami, where he had been offered a place after his silver medal in the 1972 Munich Olympics. Because his coach did not even know that the Commonwealth Games existed Wilkie had to plead for time away. He had a long, tiring journey to New Zealand, visiting his parents en route, and was 'absolutely knackered' when he finished second in the 100m breaststroke. He won gold at 200m and in the medley. 'I should have won all three,' he said, 'but I was drained. For every hour of time difference you need a day to acclimatise. I had barely any time and arrived after the rest of the Scottish team.' He prepared properly for his greatest achievement, Olympic 200m gold in a world record time, by three seconds, in Montreal in 1976. That is still widely regarded as the best ever swim by a Briton.

There was a sensational success in the boxing ring for a mighty one-man team from Saint Vincent and the Grenadines. Frankie Lucas was a very good boxer, a tough middleweight from Croydon, South London. He fought for the Sir Philip Game Club, founded by the Metropolitan Police Commissioner of the same name, which has always held strong connections with the police. Lucas was not universally popular among those who ran his sport. He had, some said, 'an attitude problem'.

When, late in 1973, England named their team for New Zealand they ditched Lucas and instead selected Carl Speare, a popular Liverpudlian. Earlier that year Lucas had beaten Speare to win the national middleweight title. He had also won the year before, following on from two great names in British boxing, Alan Minter (1971) and John Conteh (1970). Lucas could barely believe it, nor could his clubmates.

Ken Rimington, a police officer at the club, found another way to help Lucas to go for gold. Lucas had been born in St Vincent, in the Caribbean, and moved to London aged seven. So Rimington set about creating a St Vincent boxing association, and Lucas would go to Christchurch under their flag.

The next big bonus was an offer from Frank Hendry, a senior official in Scottish amateur boxing. He knew Lucas from international contests and offered him a deal: come to New Zealand at Scotland's expense in exchange for sparring with our boxers. Lucas agreed, and, said Hendry, 'He was more or less part of our team out there. Our boys cheered him on in every round. He was a hell of a character.'

He was a hell of a fighter, too. The one-man team from St Vincent, who carried the flag at the opening ceremony, won his way through to the semi-finals where his opponent was Carl Speare. Lucas beat him, just as he had in the national championship final. Next up was Julius Lupia, a talented Zambian who had been trained by the best in the business, the Cubans. 'I've come for gold, I'm gonna get gold,' Lucas told the BBC. He did.

Lucas flew back to St Vincent where, he told the boxing broadcaster Steve Bunce, he 'kicked back a bit and had some herbal relief'. On his return to Britain he became a professional, appearing in a memorable title fight against Tony Sibson at the Royal Albert Hall. A few years later he disappeared. Nobody in boxing heard from Lucas for more than 20 years and many from his circle, among them Rimington and Minter, thought he was dead. But John Conteh, of all people, had seen somebody who may have been Frankie Lucas running in a park in north London. He told Bunce, and in 2002 Bunce found Lucas, who was alive and well.

Remarkably, another boxer from the same Games was also 'killed off' too soon. The Zambian Lotti Mwale, who defeated one of Lucas's Scottish teammates, Cy Harrison, to win gold, was reported dead in 2001. *Boxing News* ran an obituary for Mwale, Zambia's greatest ever boxer, only for Mwale to call and say, 'I might be ill, but not that ill.' The magazine published an apology.

The man in charge of the Christchurch Games, Ronald Scott, was knighted a few months after the closing ceremony. The Duke of Edinburgh had been there from the start, with Princess Anne and her husband. The Queen arrived later, having visited the Cook Islands en route to New Zealand. The royals were clearly impressed: Scott received a letter from Buckingham Palace soon after the royal party had arrived home. It was signed 'Philip' and it started:

'The City of Christchurch deserves the warmest thanks and congratulations from everyone who had any part in the Commonwealth Games. The citizens made all the visitors welcome, the arrangements were superb and the weather kind. The Games have never been happier or more successful.

'I have been fortunate enough to visit New Zealand on many occasions, but I know what a wonderful impression the country and people must have made on all those competitors, officials and spectators for whom this was their first visit.'

The Commonwealth Games émigrés Keith Falla, Morgan Moffat, George Newton, Precious McKenzie, Norm Scott-Morison and Steve Hollings would all have agreed with those words.

8

Fallen hero

The history-making high jumper
who died in front of the firing squad

Emmanuel Ifeajuna became Nigeria's first international sporting hero at
the Vancouver Games in 1954. After quitting sport he co-led a military
coup, and then tried to end a civil war. He died in front of a firing squad.

The first time that Emmanuel Ifeajuna appeared before a crowd of
thousands he did something that no black African had ever done: he won
a gold medal at an international sporting event.

'Nigeria Creates World Sensation' was the headline in the *West African
Pilot* after Ifeajuna's record-breaking victory in the high jump at the 1954
Empire and Commonwealth Games in Vancouver, Canada. He was the
pride not just of Nigeria but of a whole continent. An editorial asked,
'Who among our people did not weep for sheer joy when Nigeria came
uppermost, beating all whites and blacks together?'

In the words of a former schoolmate Ifeajuna had leapt 'to the very
pinnacle of Nigerian sporting achievement'. His nine track and field
teammates won another six silver and bronze medals, prompting a special
correspondent to write, 'Rejoice with me, oh ye sports lovers of Nigeria,
for the remarkable achievements of our boys.' Sir John Macpherson,
Governor of Nigeria, a British Colony and Protectorate that was still three
years away from independence, sent a telegram of congratulation that
ended, 'We are very proud of you.'

The victory led to a campaign, the day after the Games ended, for more
investment and sponsorship in sport and the creation of a national stadium
in Lagos. Ifeajuna, feted wherever he went, would soon see his picture on
the front of school exercise books. He was a great national hero who
would remain Nigeria's only gold medallist, in Commonwealth or
Olympic sport, until 1966.

The next time Emmanuel Ifeajuna appeared before a crowd of thousands he was bare-chested and tied to a stake, facing execution before a seething, hissing mob.

He had co-led a military coup in January 1966 in which, according to an official but disputed police report, he shot and killed Nigeria's first prime minister. The coup failed, even if it had cleaned out the corrupt government. Ifeajuna escaped to safety in Ghana, dressed as a woman and driven to freedom by the famous poet Christopher Okigbo. Now, 20 months later, he was back, fighting for the persecuted Igbo people of eastern Nigeria in a civil war that broke out as a consequence of the January coup.

Ifeajuna and three fellow officers were accused by their own leader, General Emeka Ojukwu, of plotting against him and the breakaway Republic of Biafra. They denied charges of treason: they were trying to save lives, and their country, they said, by negotiating an early ceasefire with the federal government and reuniting Nigeria. They failed, they died and, in the next two and a half years, so did more than a million men, women and children of the Igbo population.

Emeka Ojukwu, until now a close friend of Emmanuel, sanctioned a swift trial. The former hero was accused of colluding with the enemy through a network of British agents and of trying to hasten Biafra's downfall: one of his colleagues, Victor Banjo, was accused of taking thousands of pounds from the British. This was all nonsense, said Nelson Ottah, a fellow disillusioned Igbo who had earned respect from afar as editor of Nigeria's *Drum* magazine. The four were found guilty, the sentence death by firing squad. Ojukwu's first instinct had been to send the plotters into exile on a plane to Lisbon. His closest advisers, during discussions that lasted into the early hours, persuaded him otherwise. Their message was simple: the people demand the death penalty.

'The public malice, in alliance with frustration, was busy heaping all the blame for all the disasters that were at the time the lot of Biafra on the heads of the four luckless men,' wrote Nelson Ottah. 'Nothing but their death would assuage the red-hot public feeling against them.' The trial was held in secret, the executions carried out 'under the glare of massive publicity'. Everybody who could stand the sight was permitted to go along and witness 'how Biafra deals with saboteurs'. Ottah saw it first hand. 'The inhabitants of Enugu, more in the spirit of a fiesta than with the air of solemnity of those about to witness a great human tragedy, started to wend their way to the place of execution – the Army headquarters – as early as six o' clock in the morning. The crowd of people on the way to this twentieth-century Calvary was so massive that thousands failed to get within eye-reach of the execution platform. The day of the execution was Sept 25 1967, and the time 1.30pm.'

There was a very short gap between trial and execution, not least because federal troops were closing in on Enugu, the Biafran capital, giving rise to fears that the 'guilty four' might be rescued. Public opinion, contrary to what had been heard in the courtroom, was that they were for the other side anyway. In his 1980 book *The Trial of Biafra's Leaders*, Ottah wrote:

As the time of the execution approached, the four men – Emmanuel Ifeajuna, Victor Banjo, Phillip Alale and Sam Agbam - were hustled forwards and, without too much ceremony, tied to their respective stakes. The administration of the rite of supreme dispensation on the four men was equally a hurried affair.

Victor Banjo, with his head out and chest erect, was a picture of bravery. Phillip Alale, although his posture was slumpy, kept on loudly protesting his innocence. Emmanuel Ifeajuna, with his head on his chest as though he was already dead, kept on mumbling that his death would not stop what he had feared most, namely, that the Federal troops would enter Enugu, and the only way to stop this was for those about to kill him to ask for a ceasefire.

A body of soldiers drew up with their automatic rifles at the ready. On the order of their officer, they quickly formed themselves into the classic phalanx of a firing squad. At another order, they levelled their guns at the bared chests of the four men who had been tied to the stakes. It was now merely a matter of seconds. Death, with its ugly grin, was about to claim the four men for its own. As a hysterical mass behind the firing squad shouted, 'Shoot them! Shoot them!' a grim-looking officer gave the command: 'Fire!' The deafening volley was followed by lolling heads.

Ifeajuna slumped. Nigeria's great sporting hero died a villain's death.

Ifeajuna had been right. By 4pm, two and a half hours after the executions, the gunners of the federal troops had started to hit their Enugu targets with great accuracy. The Biafrans began to flee: the fall of Enugu came a few days later.

Of all the many hundreds of gold medallists at the Empire and Commonwealth Games since 1930, none left such a mark on history, led such a remarkable life, nor suffered such a shocking death as Emmanuel Ifeajuna. His co-plotter in the 1966 coup, Chukwuma Nzeogwu, was buried with full military honours. He had a statue erected in his memory in his home town. His biography was written by one of Nigeria's greatest national leaders. As for Ifeajuna, the hateful verdict of that seething mob carried weight down the years. His name was reviled, his sporting glory all but written out of Nigeria's history. His name is absent from the website of the Athletics Federation of Nigeria, appearing neither in the history of the Federation nor in any other section. Occasionally one of his supporters will say Emmanuel should be honoured in death, as was his main ally in the coup. The last time anybody spoke up, in 2010, an influential former government minister replied, 'The truth is, Ifeajuna's hands were dripping with Nigerian blood before he died.'

There is no easy road to redemption for the gold medallist who inadvertently started a war and was shot for trying to stop it.

The Queen was well aware of the many far-reaching changes in global politics that lay ahead when she undertook a six-month tour of the Commonwealth from November 1953. Early in the New Year she made an important address about 'a new kind of Empire, built on the highest qualities of man – on friendship and loyalty, striving towards freedom and peace and looking towards world brotherhood'. This speech, broadcast worldwide from New Zealand, came at a time when great anxiety over the Cold War in the Western world was matched throughout Africa by growing disenchantment with imperialism. 'Nigerianisation' was a key word in a land where there was talk of nationhood and independence.

Any achievement in the world of international sport was greeted very warmly by the media and the general population, who would look on successes with great pride, as evidence of their ability to compete with other, freer countries. Nigeria's first foray into overseas sport was in 1948, when they sent athletes to London to compete in the Amateur Athletic Association Championships, and to watch the Olympic Games before a planned first entry in the next Olympiad. The following year large crowds turned up at England's top amateur football clubs to watch a Nigerian touring team, the first from West Africa, who played barefoot on hard ground, wearing boots only if it was wet. In 1950 there was cause to celebrate when the high jumper, Josiah Majekodunmi, won a silver medal at the Auckland Commonwealth Games. He also fared best of Nigeria's Olympic pathfinders, the nine-man team who competed at Helsinki in 1952. Majekodunmi was ninth, with two of his teammates also in the top 20: Nigerians clearly excelled at the high jump.

That trip to New Zealand in 1950 made its mark in Commonwealth Games history. Four black athletes and a white team manager, E. A. Miller, flew from Lagos to London in December 1949 before sailing to Auckland from Southampton. Of the 976 passengers on board the SS *Tamaroa*, 972 were white. The other four, all track and field athletes, comprised the first black Commonwealth Games team from Africa. 'We moved freely amongst the whites and they so much admired us,' Majekodunmi said on his return. 'There was no sign of discrimination. That tour was the first, and it was about the best a Nigerian could undertake. It was full of enjoyment and opportunities.' There was frustration for pole vaulter Joshua Olotu, whose wooden poles were spoiled by temperature changes en route, and who could not grip the hard track as he had no spikes. He was away for months, yet he could not once clear the bar. Nevertheless, team manager Miller was delighted with the overall effort and said, 'They were the best boys in the world to travel with. I am proud to have been manager of such a team.'

With three men having competed in that 1952 Olympic final in Helsinki, the Nigeria selectors had plenty of names to consider for the Commonwealth Games high jump in Vancouver two years later. Emmanuel Ifeajuna was not one of them until he appeared, as if from nowhere, at the last moment. Regional championships, national meetings and a match against Gold Coast (Ghana) went by in the early months of 1954 with no sign of Ifeajuna. There had been doubts about sending a team at all. In February, the secretary of the Nigerian Athletics Federation said times and distances were not good enough. 'The main point is to judge whether it is worth all the money in sending a team.' There was no structured training programme for athletes, he said, no attention to diet, no regular rest. The Federation decided Nigeria should compete in Canada regardless, and made a public appeal for funds.

Ifeajuna was not a contender until he surprised everybody at the national championships in late April, less than two months before the team were due to depart. His jump of 6ft 5.5in, the best of the season, took him straight in alongside Nafiu Osagie, one of the 1952 Olympians. There were complaints about his selection based on a single jump. At the age of 20 he was too young, some said, and would suffer stage fright. His refusal to wear spiked shoes – or, indeed, any shoes at all – added to the weight of criticism. The selectors said, 'We know best.'

There was a 13-day journey by sea to Liverpool, with light training on board, followed by a few days of more intensive work ahead of the AAA Championships at White City in London. Ifeajuna finished sixth, two places behind Osagie. There was another meeting at the same stadium a week later before the Nigerians, who stayed as guests of the Danish Embassy in London, flew to Canada with the British teams, completing the journey to Vancouver by train. They stayed at the University of British Columbia, housed next to Jamaica and Scotland.

The high jump was on day one of the competition, when complaints about high ticket prices persuaded many locals to stay at home, leaving 20,000 empty seats in the stadium. The crowd of 11,400 saw two sprint finals, the six miles, and an enthralling high-jump contest that lasted nearly four hours. Ifeajuna wore only one shoe, on his left foot. One correspondent wrote, 'The Nigerian made his catlike approach from the left-hand side. In his take-off stride his leading leg was flexed to an angle quite beyond anything ever seen but he retrieved position with a fantastic spring and soared upwards as if plucked by some external agency.' Ifeajuna brushed the bar at 6ft 7in but it stayed on; he then cleared 6ft 8in to set a Games and British Empire record, and to become the first man ever to jump 13.5in more than his own height. Amazingly, the silver and bronze also went to African athletes, Patrick Etolu from Uganda, and Osagie.

The Nigerian author, J. B. Agbogun, recalled, 'It seemed unbelievable when the news reached Nigeria. Telephones rang, people went about in the bus, in the market place, discussing the matter. Can it be true?'

There was a first gold, too, for Pakistan, a debut appearance at the Games by Kenyan runners, and three teams from the Caribbean. 'It had taken almost a quarter of a century to achieve, but at long last the Games were beginning to reflect the true ethnic mix of the Empire,' wrote the athletics historian Bob Phillips. Muhammad Iqbal's hammer throw of 55.37m won Pakistan's first title, even though his effort was more than two metres shy of the first world record set way back in 1913. If Iqbal's winning distance highlighted the permanent gulf between the Commonwealth and the rest of the world in the throwing events, it was a different story in the high jump. Thelma Hopkins, who won the women's event – a first gold for Northern Ireland – would break the world record in 1956. Ifeajuna's first gold for black Africa was a world-class performance. His 6ft 8in (2.03m), would have been good enough for a silver medal at the Helsinki Olympics two years earlier. Peter Esiri, a silver medallist in the triple jump in Vancouver, who reached the Olympic final in 1956, said Ifeajuna had 'a wonderful spring, and I would not have been surprised if he had cleared 6ft 10in'.

When Sir Arthur Porritt, the former Olympic sprinter who chaired the British Empire and Commonwealth Games Federation, presented the medals there was no such thing as a Nigerian flag, as we know it now, or a Nigerian anthem. 'Land of Hope and Glory' was played when the three Africans were on the podium. But there was, now, such a thing as a Nigerian hero in international sport.

The team arrived back home by sea on board the MV *Apapa*, which docked on 8 September 1954. That afternoon they were driven on an open-backed lorry through the streets of Lagos, with the police band on board, to a civic reception at the racecourse. The flags and bunting were out in force, as were the crowds in the middle of the course and, for those who could afford tickets, the grandstand. There was a celebration dance at 9pm.

It was a busy schedule. The following day there was a cocktail party for the returning heroes and 250 guests, among them the Governor, two archbishops, footballers, boxers and other worthies. This one was organised by the Nigerian Olympic, Empire and Commonwealth Games Association (NOBECGA). Not to be outdone, the Amateur Athletic Association of Nigeria (AAAN), held a tea party the next afternoon, Friday 10 September, at 4.40pm at King George V Memorial Park, with a dinner to follow at the Ambassador Hotel. On Sunday there was another AAAN dinner, this time at nearby Ikeja.

Oba Adele, president of Lagos Town Council, addressed the team. 'I think I can proudly say in the language of Sir Winston Churchill during the War years that never before has this country owed so much to so few.' Nobody had ever been able to win for Nigeria 'a greater honour, prestige or goodwill than you have done by your recent achievements'. Team manager Jack Farnsworth appealed to the council to provide a cinder track and better facilities for sport. Ifeajuna told reporters he had been so tired, having spent nearly four hours in competition, that, 'At the time I attempted the record jump I did not think I had enough strength to achieve the success which was mine. I was very happy when I went over the bar on my second attempt.' A film of his and his teammates' exploits was made, to be shown all over Nigeria. Not until a week after his arrival in Lagos was he able to return to his home town of Onitsha.

After a couple of weeks at home, Ifeajuna was off to university on the other side of the country at Ibadan. His sporting career was already over, apart from rare appearances in inter-varsity matches. He met his future wife, Rose, in 1955. They married in 1959 and had two sons, Emmanuel and Bay, neither of whom took up sport. Both sons, and Rose, now live in the United States.

After graduating in zoology Ifeajuna taught for a while before joining the army in 1960. He was trained in England, at the Mons Officer Cadet School in Aldershot, and was at the time, said Ottah, 'handsome, athletic, charming, avant-garde in temperament, always at the centre of things. Most likely he took to the army because it was the only organisation in Nigeria that was being run as a genuinely national institution.'

He had first shown an interest in the military in 1956 when, during a summer holiday in Abeokuta, he had visited the local barracks with a friend. The man who eventually persuaded him to sign up and train as an officer was none other than Emeka Ojukwu, who later sanctioned his execution. And the friend who accompanied him on that holiday became one of the most important figures in the Commonwealth.

Chief Emeka Anyaoku joined the Commonwealth Secretariat in 1966, the year of Ifeajuna's coup attempt. While his good friend escaped, returned, fought in the war and died in front of the firing squad, Anyaoku moved to London where he rose to the highest office in the Commonwealth, Secretary-General, in 1990. In nearly half a century of serving the Commonwealth he mixed freely with the Queen, Nelson Mandela and the great leaders of the world. For four years at university he lived in a room next door to his close friend Ifeajuna.

Why did the record-breaking champion stop competing? 'From October, 1954, when he enrolled at Ibadan, he never trained,' said Anyaoku nearly 60 years later. 'He never had a coach – only his games master at grammar school – and there were no facilities at the university. He simply stopped. He seemed content with celebrating his gold medal. I don't think the Olympics ever tempted him. I used to tease him that he was the most natural hero in sport. He did no special training. He was so gifted, he just did it all himself. Jumping barefoot, or with one shoe, was not unusual where we came from.'

Ifeajuna followed boxing, most notably the exploits of Nigerian heroes Hogan 'Kid' Bassey and Dick Tiger, and listened to news of English football on the BBC World Service. He had been a boy scout and was generally pro-British, said Anyaoku. 'I'm sure he wouldn't have objected to "Land of Hope and Glory" being played at his medal ceremony.' Ifeajuna was outspokenly critical of British intervention in Egypt, however, when the Suez crisis broke out in 1956, from which point Anyaoku became more positive about the British than his friend and neighbour. Anyaoku wrote about his own changing views, and the general perspective of the Commonwealth in his book *The Missing Headlines* (1997).

> For my generation of Africans, coming to consciousness in the post-war years, the decisive formative influence was the anti-colonial struggle. We knew precious little about the Commonwealth; it hardly impinged on our lives, except in association with the Empire, and when eventually it began to loom in the media, there was always a whiff of neo-colonialism and Anglo-centricity attached to it. The Commonwealth was then said to be knit by ties of kinship and kingship and it was by no means clear

that we, too, were within the fellowship of those bonds. The Commonwealth appeared to many of my generation as just an extrapolation of the Empire, which was going nowhere in particular.

The turning point came in 1961 when the Commonwealth, outraged by the Sharpeville Massacre in South Africa the previous year, effectively expelled the apartheid regime from its fold. That was for me the first clear intimation that the Commonwealth could go somewhere after all.

Another hugely influential voice from Nigerian history pointed out that Emmanuel, in his days as a student, had 'a fairly good record of rebellion'. Olusegun Obasanjo served as head of a military regime and as an elected president: Democracy Day, a public holiday in Nigeria, marks his first day of office in 1999 after 16 years of military rule. Besides being one of his country's great leaders he was an admirer, and biographer, of Ifeajuna's co-plotter in the 1966 coup, Chukwuma Nzeogwu.

In the biography, Obasanjo recalled Ifeajuna's role in a protest that led to the closure of his grammar school in Onitsha for a term in 1951, when he was 16. Three years after his gold medal glory Ifeajuna made a rousing speech at university before leading several hundred students in protest against poor food and conditions. He had 'an oratorical gift, and good connections, especially within academic circles', wrote Obasanjo, who later employed one of Ifeajuna's sons, an IT expert also named Emmanuel, as a special assistant.

The former president also held a manuscript written by Ifeajuna in the aftermath of the coup but never published. It stated: 'It was unity we wanted, not rebellion. We had watched our leaders rape our country. The country was so diseased that bold reforms were badly needed to settle social, moral, economic and political questions. We fully realised that to be caught planning, let alone acting, on our lines, was high treason. And the penalty for high treason is death.'

Frederick Forsyth, the bestselling author, was a correspondent for Reuters and the BBC in Nigeria who stayed throughout the civil war, after which he wrote his own account, *The Biafra Story*. He summed up the causes of the 'disease' to which Ifeajuna referred in 1966, a disease that turned a gold medallist into a revolutionary. Nigeria was a nation artificially created by the British 'where group rivalries, far from being expunged by the colonial power, had been exacerbated as a useful expedient to indirect rule' after independence in 1960. The power was in the hands of the mainly Muslim north. The main political opponents, who mostly represented the Yoruba people from the west of the country, were jailed for planning a coup in 1962, and there was widespread manipulation of census figures. 'The 1962 census inflated the population of the north for political reasons,' wrote Forsyth, 'and was discounted because, among other things, it listed more children under the age of five than all the women of childbearing age would have been able to produce if they had all been pregnant continuously for five years.'

At least there were sporting heroes for the country to celebrate, most notably the great boxers 'Kid' Bassey and Richard Ihetu, alias Dick Tiger, both of them from the eastern region. Bassey, a featherweight, won Empire and world titles in 1957, before independence. He later helped Dick Tiger, a good friend who also moved to Liverpool, and then the United States, to unite the dissenting factions of Nigeria for a while. After 'Tiger' had won the Commonwealth title, his victory over the American Gene Fullmer in San Francisco made him middleweight champion of the world in 1962 – a cause for great celebration throughout Nigeria. Dick Tiger's biographer, Adeyinka Makinde, wrote, 'It was somehow demonstrative that the country was coming on to the map of the world. He was like a torchbearer, a beacon of hope for others, who did a lot in terms of promoting Nigeria. He would engage journalists in conversations about the history of his homeland and would visit the United Nations for photo opportunities.'

At the following Commonwealth Games in Perth in 1962, when there was so much unrest, Nigeria did not even send a team. The nation was briefly reunited through sport the following year when a boxing world title was contested in Africa for the first time. It was possible only because of support from the federal government, backed up by a joint effort from the regional governments of the east, west and north. In a contest billed as 'one of the most significant international events ever witnessed in Africa', Dick Tiger pummelled Gene Fullmer to another defeat in front of 25,000 roaring fans in the Liberty Stadium, Ibadan. Tiger, an Igbo, would later return to Nigeria – to sign up for the Biafran Army in the civil war.

In 1964 the Lagos boxer Omo Oloja won a light-middleweight bronze in Tokyo, thereby becoming Nigeria's first Olympic medallist. It was a rare moment of celebration in a grim year that featured a general strike and a dirty election. Another election the following year was, said Forsyth, seriously rigged – 'electoral officers disappeared, ballot papers vanished from police custody, candidates were detained, polling agents were murdered'. Two opposing sides both claimed victory, leading to a complete breakdown of law and order. 'Rioting, murder, looting, arson and mayhem were rife. The mighty federation was crumbling into ruin before the eyes of foreign observers who had only a few years before hailed Nigeria as the great hope of Africa.' It was dangerous to go out without escort in the west of the country, even in the daytime. The prime minister, Tafawa Balewa, refused to declare a state of emergency, showing more interest in hosting a meeting of Commonwealth leaders to discuss the troubles in Rhodesia.

There was corruption in the army, too, with favouritism for northern recruits. A group of officers began to talk about a coup after they were told by their brigadier that they must pledge allegiance to the prime minister, from the north, rather than the country's first president, an Igbo.

Emmanuel Ifeajuna's group feared a jihad against the mainly Christian south, led by the north's Muslim figurehead, the Sardauna of Sokoto. Ben Gbulie, one of Ifeajuna's co-plotters, wrote, 'The political leaders had failed the country woefully. The coup would lead to the emergence of Nigeria as a beacon of hope not just for black Africa, but for the black world at large.'

The operation, codenamed Leopard, was planned in secret meetings away from the barracks. The main figurehead of the north, the Sardauna, was shot dead by Major Nzeogwu, who led the northern part of the operation. Major Ifeajuna led a small group in Lagos whose main targets were the prime minister, the army's commander-in-chief, and a brigadier, who was Ifeajuna's first victim. According to the official police report on the coup, part of which has never been made public, Ifeajuna and a few of his men broke into prime minister Balewa's home and drove him away in Ifeajuna's car. On the road to Abeokuta they stopped, Ifeajuna asked the prime minister to get out of the car, shot him and left his body in the bush. Others say the prime minister was not shot, nor was the intention ever to kill him: Balewa died of an asthma attack, or a heart attack brought on by asthma and fear. There has never been conclusive evidence either way.

Ifeajuna drove on to Enugu, where it became apparent that the coup had failed, mainly because one of the key officers in Lagos had failed to arrive as planned with armoured cars. Ifeajuna was a wanted man. He hid in a chemist's shop, disguised himself as a woman and was driven over the border by his friend Christopher Okigbo, a poet of great renown. Ifeajuna travelled on to Ghana, where he was welcomed and given a safe home by the country's rulers.

Back in Nigeria, although the coup had failed many of the targeted politicians were dead or ousted, and there was a regime change. Press coverage was remarkably favourable, at least in Lagos. An editorial in the *Morning Post*, a government paper, said, 'In the former regime corruption, graft, nepotism, tribalism were rife … Nigerians today are glad and grateful that they see the beginning of a new era.' The enthusiasm did not last long.

In May, Igbos who lived in the north of the country were attacked. In weeks of violent bloodshed tens of thousands died and a wave of refugees fled back to the east. There was a counter-coup in July in which Nigeria's interim leader, Major-General Ironsi, was killed. The northerners soon published an 'official' account that said the January plot had been led by the 'Igbos of eastern Nigeria'. Every investigator of the coup was a northerner.

Emmanuel Ifeajuna returned from Ghana to face trial and was held in the east, a 'safe' part of the country as far as he was concerned. Other plotters of the failed coup were not so lucky. Of those held captive by northerners one was tortured to death, another buried alive, others shot. As the death toll increased, the outcome was civil war. In May 1967 Emeka Ojukwu, military governor of the south-east of Nigeria, declared that the region had now become the Republic of Biafra. By the time the fighting ended in early 1970 the number of deaths would be in the millions.

Arguably, if either of Emmanuel Ifeajuna's 'plots' had been a success those lives would not have been lost. The verdicts on his role in Nigerian history are many and varied, but his detractors have held most sway. Chief among them was Bernard Odogwu, Biafra's head of intelligence, who branded Ifeajuna a traitor and blamed him for 'failure and atrocities' in the 1966 coup.

Adewale Ademoyega, one of the 1966 plotters, held a different view of Ifeajuna. 'He was a rather complicated character … intensely political and revolutionary … very influential among those close to him … generous, and willing to sacrifice anything for the revolution.' Ademoyega's view of the trial in Enugu is forthright. 'With the execution of Banjo, Ifeajuna, Agbam and Alale, Ojukwu could be said to have destroyed the only articulate and independent group who could have acted promptly to put an end to the murderous, wasteful and unnecessary war between Nigeria and Biafra. Ojukwu needed a scapegoat for his utter lack of preparation for the war.' Ademoyega visited Emmanuel Ifeajuna in jail shortly before the execution. 'Look after my wife and children,' were his last words.

One of Nigeria's foremost literary figures, J. P. Clark, compared the two main figures in the 1966 coup. 'Major Emmanuel Ifeajuna is made the villain, while Major Chukwuma Nzeogwu is the hero. The portraits are not that black and white and far apart. They both killed their superior officers and a number of key political leaders in the country in a common cause. So where lies the difference? Where the distinction? I have always found it difficult to understand why one is made out a villain and the other a hero.'

Ojukwu claimed after the executions that Ifeajuna had intended to declare himself acting governor before negotiating a ceasefire with the federals. 'I knew Emma [Ifeajuna's nickname] very well. I even believe that I was the inspiration that led him to seek his fulfilment in the Nigerian army. Emma was by nature a very restless character – something of a butterfly. He perched on subjects for very short periods. As a soldier he had no particular military qualities but as a man he was most engaging. He provoked discussions and inspired thoughts. In Biafra he rallied to me personally. When he was convicted of the conspiracy to overthrow the Biafran government he paid the price for it. I did not permit personal friendship to intervene on my duties as the Head of State.'

Two other notable sportsmen died during or just after the war. A few days after the executions, federal troops rounded up and shot an estimated 500 Igbo men and boys in the Asaba Massacre, one of the worst atrocities of the war. Among the dead was Sydney Asiodu, a sprinter who competed in the Commonwealth Games in 1966, and in the 1964 Tokyo Olympics. In 2009 an athletics foundation was launched in his name in Lagos.

Dick Tiger left Nigeria to live and work in New York after the war, during which he had been a celebrated fitness instructor in the Biafran Army. He discovered in 1971 that he had cancer of the liver: in the knowledge that he had only a short time to live he was desperate to return. 'Biafra is my home,' he said, even though there was officially no such place. 'I will die in Biafra.' His family were all dead or imprisoned, all his properties in Lagos had been confiscated – apartments, a service station, shops, a Mercedes and tens of thousands of dollars. A report of his funeral said that more than 600 sportsmen attended the ceremony though the federal government, having given permission for him to return to die, sent no representative, nor any message of condolence. At least he had a proper burial, unlike another national sporting hero.

Ifeajuna, too, lost his property during the war. A valuable plot of land was appropriated by a 'friend' who, said his widow Rose, had 'succumbed to greed'. His historic gold medal is also missing. 'I have no idea where it is,' said Rose.

When, at her parents' home near Onitsha, she heard the devastating news of her husband's death, Rose was temporarily separated from her children. They were more than 100 miles away in Port Harcourt, where Rose worked. 'How my mother and one of my brothers eventually brought them back is a story of courage, perseverance and love,' she said. There was a memorial church service for Ifeajuna in Onitsha. 'After Emmanuel died, his family and mine rallied round me and my children. So did most of his friends and colleagues. His name opened many doors for us for which we are eternally grateful.'

Emmanuel, the elder son, was IT director for the British Council before becoming President Obasanjo's Special Assistant. His brother, Bay, gained a PhD from the London School of Economics. Rose herself worked for the Nigerian civil service for 29 years before moving to the US in 1996.

The last time Anyaoku saw Ifeajuna was in 1963, when they met for lunch in Lagos before Anyaoku's departure for a diplomatic role in New York. He later moved to London, and was there in 1967. 'I was devastated when I heard the news of the execution,' he said. 'Sam Agbam had also been a close friend.' Anyaoku was reluctant to judge from a distance on Ifeajuna's attempt to end the shooting, though he did say, 'Ojukwu always seemed to enjoy the benefit of the doubt. The history of the civil war still evokes a two-sided argument. Emmanuel is a hero to many people, though they would more readily talk about his gold medal than his involvement in the war. There are people who think he was unjustifiably executed and others who believe the opposite.'

One commentator suggested recently that the new national stadium in Abuja, the Nigerian capital, should be named after Emmanuel Ifeajuna. It will surely never happen.

9

The trouble with men and women

Hard times for Dawn Fraser and Kathy Watt

Powerful, domineering men made life very hard for two of Australia's greatest sportswomen, who stood up to them. Dawn Fraser and Kathy Watt – who became good friends – are sure they would have won more often if they had had better support.

Yvette Williams was New Zealand's first female sporting star. She held the long-jump world record and won four Commonwealth gold medals in jumping and throwing events in Auckland and Vancouver in the 1950s. In-between, she gained lifelong national fame by becoming the first New Zealand woman to win gold at the Olympics, a feat that would not be matched for 40 years.

After her glorious homecoming in 1952 a horticulturist from Wanganui created a new rose. He named it Yvette Williams in honour of the Olympic long-jump champion. He soon had to think of a new name: the New Zealand Amateur Athletic Association (NZAAA) said the flower was a threat to amateur sport. 'While neither Miss Williams, nor the horticulturist, would receive any benefit from the naming of the rose after her, it might create a precedent for other cases that might not be so innocent,' declared Harold Austad, chairman of the NZAAA.

Over in Australia four years later, after Dawn Fraser had won the first of her three successive 100m freestyle Olympic titles, she had an orchid named after her. Within the next eight years there would also be a daffodil and a rose named 'Dawn Fraser' to mark some of the other achievements, many of them in the Commonwealth Games, that made her the world's most famous swimmer. Later in life there would be a road and a riverboat named after Dawn Fraser, too. The Amateur Swimming Union of Australia allowed those flowers to grow: they did not object to the names. Did that mean that they were more enlightened than the officials in New Zealand? Fraser laughs at the suggestion. 'Enlightened' is not an adjective she would use to describe the men who ran Australian swimming, nor any of the amateur sports during the decade when she made both her name and the first in a long line of enemies in positions of authority. Fraser's adjective of choice would tend more towards 'petty-minded', 'autocratic', 'vindictive', 'bullying', 'haughty' and 'uncaring', along with a few unprintable alternatives.

A more realistic example of the way it was for top achievers in Olympic and Commonwealth sport came in 1959, the year after the Australian Marlene Mathews had won both individual sprint events on the track in the Cardiff Commonwealth Games. Mathews, a hugely popular world record holder at three different distances, agreed to run an indoor three-legged race, a bit of fun in a Sydney ballroom, to raise money for charity. 'Oh no you don't,' said the Australian Amateur Athletic Union. They ruled that because the 'race' was open to anyone, including professionals, Mathews could not take part. Similar attitudes were commonplace throughout the non-Communist world at the time.

Dawn Fraser could not abide such strict adherence to the rules, even as a child. She was from Balmain, a famously tough working-class suburb of Sydney, and was aware before her teenage years that sport was run by 'the silver-spoon mob', as she called them. These men from privileged backgrounds would look down on her and would not tolerate any answering back. 'They were always men,' said Fraser 60 years later. 'What a difference a few women might have made.'

When she was 12 years old Fraser swam at a club where the senior members, those aged over 16, won prize money in their races. She was accused of once having won two shillings and was banned by the Swimming Union for two years. 'I was classed as a professional just for being a member of that club at the age of 12,' said Fraser. The two shillings had been a Christmas gift. She appealed, and lost. This was her first confrontation with Bill Berge-Phillips, the man who would eventually kick her out of the sport.

At the time of the ban Fraser and her first coach, her cousin Ray 'Chut' Miranda, were called into the New South Wales Swimming Office. Fraser told ABC Radio: 'Berge Phillips sat there and slapped his big leather desk and said, "You will never swim for Australia because you come from Balmain." I got up and slapped the desk and said, "Yes I will!" That's where I started being very rebellious towards officialdom. A couple of years later I went up to thank him, to shake hands and say, "Thank you for making me the swimmer that I am today, because you put the fire in my belly." It made me that much more aggressive in trying to achieve what I wanted to achieve.'

Another great motivator for Fraser was the memory of her brother, Don, who had first introduced her to swimming. He died of leukaemia when he was 21 and Dawn was 14. 'He was probably the most perfect man I ever met. I remember crawling through the window where he was in the hospital. He said, "You have a gift ... keep training for me." Those were the last words Donnie ever spoke to me. I lost someone that I loved very dearly at a very early age and it put my back up against the wall to take all the punches that were going to come to me throughout my life.'

Her defiant response to Berge Phillips was feisty and very impressive for one so young, but ultimately very costly. Berge Phillips, who ran his own law firm, was not a man to argue with. There was no Australian with more influence in the Commonwealth Games, the Olympics and world swimming during the second half of the twentieth century. He was a great believer in the rulebook as he showed when, at the age of 19, he stopped the American champion from taking part in a diving competition in Sydney because his costume did not conform to regulations. He worked for decades for the national swimming union, attended every Empire and Commonwealth Games from 1938 to 1990, was an executive member of the Australian Commonwealth Games Association (ACGA) for 30 years, was honoured by the International Olympic Committee and was president of FINA, the world governing body of aquatic sport. He oversaw the rise to global dominance of Australian swimmers: when he died in 2003 the *Sydney Morning Herald*'s obituary was headlined 'Father of modern Aussie swimming'.

Berge Phillips was hugely respected by fellow amateur sports administrators around the world. Dawn Fraser had her faults, as some of her own teammates would testify. Even so the lawyer's heavy-handed role in banning Fraser from swimming for disobeying team orders at the 1964 Olympics has been criticised by other, equally respected, figures in sport. Fraser won a defamation case and the ban was lifted, but it took time. By then it was too late for her to continue in Commonwealth or Olympic swimming. Ten years after Don's death she had suffered further heartbreak through the death of her father from lung cancer. In 1963 her mother died in a car crash: the driver, who survived, was Dawn. There followed a series of further setbacks in her personal life, including the break-up of her marriage and a period of heavy drinking and depression, before she eventually returned to sport in a variety of roles, one of which was mentor for Australia's Olympic teams from 1988–2000.

When, in this role, Fraser met the Australian cyclist Kathy Watt in the last decade of the twentieth century she was transported back to the bad old days of the 1950s and 60s. Here was a Commonwealth Games pathfinder – winner of the first women's road race in 1990 – and a future

Olympic champion who was suffering just as she had done herself. If 30 years of radical change had made sport more professional, more commercialised, it had not made it more feminised, at least not in cycling. Kathy Watt, like Dawn Fraser, would find herself taking on the most powerful man in her chosen sport. She, too, would feel victimised and would appear in court to claim what was rightfully hers, namely a place that had been promised to her in the Olympic team. She, too, fought and won a defamation case. And she too was spurred on by the loss of a close relative, in this case her father.

Dawn Fraser and Kathy Watt, who won 10 Commonwealth golds between them, are linked not just by the friendship that grew, along with mutual respect, from their athlete–mentor relationship in the 1990s. They were both pioneers of their time who suffered for being women in a man's world. They were isolated.

'I can't speak for what it was like in other countries, but sport here in Australia was totally male dominated for many, many years,' said Fraser. 'Looking back, give me one single thing I could change, one thing over which I had no control, and it would be putting more women on selection boards and in positions where they could make a difference. Sport needed female input.

'The men were all from the silver-spoon brigade, all well educated, but they just didn't know how to handle us. I couldn't relate to any of them. Plenty of athletes came from the working-class suburbs and the men in charge treated everybody like children. If they had given us a little more freedom, regarded us as adults, it would have made things a lot easier both in the Commonwealth and Olympic Games. This went on for years and it has only changed fairly recently. You can see with what happened to Kathy Watt that it has been very, very difficult to make progress.'

It was not only the athletes who struggled. The governing body of the Commonwealth Games carried out their duties for more than 60 years before accepting a woman on to the board. Louise Martin, a Scottish swimmer who competed in Perth in the 1962 Games, was chair of Commonwealth Games Scotland when, in November 1999, she was elected to the board of the Commonwealth Games Federation (CGF), where she has remained ever since. Martin has played a leading role in changing the make-up of the CGF, which was for decades dominated by men, many of whom would have been candidates for Dawn Fraser's 'silver-spoon brigade'.

'When I was appointed in 1999 I was the first woman ever to have anything to do with the CGF,' said Louise, who described Dawn Fraser and Kathy Watt as 'two great champions'. 'They didn't know what to do with me. It was very strange, very difficult – very much a male-dominated domain. They couldn't treat me as one of them. Someone would say "Right, gentlemen," and I would have to say "Excuse me," then they'd say, "Right, gentlemen and Louise." It took a while to break down the barriers, to make them realise that my brain is just as good, if not better, than theirs. Now we have three women on the board, and a gender-equity rule within the Federation, that neither gender can drop below 10 per cent. When the day comes that the board is mainly women and we have to vote for another man to get men back over that 10 per cent representation, that will be brilliant. It could come.'

Like Louise Martin, Kathy Watt has made a difference. She won gold medals despite a management system that she found to be 'very male, chauvinistic, anti-women and authoritarian'. After she followed her first Commonwealth victory with an Olympic gold in Barcelona in 1992 there was a boom in cycling participation by girls. The government created a new women's road-racing programme at the AIS. Watt had been helped through her difficult times by Dawn Fraser. 'She definitely made a difference, and helped in lots of ways,' said Watt. 'Dawn was inspiring. And I knew what she had been through.'

There was another man, besides Berge Phillips, with whom Dawn Fraser had several altercations – her father, Ken. The disputes caused no lasting damage, though, to a loving relationship. 'I was brought up to believe that my mother and father were my bosses and no one else. That played right through my life. My dad taught me that if you have anything to say, say it with an honest voice. I've done that all my life.'

Ken Fraser was a Scottish emigrant, a shipwright who had been a good footballer. Dawn, the youngest of eight children, had a 'wild but happy' childhood at home, in the local swimming pool and as part of a neighbourly, working-class community of waterfront people who helped one another out. Her most memorable falling-out with Ken came after a two-month trip to Hawaii in 1957, as she revealed in an Australian television interview in 2004 that showed her great affection for her parents. Fraser returned from weeks of training, and exhibition races, with 'an American accent and a swollen head'. She had travelled with her lifelong friend Lorraine Crapp, fellow Olympic champion and world record holder, and had met her idol Johnny Weissmuller, the champion swimmer who became a Hollywood star. Fraser, 19, and Crapp, 18, were feted and pampered wherever they went.

'When I came home, I remember getting up at 3am to go to the bathroom in the rain. We still had an outside toilet and as I ran down the stairs I sang out, "I wish we had an inside loo like they do overseas" in an

American accent. When I came inside I was soaking wet and here was my father standing at the foot of the stairs, razor strop in one hand, and he said, "You think you're too bloody good for this family, and you are now ready to get the first belting you've ever had in your bloody life. Drop your daks and get up to your bedroom and lay there." I got six straps on the backside.

'I didn't realise it at first, but my mother got up and she was crying. She said, "You know you've upset your father dearly." I would never do that because I just loved him, I idolised the ground he walked on. And I said, "I haven't upset Pop." She said, "Yes you have. I think you'd better pack your bags and go back to Adelaide." So I went to my bedroom and I started crying and packing my bag, because my mother meant it. So as not to show her that I was crying I got up first thing and brought my bag down the stairs. My mother and father were sitting at the table and I said, "Yeah, well, I'm going now." They never spoke to me and I got to the front door and said, "I'm not coming back!"

'I got a taxi to the airport, got my ticket to go back to Adelaide [where she had lived and trained] and I couldn't get on a plane. I got back in the taxi, went home, knocked on the front door – I didn't have a key – and my mother opened the door and I said, "I'm throwing my bag in first and I'll unpack it later, and I'll never, ever say that this house is terrible." And she just grabbed me and I cried and kissed her, and Dad had stayed home from work that day because he was so upset and I raced in and said, "One day I'll buy this house for you, and I'll put in an inside toilet for you so *you* don't have to walk out in the wet." And I did. I bought the house that we lived in, the house I was born in, and I live in it today. We have two inside loos, and a shower and bathrooms inside.'

At least that outdoor toilet was a step up on the facilities on offer at Fraser's first Commonwealth Games in Cardiff. That was in 1958, by which time she had already won an Olympic title and set several world records. Fraser and her teammates had endured a 50-hour journey from Australia so they had a bit of fun on the last leg, a coach ride from London to Cardiff. On the pretext of needing the loo, she recalled in her 1965 biography *Below the Surface*, the team pulled in at a pub and headed for the bar. It was Babycham for the girls, a sparkling perry that, Fraser recalls, was 'all the rage at the time'. In 1957 it was the first alcoholic drink ever to be advertised on British television. 'We had a few, although our team manager didn't know it.'

On arrival in Cardiff they were not impressed with their temporary home. The athletes' village was a former RAF camp that Fraser described as 'primitive'. Nine swimmers shared one dormitory-style hut where the beds, basic wire cots with thin mattresses, were lined up against the wall. They had two baths and three toilets between them – in a separate block. 'We were issued with potties in case we needed to go to the toilet during the night.'

How things changed. Compare that to one of Fraser's more recent trips, to the World Sports Awards in Austria, where she was named female water-sports athlete of the century in 2000. In a second biography, *Dawn: One Hell of a Life*, published in 2001, she wrote:

> Our accommodation in that beautiful city was at one of its grandest hotels, next to the Vienna State Opera House where the awards ceremony was to take place. The organisers were relentless in their hospitality. I was assigned a minder, whose first task was to usher me and Dawn-Lorraine [her daughter] off to the fashion house Escada to be fitted for gowns to wear on the night.

> Later that day, together with a couple of the other athletes, we were the special lunch guests of the famous Sacher Hotel. Dessert was, of course, Sacher Torte, and the whole meal was magnificent. We had our hair and make-up done at a salon in the centre of town. Later, we were off and running for one of the most memorable nights of my life. We were ushered into a private room for pre-awards drinks and *hors d'ouevres* … I was chatting with Pele and Muhammad Ali.

Later that night Fraser lay in her bed 'reflecting on the twists and turns in my life that had brought me to that point'. Looking back, while her many medals and controversies at the Olympics brought her worldwide fame, the Commonwealth Games played a large part in her life. The officials responsible for managing Commonwealth Games teams were, said Fraser, even more 'amateur' than the Olympic Federation, but the people were easier to deal with. She swam in the 1958 and 1962 Games, and had been planning to compete in Kingston in 1966 until the swimming union banned her.

Her first major disappointment was failing to qualify for the 1954 Vancouver Commonwealth Games as a 16-year-old, when she had cramps in the trials. In the 110 yards freestyle she led for three-quarters of the race only to be overtaken by Lorraine Crapp and Marjorie McQuade. 'I was struggling to get my breath but my major problem was period cramp. I was miserable and I felt like I had let everyone down.' She returned to a Sydney winter to read about two of her friends, Jon Henricks and Crapp, winning in Canada. 'I was extremely upset, but deep down I knew I had it in me, that my best swimming lay ahead.'

She was right. After her Olympic glory in Melbourne in 1956 and the United States trip in 1957 she was off to Cardiff, where she won two golds and many friends. The Australians were seen as aloof by the home crowd, who barely acknowledged their victories. Fraser won them over when she clowned around at the poolside after the finish of a men's race. She was pulled into the pool, climbed out laughing, and the crowd laughed, too. 'From then on the Aussies became much more popular.'

There was a memorable farewell before the Australians left Wales, a 'magical night'. The team went to a local pub where they drank beer and sang songs with the locals. 'I ended up in the flowerbed back in the village where I slept through the night out of harm's way.'

Fraser won four more Commonwealth golds in Perth four years later, having added a second Olympic title in 1960, when she was subsequently banned for misbehaviour. Perhaps her greatest landmark achievement came in Melbourne in the trials for the 1962 Commonwealth Games. Swimming the longer distance of 110 yards, Fraser became the first woman to cover 100m inside a minute, something she had been striving for all her career. She lowered the mark again in winning the gold in Perth a few weeks later, and held the 100m world record in that event from 1956 until 1972. She broke the 60-second barrier despite feeling fairly flat and thinking she would not swim well that night. 'When the reality sank in I felt elated. The years of training had paid off. From then on I never looked back and my swimming began to improve more and more.'

She set nearly 40 records in all: it should have been more. After a late-night prank in Tokyo at the 1964 Olympics Fraser was held by police for stealing a flag from outside Emperor Hirohito's palace. Although she was released and presented with a flag by the apologetic Japanese, and despite her being Australia's flag-bearer at the closing ceremony, Berge Phillips and the swimming union executive, fed up with Fraser's pranks and her keenness to question authority, banned her for 10 years.

The incident happened after Fraser had secured her third gold and finished her swimming. She was cleared to leave the athletes' village and stay at the Imperial Palace Hotel while shooting a film for schoolchildren back in Australia. The director invited the men's hockey team, who had just won a bronze medal, for drinks at the hotel. Fraser joined an expedition to pinch a couple of Olympic flags on the avenue leading to the Imperial Palace. The Australians were chased by police, taken to the local station and soon released. The following day the police delivered the flag and a bouquet of flowers to Fraser.

Officially, Fraser was banned for disobeying team orders: for marching in the opening ceremony when told to rest, and for wearing an unofficial swimsuit in the heats. But everybody believed it was the flag-stealing adventure that most annoyed Berge Phillips. 'He got his way by getting me out of swimming,' said Fraser. She had been in trouble in the previous Olympics in Rome and had been banned then, though not for long. As in Tokyo, Fraser had marched in the opening ceremony against team orders that she described as 'an unthinking act of petty officialdom'. She later refused to race in a relay when called in at short notice, having just eaten a large meal, and she threw a pillow at a teammate during an argument. The other swimmers ostracised her for a while.

Don Talbot, the man in charge of the team in Tokyo who later became one of the most successful coaches in swimming history, as well as the first director of the AIS, was among those who found it very hard to get along with Fraser. In his 2003 autobiography, *Talbot: Nothing But the Best*, he said that Fraser did as she wanted.

> She was not rebellious but defiant. All around Dawn there would be pettiness and bitchiness and spite. It was like she had her gang and she was gang leader. I disliked Dawn back in those days because I thought she was hurting the sport. Where she led, others followed. I had a lot of trouble forgiving her for that. She was very difficult on teams and I didn't like her or get along with her. But for all that, I thought then and I still think now that Bill Berge-Phillips was wrong in the role he played in what subsequently happened.

Despite his dislike of Fraser, Talbot spoke up for her and said the disciplinary hearing was 'an unbelievably murky story'. After the ban was announced he said, 'It's like putting her in jail. Berge Phillips was going to chase her out of the sport and he did.'

Talbot's view of Fraser the swimmer was untainted by what she did away from the pool. Fraser had an abnormally large heart. She was 'the first woman to come along with the strength of a man, and who used her upper body like a man'. Fraser was the prototype for the swimmers of today, Talbot said: 'Tall, well defined, strong, slim, and with a great feel for the water. She was well ahead of her time.'

A great deal of the credit for Fraser's success – 98 per cent of it, in her own view – should go to her coach, Harry Gallagher. 'I learned a lot from Harry besides swimming,' she said. Included in that being how to appreciate art and music, which books to read and how to write letters properly. 'I hadn't had that education.' Here was a man, unlike Berge Phillips, to whom she could relate, even if at first the two did not warm to each other – the up-and-coming coach with top swimmers in his charge, and the defiant young teenager who insisted on training with boys. At the pool she told him, 'I'm not swimming with those tarts from the private schools with their fancy uniforms. I want to get in with the blokes.' She did. Gallagher, with an amazingly sharp recall, in his ninetieth year, of events in the 1950s, said, 'That was the start of the story.'

When he moved to Adelaide to work at a pool and coach, he persuaded Fraser's parents that Dawn should move there, too. Aged 17, she worked hard in a department store and as a petrol attendant, as well as training hard, with a 4.30am start. At the outset, said Gallagher, 'Dawn was a horror. You had to guide her very subtly or she'd just do what she wanted.' Gallagher had a similarly tough working-class background to Fraser, who grew to respect him enormously. He learned a great deal from a sports science expert at The University of Sydney, long before others thought to ask, and was also close to the renowned athletics coach Percy Cerutty, the man who helped Herb Elliott to become the world's greatest miler.

Gallagher coached other great swimmers. John Henricks won three Commonwealth golds in 1954 and two Olympic titles in 1956, while Michael Wenden was a star of the 1960s and 1970s, winning nine Commonwealth golds. Wenden was a double Olympic champion in Mexico City in 1968 when Gallagher, at long last, was able to travel as an official member of the Australian team, leading them to a haul of eight medals, three of them gold. Until then he had not been invited. 'We coached the world's greatest swimmers and, unbelievably, when we went to the Games we had to pay our own way. No tickets or passes – all the officials got them. You just can't believe they treated us like that.'

Had she not been banned, said Gallagher, Fraser would have won further medals in the 1966 Commonwealth Games and a fourth successive Olympic gold in 1968. She went to Mexico City as a visitor, overweight and out of condition, and still posted times that would have won gold. Fraser herself said, 'I know I would have won it.'

'The people that banned us had no intelligence,' said Gallagher. They were 'a snobbish clique of guys, all from the best colleges, only one or two of them genuine'. They considered themselves a class above the likes of Fraser and her coach. 'They banned the greatest swimmer of all time, destroyed her life over a period of 10 years and temporarily destroyed mine. And they destroyed the image of Australian swimming.' The rest of the world, he said, was laughing at Australia.

Dawn Fraser was unable to laugh with them. The car crash that took her mother's life in the year after the Perth Games had knocked her sideways. Now this. She was away on honeymoon when the ban was imposed: because of the lengthy legal process it was not lifted in time for her to race again. She married, had a daughter, left her husband because of his gambling, sank into depression and drank heavily. At her lowest point, after her return from the 1968 Olympics as a visitor, she said, 'I wanted to die... I felt I had no friends, which was wrong, but I pushed away anyone who tried to help me.' Fraser began to dwell on her failed relationships and the ban. If it had been shorter, or if she had appealed, she may have competed again. 'I even contemplated suicide. I was a complete nothing to myself.'

Fraser recovered. She found happiness in her personal life when she had relationships with two women, one of them long-term. She ran a pub and managed a cheese shop. But her health then suffered: a spinal injury incapacitated her, as did severe asthma, which had plagued her from childhood, glandular fever and angina. Eventually, back in good health physically and mentally, she turned to public speaking and became a politician. In the 1980s, the decade when she became an MP, Dawn took up her role as an athlete mentor. She remained hugely popular with the Australian public who voted her not just into Parliament: in various polls Fraser was named the person who best symbolises Australia, and the greatest female swimmer in Olympic history. She officially became one of Australia's Living National Treasures in 1998. At the Sydney Olympics in 2000, Dawn Fraser, who had played a leading role in the Atlanta 1996 opening ceremony as one of the greatest living Olympians, was in the group of athletes who lit the flame. In 2013 she was named Australia's greatest ever sportswoman. She sits on the boards of various sporting bodies, though she resigned as president of the Australian Sports Hall of Fame shortly after they named her female athlete of the century in 1999. She gave her reasons as 'unforgivable administrative blunders and mishaps' and an unworkable relationship with administrators. Her fellow Hall of Fame director, the renowned Olympic writer and newspaper editor Harry Gordon, who was Fraser's first biographer in 1965, wrote, 'Dawn remains on affable terms with controversy. In a way, it's been almost like old times.'

An earlier verdict by Gordon summed up Fraser's life. 'Dawn Fraser is a battler in the essentially Australian sense of the word, and that makes her a most sympathetic character.' Looking back over her remarkable life, Fraser said that she had one significant personal regret above all others. In 1957, the year when she made the trip to Hawaii and upset her father on her return, she had been offered a scholarship to study and swim at Berkeley in California. 'I was the first Australian woman in any sport to be offered an American scholarship. The United States was ahead of the game in swimming at that time, and my great regret is that I didn't take it. I would have been fulfilled by education. But my father was against it, he was the boss of the family and I didn't go against what he wanted.'

Kathy Watt's father was not around to advise his daughter on her education. On 6 September 1969, Geoff Watt left his optometrist's practice in Moe, Victoria, for a training run on Mount Erica, a 4600ft mountain in the Baw Baw National Park. It had snowed in nearby Melbourne that day. Watt was caught in a storm. He lost his way, and never made it home to his pregnant wife and three young children. A search party found his body in a snowdrift early the following morning: he had died of hypothermia, aged 36.

Watt had been a fanatical runner and a fearless adventurer. He left Australia in 1959, after graduating, to travel around the world for three years. He hitchhiked across Asia, Europe, North America and Africa. He worked when he could, took in the Rome Olympics as a spectator, and accepted invitations, and one-way air tickets, to run in marathons and ultra-distance races along the way. He was a friend of the great marathon runner Abebe Bikila and the brilliant coach Percy Cerutty, an occasional training partner of Herb Elliott, and a hugely popular man.

Kathy Watt was five days short of her fifth birthday when Geoff died. He left behind a collection of diaries, photos, letters and poems. He was a role model to her despite his death, inspiring her to become one of Australia's most successful, and controversial, sportswomen.

'My dad was a huge inspiration for me when I was a junior athlete and throughout my cycling career,' said Watt, winner of the first Commonwealth women's road race in 1990, and Olympic champion two years later. 'He was a real character. He was really interested in people, and touched the hearts of many he met. After I won the Olympics it was amazing how many people told me they still had letters he had sent them.' After winning three gold medals at the 1994 Commonwealth Games Watt flew home to present the trophy for the Geoff Watt memorial run at her home town of Warragul. She still helps to organise the annual race: her father would have been very proud of her.

Watt's four Commonwealth Games appearances produced seven medals, as well as a great deal of controversy and acrimony. She won gold in Auckland in 1990 in an event for which she had not originally been selected. She felt she should have won four times instead of three in Victoria four years later, when she was in tears shortly before her final race. In 1998, in Kuala Lumpur, she was criticised for arriving too late and missing the start of the time trial, and given an ear-bashing by a Canadian for her tactics in the road race. Her return to competitive cycling, after retirement, led to an emotional farewell appearance in her home city of Melbourne at the 2006 Commonwealth Games. At the age of 41 she was cheered to a silver medal. At least Watt had been out of the headlines at the Commonwealth Games in Manchester in 2002: she had temporarily retired from competition and was working at the Games as a photographer.

Those Games in England gave Watt the chance to catch up with her great hero Sebastian Coe 12 years later than planned. Her first encounter with Coe had come at her first Commonwealth Games, in Auckland. 'I really had a ball there,' Watt said. 'I remember one day I was heading down to the athletes' restaurant with a couple of teammates when we saw a big crowd gathering. I joked that it must be the Queen, and it was. Then we bumped into Sebastian Coe, who was royalty as far as I was concerned, my ultimate sporting hero. He was busy talking to somebody else and he asked me to come and have a chat a couple of days later at the warm-up track before his race. But I won the road race the next day and when we were due to meet I was in a television studio. It turned out that he wasn't there either, because he got injured and missed his race. Twelve years later a friend introduced us at the Manchester Games and I finally got to meet him properly.'

Watt had always held a keen interest in athletics, having been a top-class runner herself before she took up cycling in 1986. She was national junior champion over 3000m, as well as an accomplished cross-country skier when she decided, because of an Achilles tendon injury, to focus on cycling from the age of 21. She bought her first bike from Sid Patterson, who was twice a silver medallist behind one of Australia's greatest cyclists, Russell Mockridge, in the Auckland 1950 Commonwealth Games.

Women's cycling was in its formative years. The first road race at the Olympics and the first women's Tour de France were held in 1984, with Olympic track races coming four years later. There were no women's events at the Commonwealth Games until 1990. 'Women had been racing since the 1950s so it actually took a while,' said Kathy. When she started out there were no female cyclists around to pass on their wisdom, no women coaches, officials or physios. When she had first approached the Victoria state cycling office to sign up in the mid-1980s Watt had been seen as a novelty. 'They asked me, "Can you bake scones?" I said, "Yes, can you?" They'd never had a woman ask before. I raced against veterans who told me they didn't even know women raced bikes.'

It was no different elsewhere. Lisa Brambani, the English cyclist who finished second to Watt in the 1990 road race, said, 'I didn't know Kathy, but I can sympathise with what she went through. The men just didn't understand the dynamism of women's racing. We were there on the programme so they sent us to race but they never, ever put any thought behind it.' Brambani was coached by Val Rutherford, one of Britain's best female cyclists of the 1950s and 1960s. 'Unfortunately it was the same nearly everywhere,' said Rutherford, a former national women's team coach and manager whose daughter, Roberta, rode on the track in the

Auckland 1990 Games. 'They didn't want women in. The men they put in charge of women didn't know much about the sport at all, never mind women's racing. It was horrendous.'

Watt was 'isolated for her gender' according to one newspaper correspondent who said, 'She was the first high-profile female cyclist in Australia, and the male officials didn't know how to handle women. They thought they could just treat her the same as another bloke.' For some this was not a problem as they became part of the national team set-up directed by Charlie Walsh, head of cycling at the AIS and national team coach. For Watt, who was outside that system, who raced professionally in Europe, and who was coached by her partner, fellow cyclist Carey Hall, it made things very, very difficult.

Watt soon made an enemy of Walsh in the way Dawn Fraser had done with Bill Berge-Phillips. This was always likely to lead to problems. Walsh was, according to *The Australian*, the nation's most respected cycling coach, the man 'credited with rebuilding Australia as a world cycling power, who guided riders to 78 Olympic, world and Commonwealth gold medals'. He won many awards himself including, like Watt, a place in the Sports Hall of Fame. At Watt's induction, alongside the cricketer Adam Gilchrist in 2012, Walsh offered her his hand. 'Can you imagine?' she laughed. 'Shaking hands with Charlie Walsh?' She could not stand the man.

Walsh, a qualified mechanical engineer and teacher, rose from local to state to national prominence as a coach in the 1980s, having been a multiple champion in South Australian state cycling himself. When he took over at the AIS he introduced revolutionary coaching practices, and set up a new system and structure with a heavy emphasis on track cycling. He was phenomenally successful. He put his faith in 'people who were really loyal, who did just what I asked of them, and who had a huge respect for the philosophy and the way we wanted to go about it'. Watt, he said, 'did well for about three months' as part of his AIS programme but then 'seemed to want to change the rules'. There was a clash of personalities between two strong characters.

Kathy raced in Europe and was coached by Hall, the former national champion. She was always confident that she could perform well on the road and the track, while Walsh preferred her to focus on one or the other. Her first encounter with Walsh was in 1988 when 'he said I had one of the best cycling techniques he'd ever seen'. Watt had been due to go overseas with the AIS team in 1989 'but it didn't happen because they thought I wouldn't fit in'. She spent that time doing cross-country skiing and running, then finished second in the national championships to qualify for the Commonwealth Games – only to be told that, unlike the others in the women's team, she had to race again in the Oceania Championships to confirm her place. She won the pursuit and the road race.

When Australians had competed in the women's Tour de France for the first time in 1988 Watt finished seventh, the team third. In the 1990 Giro d'Italia for women Watt was third. She was not selected, however, for the first women's road race in the Commonwealth Games. When she discovered that Australia could field four riders rather than the three they had selected she asked for a place. Watt had already been named for the pursuit on the track, and was told that she could ride the road race provided she acted as a *domestique*, a tactical team 'helper' for the two first-choice riders who were thought to have the best chance of victory.

'I chased people down all day, went into the lead, broke away on a hill, and waited for everyone to catch up,' Watt recalled. She was still up with the pace for the sprint finish when 'one of the Kiwis went way too early, about 500 metres out. I jumped straight to her – that skiing and running had put me in very good shape – and just kept going. I won by about a length and a half. I was punching the air as I crossed the line and the photographers captured that moment well. I might have been thinking about punching a selector's head, actually...'

Success in Auckland was followed at the Barcelona Olympics two years later by Watt's most famous triumph. She repeated the gold/silver effort in the same events, road race and pursuit, becoming the first female Australian winner in Olympic cycling, and also the first gold medallist for her nation in the 1992 Games. It created a sensation back home. 'Women's cycling back then got maybe three lines in the papers, but when I won at the Olympics there were helicopters filming the race and cameras everywhere. For the men's race later, hardly anyone showed up – it was a complete turnaround.' There was trouble, even so. Watt complained at Barcelona about inadequate coaching and support on the track, and her 'ban' from training for the pursuit until the road race was over. Few people were aware that she was helped through a difficult time by her athlete liaison officer, Dawn Fraser.

'I was very concerned with what she was going through,' said Fraser. 'Kathy's experience at those Games was terrible and this really upset me. It was the same old story with officials making the life of a focused and very strong-willed female athlete unbearable because they thought they had to control her rather than encourage her.' The two became good friends. Watt took it as 'a big compliment' when Fraser said she was one of the most focused athletes she had ever met.

Fraser was 'very helpful, inspiring', said Watt. 'We all looked up to her, knew her achievements and what she'd been through. Half the things that happened to Dawn, it's just ridiculous, just common sense it shouldn't have happened. The officials she dealt with had a very similar mindset to the ones I dealt with.

'Sometimes I would have a disagreement with a coach on what should happen and she would smooth the way a bit. It was good to have her in the Olympic Village, where she was helpful in sorting things out with the physio and the sports psychologist. There was an incident one day when we were out riding the road-race circuit in training and the police tried to get us off the route. Dawn stepped in, and the next thing we knew the police were escorting us around the roads. She really helped out there – all those little "one percenters" make a difference, they help you to get the best out of yourself. Dawn really helped in that respect.'

Like Dawn Fraser, Kathy needed somebody in authority with a different approach. 'It wouldn't necessarily have had to be a woman, but just someone who wasn't quite so authoritative. We needed different styles of coaching rather than just "Do this, and don't ask any questions". I liked to ask questions, I wanted to know why we were doing something, what the tactics were, and so on. If I was given a good reason *why* to do something it would be an extra motivation. A different mentality was needed.'

Watt was named Australian sportswoman of the year in December 1992; in 1993 she was awarded the Order of Australia. During this time she did not warm to Walsh's male–dominated AIS regime. She had studied physiology, anatomy and nutrition at university and wanted to know more about the coaching programme. 'It was very male, very chauvinistic. Charlie Walsh was against anybody not within the system, and at times it seemed impossible for "outsiders" to get into the team. At one point, in 1989, I managed to see a sports psychologist's reports on the team and they were full of words like "subservient", "submissive", "do what they're told", and so on. Anybody Charlie Walsh trained, he wanted them in his team. But all the time I just kept performing and on performance alone I got into the team too.'

At the 1994 Commonwealth Games in Victoria, Canada, Watt was imperious. She won the road race for a second time, and won the pursuit, and then the team trial. 'I attacked at an unusual spot and did well in the road race,' she said. 'I particularly enjoyed the time trial. Canada had a stronger team and should have won but we worked well. I rode the last kilometre or so by myself out in front.' Despite those three victories Watt was in tears shortly before she set out on her quest for a record-breaking fourth gold medal in the 25km points race. Her relationship with Walsh was heading for a new low point.

Watt believes that Walsh interfered with the team's instructions and it cost her the chance to win again. Five hours before the race, plans had been set out by the women's coach, Andrew Logan, at a meeting with Watt and fellow starters Michelle Ferris and Rachel Victor. Ferris, 17, and Victor would ride to help Watt win, with Victor tracking breakaway rivals and Ferris pacing her for the sprints. 'It's all part of cycling etiquette, to look after the champion,' said Watt, who held the national points title. 'We left the athletes' village having agreed at the meeting to ride to the tactics Andrew had devised.'

But, as Ferris confirmed, Walsh later told Ferris and Victor to ride their own races. 'By telling everyone to race for themselves, he was really telling us to race against each other, which prevented Australia from winning a medal,' said Watt immediately after the race. She was in tears when she realised what was happening 90 minutes before the start. Unable to focus properly, and without support from her teammates, she finished fourth. 'I'm no whinger, but Charlie clearly went over the top. He had no right to butt into or interfere with the women's programme. He's not the women's national coach – Andrew Logan is.' Watt had complained of Walsh's 'interference' at Barcelona, too, and after a meeting with Ray Godkin, head of Australian cycling and also of the nation's Commonwealth Games Association, she said, 'I've been given a written guarantee that stops Charlie from meddling in the women's endurance programme.'

If that was bad, 1996 was even worse. The team for the Atlanta Olympics gathered for a pre-Games preparation camp in Texas – without Watt. 'I don't want to go anywhere near Charlie Walsh,' she told the *Herald*. 'He has told me he doesn't like me as a person and I feel if I attend the camp I will be surrounded by negative and unhelpful people.' When Walsh 'deselected' Watt from the pursuit, naming her arch-rival Lucy Tyler-Sharman in her place, Watt challenged the decision in court. The issue, said her coach-partner Hall, was 'ensuring that individual riders who did not train with Walsh were still able to represent Australia. Charlie's a very successful coach, and I hope the guy does well in these Olympics. But you don't have to be under Charlie Walsh to get in the national team. It shouldn't be a closed shop.' Watt won the case. To the dismay of Walsh and his supporters, she was reinstated.

Once again Fraser was on hand for Watt. 'She was having a terrible time with her team and coach ... she was being psyched out by officials after all the conflict surrounding her selection, which sometimes goes on when an athlete is very gutsy and independent. The official can't bear not to control them, so they play mind games. It really upset me to see her in that situation, so I talked to her for quite a while and didn't get back to bed till about 2am.' Those recollections are from Fraser's 2001 autobiography, the back–cover photo for which was taken by Kathy Watt. 'I'm very proud of that,' said Watt.

Walsh felt that Watt was taking on too much in Atlanta: she competed in three events but did not win a medal. Tyler-Sharman, who watched the pursuit from the stands, showed her form later in the year when she finished second at the world championships in Manchester. She won the world title in 1998. Walsh still maintained, years later, that Australia's best rider on form had been denied her chance. After the race he told reporters that Watt had damaged Australia's Olympic prospects by contesting his choice of riders: when his views were published Watt sued the *Herald Sun* for defamation. She felt her reputation had been damaged, and was right, judging by a poll in 1997 in which a magazine's readers voted her the athlete they most loved to hate. A newspaper report in 1998 – the year when Watt stayed apart from the rest of the team at the Kuala Lumpur Commonwealth Games – said she had 'a poisonous effect' on teammates. Watt broke down in tears in a supreme court witness box when the case was heard in 1999. 'Charlie Walsh was saying I wasn't helping Australia win medals, but I was just trying my best,' she said. 'And I followed the processes set out by the Australian Cycling Federation.' Watt won her case: the newspaper apologised.

The in-fighting and turmoil in Kuala Lumpur in 1998 brought even more bad publicity to cycling. For the first time the Australians sent home an athlete from the Commonwealth Games. Tyler-Sharman accused Walsh and his team of sabotaging her chances when she was made to ride with unfamiliar pedals in her pursuit semi-final. She said, 'There are three words to describe my relationship with Cycling Australia this year: antagonism, ostracism and undermining. In Australian cycling there are people who either are incompetent or full of malice.' She would not retract her comments or apologise, at least not until later, and was sent home.

Watt was involved in another controversy, starting 29 seconds late in her best event, the time trial. Having stayed away from the team in separate accommodation because of her relationship with Walsh, she and Hall were responsible for her preparations. At the start her shoe buckle had jammed, she said, an explanation that did not placate Godkin, the head of Australian cycling. After Watt had made up ground to finish third, Godkin said, 'I am absolutely disgusted. This is the last time people will be allowed to operate outside the team. They're either in the team or not in the team.'

Because of the many acrimonious disputes, a review of Australian cycling was held. Watt complained of victimisation, saying she had been denied funding, and several riders, according to a report in the *Age* (Melbourne), said there was a 'closed shop' atmosphere. 'If they fell out with Walsh, they had little chance of being picked for Australia, and the coach had far too much power. The strong alliance between Cycling Australia president Ray Godkin and Walsh was also scrutinised.' Another report said that while Walsh was acknowledged as 'a supreme tactician and master coach', his authoritative manner had led to a breakdown in relationships with many cyclists, 13 of whom were named. The prevailing attitude was that 'if a rider is not coached by Walsh, he or she is no good'. In an interview 10 years later, Godkin conceded that there may have been some truth in that claim.

The review made no great difference. Charlie Walsh, with his great record of achievement, remained in charge until after the Sydney 2000 Olympics. Watt tried to gain a place in the Sydney team on performance but was not selected. This time her appeal in court failed. The aftermath of all the disputes led to an additional requirement for Australia's riders at the Manchester 2002 Commonwealth Games: they must have 'the psychological focus appropriate to the event'. Watt had a focus of a different sort. Having studied photography as well as science she was in the early stages of her career as a sports photographer. She also runs a bike shop and a personal fitness business, and takes groups to the Tour de France.

With Walsh gone, Watt returned to competitive riding in 2003. She did not make the team for the 2004 Olympics so she targeted the Melbourne Commonwealth Games. Victory at the national championships, two months before the Games, would guarantee a place in the team. 'I knew it wasn't up to selectors, so I went for it.' At the age of 41 Watt won the time trial, defeating the Olympic road-race champion, Sara Carrigan. 'I was really motivated,' she said, 'because the time-trial course goes right by my bike shop at Black Rock. I've probably ridden that road thousands of times.' In the big race, Australia finished 1-2-3, with Oenone Wood taking the gold, Watt silver and Carrigan bronze.

'I got heaps of support from crowd, people cheering the whole way, people who use the bike shop or who know me,' said Watt. 'There were signs painted on the road, funny slogans. I was hoping to win gold, but it's good Australia made it 1-2-3.' Wood and Carrigan both agreed that Watt has been an inspiration to others. 'It's really impressive,' Wood said. 'It's motivating for a lot of women who've pursued a career and decide to get into the sport. Kathy's shown you can come back even stronger.'

After Watt's 1992 Olympic victory, sports minister Ros Kelly ensured that women's road racing had its own programme at the AIS. There was a boom in participation on the track and the road. Among the young girls who saw Watt as a role model were the sisters Kerrie and Anna Meares, who decided to try track cycling after watching Watt's triple-gold exploits in 1994 on television. Anna Meares has since won four Commonwealth golds, two Olympic titles and 10 world championship races.

'Seeing Kathy Watt win gold for Australia on the track was an enlightening moment,' said Meares, who followed the Commonwealth Games in Canada from the family's country home in Middlemount, Queensland. 'I come from a family who love sport and we are all very active. My three elder siblings and I had already been competing in and winning club, state and national BMX titles, and growing up in the country we rode our bikes everywhere. But track cycling was new to me. I had never seen a velodrome before let alone anyone who competed on it. I remember how cool it looked on TV, how exciting it was to be cheering Kathy on to win, how inspired I was. Kathy was cool and she was fast in my eyes. I had never heard of her before then but she sparked my interest in track cycling. She was an amazing athlete, I respected her ability, and she was my first role model in this sport I love.

'After I made my first Olympic team in Athens in 2004 and returned home, I had a surprise phone call from Kathy Watt congratulating me. I didn't know what to say – I was so much in awe that she had personally made the effort to contact me. Nowadays I almost work with Kathy, as she is at most if not all the big international events I compete in, as a photographer. It's strange … my idol as a little girl now photographing me doing what she did all those years ago.'

'People have often come up to me and said they started out because of me,' said Kathy Watt. 'I think I can say I put women's cycling on the map in Australia.' She did.

10

South Pacific

How a future president started a sporting boom

When Marcus Stephen – a future president of Nauru, the world's smallest republic – won Commonwealth gold in 1990, he started one of the most remarkable booms in sporting history. Within a decade there were more international weightlifters in Nauru than in China – and thanks to nomadic coach Paul Coffa, many more Pacific Islands followed Nauru's lead.

Before 1995, Friday night in one part of the Pacific Ocean country the Republic of Kiribati was Saturday night in another. There was a 23-hour time difference within the boundaries of the remote, sparsely populated nation made up of dozens of islands and atolls, many of them uninhabited. Because the equatorial islands are clustered around the International Date Line (IDL), and the waters of Kiribati stretch from west to east as far as London to Cairo, or Perth to Melbourne, sailors could be forgiven for not knowing which day of the week it was.

The bright minds in Kiribati's government saw an opportunity that would bring global fame and a nice sum of money to their nation. They gained approval to shift the IDL and bring all their islands into the same time zone, thereby ensuring that Kiribati would be the centre of attention in five years' time as the first country in the world to welcome in the new millennium. An uninhabited atoll, renamed Millennium Island, was the place to be at dawn on 1 January 2000.

Kiribati put a price on the TV rights for the special sunrise. The BBC were among those who paid. They sent a team, with their own supplies of food and water. It took some of them weeks to travel to Millennium Island and back, during which time they found themselves farther away from land than they had ever been. The last leg of the journey alone was five days at sea within Kiribati's boundaries.

All of which shows just how hard it can be to find your way to, and around, the remotest member nation in the Commonwealth. Not the ideal place, one may think, to host an international sporting competition. That is what they did, however, within a couple of years of their big millennium moment. The Oceania Junior Weightlifting Championships in 2001 became the first and – to date – only sporting event of note ever staged in Kiribati. The three days of action, televised throughout the Pacific region, drew the largest crowds for years in Tarawa – the main island – and provided wonderful memories for those who were there.

Sadly, New Zealand were not among the 16 national teams who found their way to the Championships. 'It was so many flights and boat rides, we couldn't make it,' said a regretful Richard Dryden, New Zealand's national weightlifting coach. 'I've heard all about it from the teams who went. They all said it was amazing.'

So they did. Matthew Curtain, an Australian lifter who became one of the sport's leading administrators before being appointed a director of the Commonwealth Games Federation, said Kiribati in 2001 was a 'once-in-a-lifetime experience'. The athletes were treated like rock stars, he said, with local people asking them to pose for photos and sign autographs.

Four days before the championships began there was no competition venue. Local craftsmen swiftly constructed a massive, custom-built traditional hut – made entirely from trees, leaves and coconut twine – that accommodated the lifting stage and more than 2000 people. This was not big enough to cope with demand, so they added six extra rooms around the arena, all with televisions, and erected a giant screen on the nearby tennis courts. There were more than 3000 people watching every session, most of them sitting on the floor. Some arrived two hours before the action started to be sure of a place. The VIP seats were taken by, among others, the president of Kiribati, his ministers and foreign High Commissioners. The championships were televised live by the Sports Pacific Network. Curtain, who was in charge of the highly successful London 2012 Olympic weightlifting programme, said, 'That was the only event since Kiribati where I've seen such enthusiastic spectators.'

Paul Coffa, who was then, like Curtain, based in Nauru – 450 miles east of Kiribati's main island – and who runs the Oceania Weightlifting Institute, looks back on those championships with great fondness. 'It was sensational,' he said, 'an incredible sight. People came in by boat from some of the other islands and the arena was packed for every session. You could not even walk through the crowd, they were so crammed. What a picture it was in the moonlight. Magical.' David Katoatau, who competed in those Junior Championships and who has high hopes of becoming

Kiribati's first ever Commonwealth Games medallist, said there had never been anything like it in his home nation before or since. Nor have there been crowds – at a sporting fixture or any cultural or musical event - to match those of 2001.

The people of the Pacific Islands have provided many more memories for those involved in weightlifting. Before those 2001 Championships in Kiribati, the 1998 Commonwealth and Oceania Championships hosted by Nauru attracted nearly 30 nations and huge crowds, and featured a motorcade around the tiny island that doubled up as the opening ceremony. There was a $50,000 firework display and a banquet at the finish.

Weightlifting has continued to grow in popularity throughout the Pacific. In 2004, three years after Kiribati's big event, the Oceania Institute opened in Samoa, backed by sponsors' money, as well as funding from the Olympic movement and the International Weightlifting Federation. When Samoa hosted the 2006 Oceania Championships the 4000-capacity arena was packed for every session, even when there were three of them in a day.

Richard Dryden, who has taken New Zealand teams all over the Pacific, first saw the islanders' appetite for weightlifting in 1996, also in Samoa. 'I've been several times to various islands and when the crowds arrive it's like everyone's on holiday, they just go crazy. It's very emotional – a bit like the most committed All Blacks fans. It can be quite nerve-racking for our athletes, if they've never lifted outdoors, with people right in your face, especially if a local lifter is doing well. The support is incredible.'

Back in the mid-1990s, New Zealand and Australia started having significant concerns about the competition they were going to face from the Pacific nations. The islands had great opportunities ahead of them, which could diminish the success of the two most dominant countries in the sport in Oceania, most notably in the Commonwealth Games. 'The islanders' natural physique is good for weightlifting,' said Richard Dryden. 'They're big but not necessarily tall, strong, with powerful legs. It became clear that, with the right environment and good coaching, they could be very, very good.'

His assessment is spot on: those enthusiastic supporters have had plenty to cheer in recent years; there have been Commonwealth gold medals aplenty, podium places at the world championships and an impressive list of Olympic appearances, with every indication that there is more to come. 'I think we'll see a Pacific Islands weightlifter on the dais at the Olympics, for sure,' said Dryden. 'It's just a question of that special athlete popping up, the one who can take everything a bit further. It's a remarkable phenomenon, the rise of the islanders. I can't really think of anything else like it anywhere in the Commonwealth.'

Nor can anybody else. Since 1990, when Marcus Stephen won Nauru's first gold medal in the Commonwealth Games, the boom in weightlifting in the islands of Oceania has been quite extraordinary. At one point Nauru, with its 9500 inhabitants, had more competitors logged with the International Weightlifting Federation than any country in the world, including China and Russia. The size of the crowds, the numbers who take part, the list of achievements and the besting of Australia and New Zealand as the regional masters have all been impressive enough, but it goes beyond that. Where else in the world would babies be named after famous weightlifters, and cabinet meetings discuss the most efficient technique in the clean and jerk, as they once did in Nauru? 'Almost every president and prime minister in the region is knowledgeable on weightlifting,' said Stephen, who should know, as he was himself president of his country for four years.

The barbell boom of the Pacific Islands has been fuelled and funded by Nauru's rich phosphate deposits, and by a number of institutions, sporting and otherwise. It would probably never have happened without the existence of the Commonwealth Games, which have provided the stage for the athletes to earn their glory, and it would definitely never have started but for the efforts of two men who met by chance near Melbourne in 1986, Marcus Stephen and Paul Coffa. Stephen led the way by winning the first of many gold medals in Auckland in 1990 and, more significantly, helping to tempt Coffa away from his homeland of Australia. Coffa shipped out in 1994 immediately after leading Australia to 14 gold medals in the Victoria Commonwealth Games as head coach. Since then, he has lived a nomadic life while building a formidable weightlifting empire. The results of his work are clear for all to see.

Australia won gold, silver and bronze medals in Olympic weightlifting in the 1980s and 90s, in addition to a huge pile of Commonwealth titles. At the London Olympics in 2012 Australia fielded two lifters, New Zealand one. In comparison, five Pacific Islands with a combined population considerably lower than that of Adelaide or Auckland sent 13 men and women to the Olympics. In Delhi, at the 2010 Commonwealth Games, New Zealand won no golds, Australia two – one fewer than Samoa. Nauru has won in 20 years as many golds as New Zealand has amassed since weightlifting became a permanent Commonwealth sport in 1950. The Samoans and Nauruans could not have done it without Coffa's coaching; and Coffa would never have been there but for his encounter with a schoolboy who became the leader of his country.

Political leaders who have involved themselves in sport are not uncommon. Vladimir Putin is a black belt at judo and a lover of martial arts. Barack Obama's golf is good enough for him to have played respectably alongside Tiger Woods. Some of Obama's presidential predecessors were also capable golfers, among them John F. Kennedy, Dwight Eisenhower and George W. Bush. Silvio Berlusconi oversaw the most successful period in the history of A. C. Milan, one of the world's most famous football clubs, as president and owner. Those leaders past and present of Russia, the United States and Italy are not in the same league, however, as the world's best sporting head of state.

That title belongs without question to Marcus Stephen, cabinet minister and former president of Nauru, a country that may lack the global influence of America and Russia but which was once said to be the second richest in the world thanks to phosphate deposits built up over millions of years. Stephen's first Commonwealth gold medal in 1990 in Auckland, just three days after Nauru had been accepted as a member of the Commonwealth Games Federation, led to a public holiday being declared. He won another six golds and five silvers over the next 12 years, finished runner-up in the world championships and made three Olympic appearances, one of them for a 'neighbouring' island that is nearly 2000 miles away.

Marcus Stephen has influenced Nauruan life in other ways. Before he started winning medals, boys on the island would be given a local forename by their parents: Ruben, Kenas and Derog were among the popular ones. Within a short while of Stephen's peak performances in the late 1990s, when he followed his three Commonwealth golds in Kuala Lumpur with a world championship silver in Athens, a few new names became popular. Not just Marcus, or Coffa, after his coach, but Pyrros, Dimas and Naim, too – after the great Greek and Turkish lifters Pyrros Dimas and Naim Suleymanoglu. 'It was incredible,' said Coffa. 'It wasn't just the new names. You just could not believe that while you drove around the island you would see young kids with broomsticks on the sidewalk practising the snatch, or in their front gardens trying the clean and jerk.'

By 1998 Nauru had made such an impression that Juan Antonio Samaranch, president of the IOC, flew to the island. 'At that time,' said Coffa, 'the International Weightlifting Federation said that of all the countries in the world, the one with the most lifters in international competition was Nauru with 54. More than China, Russia, Bulgaria, Greece – countries that dominated the sport.' In participation too the world's smallest nation was number one in the world, with more than 1.5 per cent of the population registered as weightlifters.

Before Stephen took up the sport there was no such thing as weight-lifting in Nauru – no gym, no equipment, nobody was interested. 'People played a bit of cricket, basketball, athletics, Aussie Rules,' said Stephen.

Sport and politics are clearly a potent combination in Nauru: Aussie Rules is said to have been introduced to the island in the 1960s by the country's first president, Hammer DeRoburt.

Nauru gained independence in 1968, by which time much of the island had been transformed into a giant phosphate mine. It had been inhabited by Micronesian people for 3000 years, until it was annexed in 1888 by Germany, who then lost Nauru in the First World War. Phosphate mining had already begun by then. The minerals – highly valued for fertilising soil – and the profits headed to Australia, New Zealand and Britain, who had jointly been given control by the League of Nations. After independence the people of Nauru took over the phosphate operations and enjoyed great wealth until the deposits ran out in the final years of the twentieth century. During the boom period Nauru owned ships and a five-plane airline, as well as a huge stock of property in Melbourne, where the 52-storey Nauru House was the tallest building in the city.

Nauru House, like so many assets long since sold off, played a role in the weightlifting boom. One Saturday evening in the late 1980s, after a youth championship in nearby Ballarat, a 17-year-old Marcus Stephen was given a lift home by Paul Coffa. He asked to be dropped off in Melbourne's business district. 'Nobody lived there – it was all office blocks,' said Coffa. 'I thought he was pulling my leg.' Stephen was headed for the top floor of Nauru House, where his father, a government minister, was staying. Until then Coffa had assumed Stephen was Australian. 'It was news to me. I had no idea where Nauru was. I'd never heard of the place.'

Stephen, like many teenagers from Nauru, had been sent to Melbourne for his education. At first he found it a big culture shock. 'It was a lot colder than Nauru. It was also the first time I'd ever seen escalators and elevators and I was amazed that such things existed. I used to go to Nauru House just to travel up and down in the elevator, for the thrill of it. To start with it was just study, sleep, study, sleep. But I got used to it and I did a lot of sport.'

He was among the school's best at cricket, rugby and Aussie Rules. Little did he know that, after he impressed Coffa in a weightlifting trial, the coach quietly and sneakily persuaded his teachers to bar him from team sports so he would focus on what he did best. 'I was only allowed to do weightlifting. I had done well in a talent identification programme try-out, but I wasn't really interested. It wasn't till a year later that I found out what had happened. Paul thought I had great potential.' Stephen himself was not so sure at the outset. 'I had no idea I'd be any good but Paul could see there was plenty of improvement to be had. I was 16 when I started, and didn't consider myself particularly strong. I only weighed about 50kg but

I could lift a lot for a small guy. I won the clean and jerk regional championship and was invited by the Victoria Weightlifting Association to sign up, with Paul as my coach.' He trained three or four times a week to start with, building up to 11 sessions at his peak. 'Work hard, train hard' was his motto. His first international appearance was in the 1987 Oceania Championships in Canberra.

For the first few years Stephen trained with Australian lifters and, until Coffa quit as coach in 1994, was treated as a member of their team. 'He was one of us,' said Coffa. He completed his school years and then went to university in Melbourne to study business accounting.

Nauru had no membership of the Commonwealth Games Federation until three days before the 1990 Games in Auckland. There had been no need to join, as Nauru had never sent an athlete to the Games before. When it became clear that Marcus Stephen was good enough to compete, the Nauruans asked about membership. They were told their acceptance was a formality – but they would have to wait until the next meeting of the Commonwealth Games Federation in Auckland.

A small deputation from Nauru travelled to New Zealand, where Stephen was cleared to lift in the 60kg category. Although he had improved, he did not expect to be on the podium. 'I was ranked fourth or fifth and didn't expect to win a medal – maybe a bronze in the clean and jerk if I was lucky. When I won a gold and two silvers it was a real shock. I had kept improving, I lifted well and some of my rivals missed their lifts. Even so, I was still disappointed. I'd have won all three golds if I'd made my last lift in the clean and jerk. I got the bar above my head but I lost it forward. That miss got stuck in my head, and I told myself I'd definitely win all three in four years' time.' He did.

He was cheered in Auckland by a noisy group of 35 friends and relatives, among them his father, Lawrence, and mother, Sunshine. The news of his gold medal was relayed back to Nauru by phone. 'The whole island went crazy. They even declared a holiday. I was young then, 20 years old, and I didn't appreciate that I had achieved something extraordinary for Nauru.' In his naivety he also turned down an invitation to lunch with the Queen, who had travelled to Auckland. He said the function would clash with his training programme.

'I was a very young man and my ambition was to do well in weightlifting and for my country. That was my priority. When I look back on it now, I truly regret it and I should have taken the invitation. I would have treasured it for life. But I was very lucky to be given a second chance to have lunch with the Queen in 1994 in Victoria, during the Commonwealth Games there. I gave her my apologies. I was also very privileged to meet the Queen again at the 2010 Commonwealth Games in India, as Head of State. She was fantastic – she remembered me as an athlete, where Nauru was, her visit on a royal tour in 1982, our population and so on.' Given her convivial encounters with Precious McKenzie over the years, detailed elsewhere in this book, it appears Her Majesty Queen Elizabeth II is something of a weightlifting fan.

Stephen stayed in Australia for four more years after the Auckland Commonwealth Games and continued to train under Coffa, who was beginning to tire of press criticism and bureaucratic disputes. He had seen an opportunity, when the Berlin Wall came down in 1989, to persuade several top lifters from Soviet Bloc countries to emigrate to Australia. They formed the core of the national team, leading to headlines that Coffa was 'buying medals' in the Olympics and Commonwealth Games. He found it increasingly difficult to secure funding for a sport tainted by drug-test failures, most notably in Eastern Europe – 'We had world champions, and we couldn't even get a single dollar' – and quit after the 1994 Commonwealth Games in Victoria, Canada. Next stop, Nauru.

Marcus Stephen had travelled to Canada in 1994 as favourite. Luckily for him, his rivals were unaware that he had badly injured himself in Sicily at a pre-Games training camp. He had damaged both wrists and could not lift anything above his head for two weeks. 'If they had known, they might have put the pressure on a bit. As it was they all thought they were just lifting for silver and bronze.' The problem was so serious that Stephen was unable to do any strenuous lifting in the days before the Games. Coffa told the Indians, whose top lifter might have won, that it was Stephen's usual tactic not to lift before a big contest. 'If he hadn't been able to lift 90kg in the snatch we would have withdrawn,' said Coffa. Stephen wrapped an entire roll of white tape around each wrist and managed to perform as if nothing was amiss, lifting 115kg. In the snatch he lifted 5kg more than India's Raghavan Chandrasekharan. He beat the same man by 2.5kg in the clean and jerk, and 7.5kg overall to make good on his promise and win all three golds. He knew there was better yet to come but he was leaving Australia and heading home to Nauru, where there were no coaches, no gyms and no weights. The only option was to take Coffa with him.

Francesco Coffa and his family emigrated from Sicily to Melbourne in the 1950s. His sons, Paolo and Salvatore, became Paul and Sam in their adopted country. Sam worked as a doorman at the 1956 Olympics in Melbourne, in the weightlifting arena. He fell in love with the sport and over the years the Coffas transformed their local youth club in Hawthorn into a powerhouse for weightlifting. Sam won six national titles, finished sixth in the 1962 Commonwealth Games in Perth and became one of the most senior administrators in Australian sport. He is president of the Australian Commonwealth Games Association, a vice-president of the International Weightlifting Federation and is on the executive board of the Gold Coast 2018 Commonwealth Games organising body. Paul was a good lifter and has become a top administrator too. The field in which he has most excelled is coaching.

His nickname, 'The Brute', is appropriate because he works his lifters very, very hard. He regards time spent with physios and masseurs as time lost. After more than a decade of coaching Pacific Islanders he hosted a couple of Australian lifters at his gym ahead of the Melbourne 2006 Commonwealth Games. He was shocked. 'They just broke down in three days. They were crying, literally crying.' When Australia organised a training camp in Fiji, nearly half the team withdrew.

The biggest difference between the 20 lifters at the Oceania Institute, from 11 different islands, and those in Australia and New Zealand is that Coffa's best performers are full-time athletes. They do not need to work, do not attend university, and are not distracted by computers, television and other technological gadgets, at least not to the extent of young athletes in many other parts of the world. The institute has moved around the Pacific with Coffa – from Fiji to Samoa to New Caledonia. The French Government helped to fund the headquarters in Noumea, as New Caledonia is an overseas *departement* of France. 'It's like a little hotel, and it's a hundred times better than anything most of these lifters have on their own island,' said Coffa. The best lifters are funded by their own national Olympic committees, who pay them a small weekly allowance. Accommodation and facilities are free, as is Coffa's coaching since he left Nauru in 2001. 'For more than 10 years I haven't received a single dollar in coaching fees,' he said. 'I was very well looked after in Nauru, well paid. I'm lucky to be able to do it. It's very rewarding. For example, Samoa had never won a gold medal in the Commonwealth Games before Delhi in 2010, and they won three in weightlifting. Can you imagine the feeling? And getting a young kid from Kiribati, who was training at 6am on the beach because it's too hot later in the day – so hot you couldn't touch the bar – and training that kid until he becomes a realistic medal hope for 2014, that's a big, big thing. It's hugely gratifying.

'Pacific weightlifters are warriors who love the scent of battle. They crave the sweat, the pain, the adrenaline and the fight of each lift they muster. To miss a training session is taboo for them. The desire to master the weights pushes them well over the capabilities of the average weightlifter. The way they are built, they have very strong joints and hardly ever get injured. And yet they consider themselves inferior to lifters outside the Pacific region. All they can do is admire other lifters at a distance and wish they were as good, never realising that they may be just as good or better. It's a pity to see these athletes feel inferior.'

When Coffa started in Nauru his task was not just to coach weightlifters. Within months of his arrival he had created the Nauru Olympic Committee. This enabled Stephen to compete for his homeland in the Atlanta Olympics in 1996. It had not been possible four years earlier, so in the 1992 Barcelona Games he represented Samoa. The president of Nauru and the prime minister of Samoa were close, which helped to speed up the paperwork. 'The links between the Pacific Islands are strong and they help each other when they can,' said Stephen, who finished ninth in 1992, failed to complete his lifts in 1996, and was eleventh in the Sydney 2000 Olympics, where he was Nauru's flag-bearer at the opening ceremony. When any lifter from the Oceania Institute is competing, whatever their nationality, all the others will be there to offer support, said Stephen. 'If anybody wins a medal, everybody in the Pacific region feels we won it together.' Heads of State, government ministers and officials from other sporting bodies will come along to support their lifters.

Coffa first thought about leaving Australia at the Barcelona Olympics. Vinson Detenamo, Nauru's vice-president and sports minister, took Paul to dinner and suggested he consider working in Nauru, where there were many more young people built like Marcus Stephen. The country's youth were desperately keen on sport and needed help. 'So I took up the challenge two years later,' said Coffa. 'By that time I really needed a change in my life. In October 1994 my family packed up and left – my wife, and three kids then aged five, two and one. We were provided with a beautiful home with a swimming pool, plus two cars and a minibus. We were looked after very, very well.'

On his arrival Coffa found that 'sport barely existed at all' in Nauru. There was no equipment, nowhere to train, not even a set of weights. He made his views known, and on the next flight from Australia there were 10 sets of Olympic weights. The government gave him two classrooms to convert into a training centre, which became a permanent base. 'Within a week we had possibly the best weightlifting facility in the Pacific. Two weeks later the President opened the Nauru Weightlifting Centre and from then on we were ready to rock'n'roll, with 50 youths training day after day, every one of them already built like a weightlifter.' School timetables were changed so the best lifters could train twice a day. Within a couple of years Nauru dominated the sport in the region. Samoan lifters came to train in Nauru, and Coffa had started to build the foundations for the Oceania Institute. 'Nauru became a powerhouse of weightlifting and other islands followed.'

By the end of 1995, Nauru had sent four lifters to the World Junior Championships in Poland, and three to the World Championships in China. A women's team, the Dolphins, and a youth team, the Skipjacks, were formed. More than 100 lifters of all ages were training twice a day. Within three years of the start of the programme, almost every junior record in the Oceania region was held by a Nauruan lifter. Gold medallists in international contests were rewarded with payments of A$30,000 to A$50,000 from the government. The world of weightlifting began to take notice and the International Federation sent all its top officials to the Commonwealth and Oceania Championships in Nauru in 1998. Stephen won three more Commonwealth Games golds, in the 62kg class, in Kuala Lumpur later in the year and followed up with a silver in the same weight category at the world championships in Athens in 1999, in the clean and jerk. 'That was an incredible performance,' said Coffa.

At those 1998 Games Stephen had faced a big challenge from a former Soviet lifter who was now Australian, Yurik Sarkisian. 'He was really good,' said Stephen, 'but I was at my peak around that time and was strong enough to face anybody.' Stephen's featherweight records from the late 1990s were the only Commonwealth weightlifting records that, heading into the Glasgow Games, had lasted since the previous century. Sarkisian gained revenge in Manchester four years later, relegating Stephen to the silver medal position in the snatch, the clean and jerk and the combined. Stephen retired after Manchester having won seven golds and five silvers in his four Commonwealth Games appearances.

By the time of Marcus Stephen's farewell he had lost Paul Coffa as his coach. Nauru, remarkably, had won the bid to host the 2001 weightlifting World Championships. Taiwan, a political ally, had helped with the funding and the arena was nearly completed, as was a 64-dwelling athletes' village. 'When the final instalment was to be withdrawn from the bank for the completion of the stadium and the village, the president at that time, who has since died, used the money for other purposes and left the championships in a mess,' said Coffa. Nauru had to withdraw its offer. 'It was a great disappointment to me, it was unforgivable. Within two weeks I packed up and left Nauru. Unfortunately all good things come to an end.' Coffa still has great memories of 'living the dream' in Nauru. He has remained close to Marcus Stephen and coaches Nauru's best lifters from his bases elsewhere.

Coffa's next stop after Nauru was Fiji, where he built a beachside house and intended to retire. He missed the coaching, so he started taking on local lifters. That went well and the Oceania Institute was born in 2002. Several islands were soon sending their best prospects to train with Coffa. When he moved again to Samoa five years later, and then on to Noumea in New Caledonia, the institute and the Pacific's top lifters went with him. They train seven hours a day, every day, during which the top women will lift a total of 15 tons and the men 20 tons. Current and former lifters are trained as coaches, funded by the Olympic movement. 'If we don't win five or six gold medals in Glasgow something will be wrong,' said Coffa, who intends to stay in Noumea at least until the 2016 Olympics. 'After that, we'll see.'

He felt at home as soon as he left Australia. 'I got to like the way of life, the environment, the culture. My family settled well in the islands. I really enjoy what I'm doing. My wife teaches PE in schools and helps to teach the lifters English, among other things.' Educating young lifters has been a big challenge. Working on plantations, fishing and otherwise providing for the extended family take precedence over schooling for many islanders, said Coffa. 'Their education can be limited, and that hinders their ability to communicate.' Another disadvantage, linked to lack of education, is the high percentage of teenaged girls having children. 'I have had lifters who, at 14 and 15 years of age, have already had a child. They are so talented in lifting yet you lose them at such an early age.'

There was a terrible case in 2005 of an Oceania Institute lifter being jailed for manslaughter in Australia. Quincy Detenamo, who competed at the 1996 Olympics and finished sixth in the 77kg category in the 2002 Commonwealth Games, killed a woman during an argument in Melbourne. Detenamo, whose relatives include the former minister Vinson Detenamo – the man who persuaded Paul Coffa to move to Nauru – and Commonwealth medallist Itte Detenamo, was eventually sentenced to nine years' imprisonment. Coffa and his fellow lifters were 'shocked and devastated' by the case but, after Detenamo's release, they have helped him to put his life back in order. Detenamo is now a qualified weightlifting coach working with Nauru's best lifters. 'He paid the penalty and is now going ahead with the rest of his life,' said Coffa. 'I am happy to see that he is involved in coaching.'

Lack of equipment is another challenge. On Kiribati, weightlifters train on the sand: Coffa calls them 'coconut lifters' because they train under coconut trees for shade. 'They have no platforms, no squat racks, and no weightlifting boots. It absolutely amazes me how they can lift so much under these conditions. One of the lifters from Kiribati who came to the Institute to train could not jerk more than 150kg with shoes. Yet without shoes, he clean and jerks 170kg.'

Diet is important. New Zealand's Richard Dryden recalled Coffa talking to him about his fears of the lifters finding their way to a Kentucky Fried Chicken restaurant on a visit to Australia. 'They'd eat it morning, noon and night if they could,' said Dryden. 'And those guys can eat!' The simple diet in the islands comprises mainly rice, taro (root vegetable), fish and coconut. 'Very simple, but they eat in large quantities and as a consequence they increase their body mass at a very early age,' said Coffa, who stressed the importance of keeping the lifters within their own culture. 'Take them out and they won't succeed. Look at what happened with Cameroon.' The West Africans won nine weightlifting golds, men and women, at Manchester 2002 where, said Coffa, they 'looked exceptional, a fantastic team of lifters'. They went to Paris to train, became 'distracted by the bright lights' and most of them were never heard of again.

When Coffa left Australia the nation's weightlifting prospects suffered, as his brother pointed out. 'That's when our problems really started,' said Sam Coffa. 'Paul is a great inspiration, a very demanding bloke, and when you lose a person like that it is a very big blow.' The same thing happened to a lesser extent in Nauru, where Stephen said, 'We owe it all to Paul – there is nobody quite like him. He has devoted his life to his sport.' The numbers have dropped since Coffa left. Weightlifting is still the most popular sport but, said Coffa, 'Today they struggle for money, the phosphate has gone. Marcus is still confident and he's working hard to get it back, but the power has shifted from Nauru.' Samoa and Kiribati are coming to the fore. Besides Kiribati, four other nations who have never won a Commonwealth medal in any sport will have high hopes in weightlifting at Glasgow 2014 – Niue, Solomon Islands, Tuvalu and Vanuatu.

Paul Coffa's 'infectious passion and enthusiasm' drew praise from the head of weightlifting's world governing body, Dr Tamás Aján. Coffa should be 'well proud of his selfless accomplishments over the last four decades' said Dr Aján, president of the International Weightlifting Federation and a member of the IOC. 'Without doubt, Paul Coffa has been, and continues to be, the most important official within the Oceania and Commonwealth Weightlifting Federations.

Nauru's best days are over, judging by views expressed by visitors in recent years. Alexander Downer announced in 2008 that the worst place he had visited in his 11 years as Australia's foreign minister was Nauru – followed by Kiribati. Tony Wheeler, founder of the world's most popular travel publisher, Lonely Planet, wrote a chapter on Nauru in his 2013 book *Tony Wheeler's Dark Lands*. His hotel looked like a squatter camp, the island was stricken by power cuts and water shortages, and nobody wanted to visit a country where the influx of tourists averaged 13 per month, he wrote. He toured the refugee camp that, when the primary phosphate deposits ran out in the 1990s, became a new source of income for Nauru. Australia sent boatloads of Asians here as part of their 'Pacific Solution' – a holding camp for asylum seekers while their paperwork was processed. It opened in 2001, closed in 2007 and reopened in 2012. Wheeler wrote, too, of the now defunct Nauru banking system that once featured 400 banks, all run from the same PO Box address. The Russian Government estimated that US$70 billion of mafia money was laundered via Nauru, and an English con man was sentenced to 12 years in prison for using Nauru banks to defraud the Inland Revenue of more than £70m. There are no banks now. Nauru was not a bad place, however, concluded Wheeler: it was more 'misguided, credulous and exploited'.

Richard Dryden, the New Zealand weightlifting coach, has returned to Nauru a few times since his first visit in 1996, when the phosphate mining left a lasting impression. 'I thought it was like being on the moon,' he said. 'There were craters everywhere – all the good had been sucked out of the land. Because so little was grown, the plane to Nauru was one third full of passengers and two thirds full of food and supplies. It was a bizarre place – but the people were incredibly warm, so positive, friendly, carefree. And we had a great party at Paul Coffa's house.'

What does Marcus Stephen say? That Nauru has moved on from the days of bad investments and crooked investors. That the offshore banking was set up as a revenue source quite legitimately, as it has been elsewhere, and that some of the bigger countries who have bullied Nauru should also take the blame for what happened. 'If they are going to point the finger they should also look at themselves, at where the money originated from.' Nauru is off the international blacklist and, in a recent report on the Pacific region commissioned by the Australian Department for International Development, it came out on top in terms of accountability, transparency and delivery of projects.

'There are so many good things nowadays that we as a country are very proud of. We made mistakes in the past but who hasn't? We have developed, we have learned from our mistakes and we have introduced stronger legislation and amended our constitution. We may not be as rich as in the 1970s but we are very comfortable now with what we have. As a race we are kind and very modest.

'I love my country, I love island life. It is not New York, London or Melbourne. It is a Pacific island, one that was given the name of "The Pleasant Isle" by the whalers in the old days. It's a beautiful island, beautiful sunrises and sunsets every day, warm weather all year around. Fantastic fishing, which I enjoy very much. I go out fishing almost every day. I just love it. Family are good, what more do I want? I am a very lucky man. Nauru is Nauru. To me it is paradise.'

Stephen will have been a member of parliament (MP) for 14 years at the end of his current term in 2016, when he will surely be elected again. His stardom helped him to win voters' support and his experiences in sport were an advantage when, in 2007, he was elected president. 'To have travelled the world opens one's eyes. To have good discipline and work ethic is a winning formula. Sport gave me confidence to take on the big challenges.' This may have entailed speaking persuasively at the United Nations or an international forum, negotiating foreign policy and aid, or writing on climate change for the *New York Times*, as he once did. He met President Obama and his wife, Michelle, on one of his official visits to the United States. 'I am never overawed and love taking on a challenge if it helps my country. My sporting achievements showed that someone from a small island of 10,000 people, if they put in the hard work, can take on the world. What are the odds? I achieved a lot in my career. Not many have done what I did.

'We are a Commonwealth country and we are proud of the history and association. We are grateful for the many years under Australian administration and also the British through the British Phosphate Company, who left a huge legacy for us to enjoy and to help develop Nauru. We are very lucky to have the resource, and our oceans are very rich in fisheries resources too.'

His four years of presidency ended when Stephen resigned during one of many arguments over corruption in phosphate deals. He had been accused of trying to gain financially from a contract with a Thai company. Stephen denied any wrongdoing, said the accusations were 'unwarranted and mischievous' but resigned 'because the office of the president was being devalued'. He remained in government as a senior minister and could return to the presidency in future.

During his tenure, he said, the government established an efficient internet service and mobile phone network on Nauru, and restored stability to the airline. Developed countries would take those services for granted, Stephen said – along with fresh water and electricity.

'We never had them but we made it happen. We improved the quality of life. It gets a bit complicated, but in short, looking back, we did a hell of a lot of good things. Politicians can twist words and take things out of context, and of course there have been some bumpy rides, but this is part and parcel of politics – just like in sports.'

Politics in Nauru is not run on party lines, just 'groups of common interest'. New or broken alliances with fellow MPs can and do lead to constant change. At the time of Stephen's resignation, Nauru had three presidents within a week. He said after the 2013 elections, 'I can be opposition now but down the track I can be re-elected president – who knows? It has happened many times.' Stephen was appointed minister for fisheries, minister for the Nauru Phosphate Royalties Trust, minister for commerce, industry and environment, and Minister for Home Affairs and Public Service. He is a member of the International Weightlifting Federation executive board, vice-president of the Pacific Games Council, president of the Oceania Weightlifting Federation and head of Nauru's Olympic committee.

Weightlifting is still his great love, and is still the island's favourite sport. 'We keep coming up with good lifters and winning medals, and the people expect weightlifting to deliver year in, year out. Jamaicans and other Caribbean countries are good at sprint races, Africans in long-distance running. Given the right support and proper resources, proper coaches, the Pacific can and will be a force in weightlifting. We are a natural at it. It is our gift.'

11

Miracle mile

Biggest audience ever for Bannister v Landy
– then a horror show

The world's biggest audience for a single sporting contest tuned in to follow the 1954 mile race at the Commonwealth Games in Vancouver, effectively a match between Roger Bannister and John Landy. Twenty minutes after Bannister's triumph the packed stadium fell silent during a sickening finale to the marathon.

On the afternoon of Saturday 7 August 1954 two of the best female athletes of the twentieth century shone at Vancouver's Empire Stadium. Newlywed Marjorie Jackson, a future state governor of South Australia, was running her last race before retirement at the age of 22. She flew down the straight on the final leg of the sprint relay to overtake England's Anne Pashley on the line, finishing with a career tally of seven Commonwealth golds, the Olympic 100m/200m double, six individual world records and global recognition as the world's foremost sprinter.

Jackson was the first Australian woman to win an Olympic gold medal in athletics. The first New Zealander to do so, also in Helsinki in 1952, was Yvette Williams – probably the world's best all-round athlete in the days before the pentathlon. She made her case by winning two events at the same time on that Saturday in Vancouver. The discus and long jump had been due to start an hour apart but the discus was delayed because of the late arrival of the Duke of Edinburgh.

'It caused a major problem,' said Williams, who had already won the shot-put and run sixth in the sprint hurdles final. 'The long jump was held on one side of the stadium and the discus on the opposite side, 100 metres or more away. So I had one long jump then had to dash across the stadium, change from my long jump spikes to my discus throwing shoes, have a throw, then race back for another jump.' This continued throughout the afternoon. Twelve dashes across the stadium, 11 changes of shoes and two gold medals. 'Considering the circumstances, winning those two events at the same time was one of the best performances of my career.'

Their efforts gained nowhere near as much publicity as Jackson and Williams deserved. *The Times* in London gave each woman a brief paragraph at the foot of their report. Even in Australia news of Marjorie Jackson's farewell achievement was buried away. The reason was simple: bad timing. If they had run, jumped and thrown on any other day of the Commonwealth Games their medals would have been much bigger stories. All the headlines, newsreels and radio broadcasts from Vancouver on that sunny August weekend focused instead on two events that completely overshadowed all others – Roger Bannister's victory over John Landy and the sickeningly dramatic collapse of Jim Peters in the marathon shortly afterwards. It was billed as 'Triumph and Tragedy' on front pages worldwide. The two men represented both sides of the divide in English athletics: Bannister an Oxford academic who was very much part of what Peters and others called 'the university crowd', Peters a working-class Londoner with 'a tough Cockney attitude'. It was without question the most remarkable single session of athletics in the history of the Empire and Commonwealth Games.

If the Americans, as detailed elsewhere, unwittingly played an important part in the creation of what became the Commonwealth Games they also had a significant role in making the 1954 mile one of the most famous races ever run. Such were the effects of that celebrated 'miracle mile' or 'mile of the century' that American writers identified it 50 years later as a landmark event, one that highlighted the extent of sport's growing commercial appeal and the 'celebrity culture' that would go with it.

'It struck one of the first notes of sport's future,' wrote Neal Bascomb in his book *The Perfect Mile* in 2004. Bascomb's view echoed that of *Sports Illustrated*, the magazine that was launched in the United States a week after the 'miracle mile'. In a special report in 2003 *Sports Illustrated* said the race had been a highlight in a year that 'marked the beginning of an intriguing confluence of people and circumstance, talent and ambition, that fundamentally changed sports'.

It was 93 days since Bannister had gained worldwide fame by becoming the first man to run a mile in less than four minutes. It was 47 days since Landy had run even faster. Here were the only two milers ever to have beaten four minutes, an Englishman and an Australian going for gold in what *Sports Illustrated* described as 'the most widely heralded and universally contemplated footrace ever run'.

What made it so was the Americans' interest. More than 500 American radio stations broadcast live commentary, as did the BBC and many others

around the world. The audience was taken to a new high by the presence
of American television crews. The sub-four-minute 'dream mile' had
been talked about in the United States as much as anywhere for some 20
years, so – for the first time – a one-off sporting event with no Americans
involved was shown live on US television. NBC built a number of radio
relay towers between Vancouver and Seattle so the pictures could be
transmitted throughout the United States.

The Americans, unlike most Europeans, were enjoying a post-war boom.
They had the biggest cars, the biggest stars of stage and screen, and the fattest
wallets thanks to a buoyant economy that had never performed so well. The
world's new superpower had confidently predicted that one of their own
would be the first man to break the four-minute mile barrier. Their hopes
had been pinned on Wes Santee, from Kansas, who was training to join the
Marines. 'The honor of running the first four-minute mile will be lodged in
the USA,' wrote *Track and Field News* after one of Santee's many near misses.
'I'll run it, you can be sure of that,' Santee had told a journalist. 'I'm as
certain I can run the four-minute mile as you are that you can drive your
car home.' Perhaps the car ran out of petrol, for Santee, who broke the
1500m world record a month after Bannister's famous feat, never did go
under four minutes for the mile – nor did any American until 1957. Santee
was merely an onlooker for the 'miracle mile' as a commentator for NBC.

In the words of *Sports Illustrated*, who named Roger Bannister as their
first sportsman of the year, his mile inside four minutes and Sir Edmund
Hillary's 1953 ascent of Mount Everest 'were part of the spiritual rebuilding
of postwar Britain'. Bannister's feat in Oxford was quickly followed by a
'victory tour' in the United States, organised by the Foreign Office.
Bannister was just the man to show the Americans that Britain was still a
force to be reckoned with: an estimated 75 million viewers watched his
interviews. The television audience for the 1954 'miracle mile' was
estimated at 100 million.

Bannister would give up athletics later in the year to devote more time
to medicine, as he had always planned. He had qualified as a doctor eight
weeks before the Commonwealth Games. Running was nothing more
than 'an exciting distraction' to him despite the fact that it brought him
lifelong fame. Peters had wanted to continue in the hope of an Olympic
medal in 1956 but was, in his own words, 'lucky not to die that day'. The
man who held the marathon world record for more than six years from
1952 was so badly affected by his experience in Vancouver that he never
ran another race. Jim Peters lived a long and fulfilling life, but he
occasionally suffered giddiness and his 'Vancouver headache' right up to
his death in 1999.

John Landy was the first great Australian middle-distance runner. He, too, would have quit had he won in Vancouver – like Marjorie Jackson and Yvette Williams, both of whom married and retired from athletics in 1954. Landy took a teaching job for a while but returned to the track for the 1956 Olympics in his home town of Melbourne. He had suffered a cut on his heel in Vancouver and was injured again before finishing a disappointing third in the 1500m in Melbourne, but he never complained. Nearly six decades after the 'miracle mile' he said, 'Looking back, I would always have taken that Vancouver race over Melbourne. Of course, it would have been nice to win the Olympics in my home town, but Vancouver was a watershed race. If I had won that everybody would have said it should have been me who broke the four-minute mile. It was an almost unbelievable set of circumstances. That race had all the ingredients of a world title fight. I don't think I'd have ever run again if I had won.' Bannister said that 'breaking four minutes before him would have meant nothing' had he lost to Landy in Vancouver. 'The pressure was unbearable. Beating John Landy was my defining race.' A statue of Bannister overtaking Landy on the final bend was unveiled in Vancouver in 1967.

The *Daily Telegraph*, on the morning of the 'tremendous duel between the two four-minute milers', announced: 'This is the perfect race, in that it is a personal struggle rather than a contest against the stopwatch. The whole world is awaiting the outcome.' Landy was seen as the slight favourite.

Bannister had used his medical knowledge to his advantage on the track. From the age of 16, when he was offered a place at the University of Oxford, he studied breathing, physiology, the transfer of oxygen to the muscles and anything else that may aid a middle-distance runner. He had planned everything meticulously for the 1952 Olympics only to be undone by a change in conditions. An extra qualifying round was added to the schedule: he knew his body could not cope with three 1500m races in three days. He finished fourth.

That Olympic 'failure', Bannister's perceived lack of tactical nous, his refusal to appoint a coach and Landy's much quicker time over the mile appeared to give the Australian the edge in Vancouver, though he never rated his own chances at better than 50–50. Bannister's historic sub-four-minute run in May, on a track in Oxford that is now named after him, was achieved at a low-key meeting and would not have happened but for the help of his friends Chris Brasher and Chris Chataway, who ran as pacemakers. At an invitation meeting in Turku, Finland on midsummer's day Landy had beaten Bannister's time by 1.4 seconds, a huge margin that would equate in distance to about 10 yards.

Besides helping Bannister in Oxford, Chataway, the gold medallist over three miles in Vancouver, was the spur for Landy in that race in Finland. Landy, invited to run in Scandinavia, spent several weeks there. He had seen it as ideal preparation for Vancouver only to find that there was little serious competition in a series of easy wins. That changed when Chataway persuaded organisers to switch a 1500m race to a mile and flew over to run against Landy in Turku. Chataway challenged for the lead for more than three laps of a race in which the brilliant Australian also set a 1500m world record. That was more bad news for the Americans, as the man who lost the 1500m record was Santee, who had set it only 17 days earlier. Chataway was also part of the 'university crowd' who liked to have a good time: he was astonished that Landy did not want to go out on the town in Turku for a serious celebration of his achievement. Landy said, 'I went home early that night thinking "That's history, now I've got to work out how I'm going to beat Bannister".'

Touts were asking $100 Canadian (more than $850 or £450 in today's terms) for tickets to see the big race, which attracted a full house of 35,000. Among them were two Americans who drove up from Oregon – newspaper publisher William W. Knight and his 15-year-old son, Phil. The race sparked Phil Knight's interest in running, which led later to his founding of Nike, the world's leading sportswear company. 'That race was a big inspiration to me,' said Phil Knight 50 years later.

British listeners tuned in at 10.25pm on Saturday night to listen to Rex Alston's commentary on the Light Service: it was already Sunday morning in Melbourne when the starter fired his gun. With a lap to go, Briton and Australian alike must have expected the front-running Landy to win. 'Can Bannister catch him?' asked Alston. 'There's none of his famed spurt at the moment. Landy is drawing slightly away. Yes, Landy has a lead of three yards. It's 220 yards to go and I don't believe Bannister is going to be able to catch him. Landy is running beautifully.'

Bannister, too, had his worries at halfway. 'Landy was a long way in front and looked like staying there,' he recalled. He was not slowing down; the Englishman's confidence dipped. Bannister abandoned his carefully planned tactics on the third lap. He would have to run to Landy's time schedule, not his own. 'That was the turning point,' he said.

It worked. A few seconds later Alston was telling his listeners, 'Bannister is coming up on him now, 150 yards to go and Bannister is gaining ever so slightly with each stride … 130 yards to go and Bannister is coming up on Landy's elbow.'

Landy knew that Bannister would have to run a few yards more to overtake him on the outside and, expecting a challenge on his inside, he turned his head to look over his left shoulder. In his 1955 autobiography *The First Four Minutes*, Bannister wrote: 'The moment he looked round he was unprotected against me and so lost a valuable fraction of a second in his response to my challenge. It was my tremendous luck that these two happenings, his turning round and my final spurt, came absolutely simultaneously.'

Bannister went ahead. His finishing kick took him clear by five yards at the line. His 3 minutes 58.8 seconds, more than half a second faster than his Oxford run, was 0.8 seconds ahead of Landy. For the first time in any race two men had run a mile inside four minutes. Bannister collapsed, exhausted, into the arms of the England team manager, Leslie Truelove, after breaking the tape. He was carried through the crowds milling on the track before he recovered enough to jog after Landy, whom he hugged in congratulation. The last lap had been one of the most exciting moments of his life, he said. But the euphoria did not last long. Twenty minutes later, Bannister recalled, 'all was forgotten as the dazed figure of Jim Peters, in the last stages of exhaustion, appeared at the edge of the stadium'. The *Guardian*'s man on the spot, Frank Keating, captured the moment:

Hardly had the cheering died away after the Bannister–Landy mile when a frail-looking figure in white shorts and vest tottered into the stadium. The crowd of 35,000 rose to cheer the marathon winner home from his gruelling 26 miles–plus run. But Peters was not home yet. His head rolled from side to side as he gasped for breath and he fell to the track with a lap still to go. For a full two minutes he lay motionless. A hush fell on the horrified crowd. Police and doctors gathered round, knowing that to help him meant his disqualification. Other events came to a halt and the athletes saw the gallant Peters climb unsteadily to his feet. He tried to run on but almost immediately he was down again. The courage which has driven Peters more than the distance round the equator since he took up marathon running again brought him to his feet. From side to side of the track he reeled in his agony. Down again and then up. A few anguished paces and down again.

Fifteen minutes after he entered the stadium he had covered only 150 yards. He must have fallen twenty times. At last he crossed what he thought was the finishing line. Mick Mays, the English masseur, wrapped his arms around the exhausted runner and carried him from the track. Mays, too, had mistaken the finishing line. There was still 220 yards to go. The line Peters had crossed was that which had been used for the finish of the mile. Six doctors, including Bannister, crowded round the disqualified Peters, and he was given oxygen.

Keating wrote again about the Vancouver race in *Observer Sport Monthly* more than half a century later. Looking back, he described it as 'a grotesquely hideous ballet' and 'a pitifully tottering dance of death'. A Canadian reporter was physically sick as he watched from the stands. The *Daily Express* said more than 20 women fainted. Keating recalled:

> High in the pressbox, Peter Wilson of the *Daily Mirror* fed another sheet into his typewriter: 'Two steps forward, three to the side. So help me, he is running backwards now ... oh, he's down again ... The nauseous spectacle of a semi-conscious man being allowed to destroy himself while no one had the power or gumption to intervene.' When some from the grandstands, unable to bear it, began to shout for a stop, the stadium announcer crassly called for order and 'a respect for sportsmanship'. Peters, his skin a deathly mottled grey and a collar of foam streaming from his mouth, was borne away on a stretcher. He never ran again.

The stretcher bearers were needed for the medal ceremony, too. The third-placed finisher, South African Johannes Barnard, had to be carried to the podium: his feet were so badly blistered he could not stand up. Four years later Barnard's finishing time was half an hour faster as he took the silver medal in Cardiff behind Australia's Dave Power. Jim Peters's great friend and rival, Stan Cox, was another victim of the Vancouver heat. Reports said Cox had run into a telephone pole at the twenty-third mile though the eventual winner, Scotland's Joe McGhee, said this was not entirely accurate. 'He just collapsed, and held on to the pole as he sunk to the ground,' said McGhee. When Cox came back to his senses he asked onlookers to take his shoes off: his feet were burning. 'Did Bannister make it?' he asked. When told that he had, Cox replied, 'God bless him,' and then said he had to finish the race because he couldn't 'let England down'. Instead he was taken to hospital. Bannister went along too to check on his teammates' progress. He would stay with Peters until he was safely home in England, travelling with him on the long flight 'because he might need assistance'.

Within hours of the end of the Games, which finished later that afternoon, Bannister was receiving telegrams from all over the world and, according to Frank Rostron in the *Daily Express*, 'fending off telephone calls, dodging society hostesses and basking in the adulation being showered on him' as the world's most celebrated athlete. 'No one, athlete or spectator, man of the Empire or fan from over the US border, could fail to feel his pulse quickening with admiration for Bannister,' Rostron wrote. In the *Mirror* Peter Wilson dwelled more on the predicament of Jim Peters when he wrote, 'Sport should never revolt you, make you squirm, force you to close your eyes and feel dirty and ashamed … as though you had paid a black market price to be a spectator at a public execution.' Letter writers to Canadian newspapers said marathon running should be banned. It was announced in Melbourne – the host city for the 1956 Games – that because of what happened in Vancouver, the start time of the next Olympic marathon would be put back until 3pm or later.

Bannister had told Frank Rostron in the *Daily Express* that his own experiments had shown him to be capable of three maximum-effort runs in a year. Those efforts were: the four-minute mile in May, the 'miracle mile' in August, and the European Championship 1500m in Berne, Switzerland three weeks later. Bannister won again in Berne. At the age of 25 he then promptly retired from athletics, just as he had planned. Now he was ready for the important part of his life: raising a family and furthering his career in medicine.

The miler's education was a world apart from the marathon man's. Jim Peters 'roamed wild' for many months when his parents moved to a new council estate in Essex. He missed an entire year of schooling aged eight to nine. He left to find work soon after his fourteenth birthday. At the age of 17 he started to work for an optician who helped him to gain qualifications. Eventually he would run his own business, branching out in the year of the Vancouver race.

Jim Peters, underweight and anaemic throughout his teenage years, wanted to be a professional footballer. He was good, but not quite good enough so he took up running, too, winning the London boys' cross-country title. When he was conscripted – he would become the army's first sergeant optician – he took his boots to professional football matches at Southampton and Aldershot hoping to be called into action. Had it happened, he would have lost his amateur status and with it the right to compete in athletics. Peters did not give up on his dream of being a footballer until the war was over.

Within three years of the Allies' victory, Peters had become an accomplished long-distance runner. When he ran in the 10,000m at the 1948 London Olympics, he crossed the finish line alongside the great Czech champion Emil Zátopek – but sadly he had another lap to go. 'I felt I had let the country down,' he said. Stan Cox ran in that race, too.

By the time of the next Olympics Peters had trained relentlessly for three to four hours every evening. He spent so much time running, he told Rachel Cutler in an interview for the British Library's *Oral History of British Athletics* series in 1996, that his wife asked him if he was having an affair. No, he was just pounding out the miles, improving his times so much that he broke the marathon world record a few weeks before the

1952 Olympic Games in Helsinki – only a year after running the distance for the first time. He went to the Olympics as favourite. He had a frightening journey when the plane taking him to Finland was struck by lightning. He suffered cramp for the first time in his life and failed to finish. The greatest long-distance runner of the time, Emil Zátopek, running the distance for the first time, completed a unique treble of 5000m, 10,000m and marathon.

Peters decided to carry on running, training at lunchtime as well as in the evening – and always running in plimsolls, primitively flimsy footwear compared to modern running shoes. In 1954 he had a serious discussion about training with a visitor to England: John Landy. He won the Polytechnic Marathon in London for a third year in succession, all three of them in world-record time. The plan was to win at the Commonwealth Games in Vancouver and have one more try for Olympic gold in Melbourne in 1956. In his early years he had been 'a tiny little fellow full of heart, a tough Cockney boy', he said. He showed how tough he was by coping with the punishing training schedule that reduced his weight from 10 stone 2lbs at the 1948 Olympics to 8 stone 10lbs for his last, fateful race at the Vancouver Games.

Peters arrived three weeks early to train three times a day. The rowdier members of the 'university gang' were a distraction. 'They made a lot of noise after enjoying a night out – every night – so we had coconut matting put down in the huts to keep the sound down. The university types had a completely different outlook.'

When Peters studied the marathon course he found it was too long by three-quarters of a mile. It was shortened to the correct distance but was still 'the toughest course I'd ever seen'. The race was made even tougher by a start time of noon: only six of the 16 starters would finish. 'It was the hottest part of the day,' said Joe McGhee, whose winning time was 2 hours 39 minutes 36 seconds. 'Sweat was dripping from us before we even started. A Yugoslavian tried to gatecrash the race at the start and was politely told Yugoslavia was not part of the Commonwealth.' Jim Peters yelled at officials, 'Get this madman out of here!' McGhee said later that Peters had run 'an unintelligent race' and could not blame the weather alone. A world record was out of the question, so Peters could have run half a minute slower for every mile of the race and still won. 'He didn't slow down,' said McGhee. The South Africans had predicted that Peters would burn himself out and fail to finish.

Three Australians dropped out early and McGhee was left behind at about ten miles, and then it was Peters and Cox out in front. Peters had no idea that he was so far ahead when he came to the last half-mile. He was 17 minutes clear of McGhee, yet he thought Cox was his nearest pursuer a few hundred yards away. Had anybody told him he would have 'trotted in slowly' and finished, he said. He had taken no water during the race for fear that it would cause diarrhoea. He remembers falling over on the track and thinking, 'Oh dear, it's another Dorando.' Then his mind went blank until he came round in hospital. He fell 12 times in all.

Dorando was the Italian marathon runner Dorando Pietri who, like Peters, came close to death when he collapsed on the track at the end of a race. It happened at the 1908 London Olympics, where Pietri fell five times. 'I was literally a dead man,' Pietri said later. 'My heart had moved half an inch out of place with the strain of the run. The doctors brought me back to life by massaging my heart into place.' Pietri crossed the line first but because he had been helped to his feet by officials he was disqualified. The heroic failure earned him worldwide fame and fortune: he turned professional, ran in lucrative exhibition match races in the United States and set up his own bakery back in Italy. Pietri was presented with a special silver cup by Queen Alexandra in recognition of his efforts. Peters, too, was awarded a trophy by the royal family. The Duke of Edinburgh presented him with an honorary gold medal in December 1954 inscribed: 'J Peters, a most gallant marathon runner'. To Peters it was 'the most treasured of all my trophies'. By the time he accepted it he had received more than 3000 fan letters.

When he had first regained consciousness in hospital Peters thought he had won. 'When I asked a nurse, she said, "You did great, Jim, just great", so at least I went back to sleep a winner, didn't I?' His wife, Frieda, was staying with friends on England's south coast who did not have a telephone. While a Canadian radio station was erroneously telling its listeners that Peters had died, a British journalist managed to persuade the police to find Frieda and tell her that her husband was conscious and recovering. Visitors to his bedside included McGhee and Bannister. 'Roger Bannister told me it was a miracle I'd survived. I must have been dehydrated for miles.'

After Bannister and team manager Leslie Truelove had taken Peters home he went to see Sir Adolph Abrahams, an eminent doctor who had studied the effects of training on athletes' health. Abrahams, brother of the 1924 Olympic champion and athletics administrator Harold Abrahams, treated Peters without a fee at his Harley Street practice. 'He gave me a lot of attention after Vancouver,' said Peters. 'He couldn't find anything wrong with me but said "You should retire gracefully, you've done your whack", so I did. I knew I wouldn't have much chance in Melbourne.'

When he was invited back to Canada later, to appear on television, Peters told his host that he did not regard the Vancouver race as a failure.

'It was part of my life and now I was focusing on business.' Jim Peters ran a successful optician's business until retirement.

Roger Bannister had a great career ahead of him when he stopped running. When he was an athlete the acronyms CAN and GER may have appeared on a runner's vest or a results sheet for Canada and Germany. But to Bannister they had long meant something completely different: CAN is 'central autonomic circuits'; GER is 'gastro-oesophageal reflux'. Both feature in Bannister's 1983 masterwork, *Autonomic Failure, a Textbook of Clinical Disorders of the Autonomic Nervous System*, which has been updated many times. The publication of that textbook was one of the highlights of Bannister's 40-year career in academic medicine. 'That represents a lot more work than the four-minute mile,' he said.

'Running was only ever a small section of my life. If I'd had to give something up it would always have been running, never medicine. Medicine was my life.' In an interview in the *Guardian* 50 years after the 'miracle mile' Bannister spoke of how the events of 1954 had been a hindrance in his medical career.

> I had always wanted to become a neurologist, which is one of the most demanding vocations in medicine. Where do you stop, after all, with the brain? The work seems unending. After qualifying as a doctor you face nine more years of training. There were only 170 neurologists in Britain then and, whether spoken or unspoken, there was this insidious feeling. How can Bannister, a mere athlete, probably spoilt by all the publicity and fame, dare aspire to neurology? But I'd done a lot of research and my academic record was very good. So I had to alter the perception people had of me in my profession by being totally dedicated.

> I remember being invited to the Olympics in Tokyo in 1964, and turning it down. I could just imagine these brain specialists stalking the hospital corridors and asking, 'Where's this Bannister fellow?' As soon as someone said, 'Oh, he's in Toyko', it would've felt as if they'd been right about me all along. I was nothing but a runner.

John Landy, too, enjoyed a distinguished career after athletics. He became state governor of Victoria, headed rural science research for Imperial Chemical Industries (ICI) in Australia, served on various sports bodies, and was Australian Commissioner for the Vancouver 1986 Expo.

Bannister, like Landy, was still involved in sport, as the first chairman of the Sports Council. He worked hard to encourage mass participation and to discourage the use of performance-enhancing drugs. He was knighted by the Queen in 1975 for services to sport. He became Master of Pembroke College, Oxford, and in 2005 received an honour that meant more to him than any from sport: a lifetime achievement award from the American Academy of Neurology.

Running was no more than an 'exciting distraction' to Bannister, who 'almost hated it' at the height of his fame because of all the publicity. 'Somehow I felt this prostituted my running. It left me no freedom or joy to run as I pleased.' His heroes as a teenager were not sportsmen but Nobel laureates – Marie Curie and Louis Pasteur. When he took to running seriously there was one man he admired above all others: the New Zealand miler Jack Lovelock, a gold medallist at the 1934 Empire Games and Olympic champion over 1500m in 1936.

Bannister and Lovelock had much in common: they studied medicine at the same Oxford college, worked at the same London hospital, both held the mile world record, and both gave up running to focus on their work. Lovelock's tactical advice to Bannister in 1949, about surprising opponents with a well-timed increase in tempo, stayed in his mind right to the end. Bannister said Lovelock, whose analytical, scientific study of running was unique, was 'the best miler ever' and 'the first modern athlete'. On his retirement from athletics Lovelock sounded just like Bannister. He said, 'I have a lot of work to do and running doesn't go with medical work. I've got some wonderful memories to look back on, but sport is a very small part of a man's life. After all, we are here to work.' Lovelock moved to New York, where he died aged 39 in December 1949. He left work early, feeling unwell, and fell under a train on his way home to his wife and two young daughters.

Bannister gained global fame for a run that lasted just under four minutes. It always rankled with him that his 40 years of research and practice as a neurologist counted, to the wider public, for comparatively little. 'Sport is simple, black and white,' he once said. 'Medicine is complex, indescribably difficult. Running is a part of life. It's not really life as a whole, is it?' Perhaps *Sports Illustrated* was right: Roger Bannister may have been sport's first victim of 'the cult of celebrity'.

12

Con man

Robert Maxwell and the missing millions

Politics intruded into sport in such a way in 1986 that the Edinburgh Commonwealth Games – boycotted, broke, and run by a group of hapless amateurs – faced the threat of cancellation. Enter 'the white knight' who saved the Games and effectively made a fortune in the process.

Rarely, if ever, has a Games produced a cast list of champions to match that from Edinburgh in 1986. Greater fame lay ahead for many gold medallists, among them Lennox Lewis, who would become – in the view of some judges – an even more accomplished world heavyweight champion than Muhammad Ali. Steve Redgrave, later to be knighted as Britain's finest Olympian, won three times as rowing made its farewell appearance as a Commonwealth sport. Scotland's only winner on the track was the 10,000m runner Liz Lynch, who became a world champion as Liz McColgan five years later. Sally Gunnell's winning debut in the big time was a foretaste of record-breaking hurdling achievements in the Olympics and World Championships. Linford Christie was beaten in the 100m by Ben Johnson, whose glory days would end two years later in probably the biggest drugs scandal in sporting history.

Other winners had already been world-beaters. Steve Ovett, one of the best middle-distance runners of the previous decade, left the 800m and 1500m to another of the all-time greats, Steve Cram, and ended six years of injury and underachievement with a gold medal at 5000m. Daley Thompson won not only his third straight decathlon gold but a silver in the sprint relay, too. The big story in the swimming pool was a first ever defeat over 200m for Canada's brilliant breaststroke star, the world, Olympic and Commonwealth champion Victor Davis. England's Adrian Moorhouse, the man who beat him, would win Olympic gold in 1988.

Who, then, was the most written-about figure as the Scottish capital became the first city to host the Games for a second time? It was none of the above. Regardless of the quality of the sport, the undisputed champion of headline-making at Edinburgh 1986 was a Jewish Czech war hero whose mother died in Auschwitz. He spoke 10 languages despite being the self-educated son of a peasant farmer. He made a fortune from publishing, allegedly helped along by Britain's secret service, was an MP for six years but was 'not a person to be relied upon to exercise proper stewardship of a publicly quoted company' according to the Department of Trade, who investigated his dealings. He owned Pergamon Press, the world's largest scientific and educational publishing company, Mirror Group Newspapers, two football clubs, and a massive ego. Lampooned in the satirical magazine *Private Eye* as 'the Bouncing Czech' and 'Cap'n Bob', he craved international status as a political figure. He was born Jan Ludvik Hoch: he was better known as Robert Maxwell.

These were the most bizarre, most troubled Commonwealth Games ever staged. Edinburgh was boycotted and broke. More than half of all Commonwealth nations stayed away, as did the much-needed sponsors who might have kept the organisers out of debt. If Britain's Prime Minister, Margaret Thatcher, was the villain – there was no shortage of people keen to cast her in that role – then Maxwell claimed to be the hero. The press called him 'the white knight' when, with five weeks to go to the opening ceremony, Mirror Group Newspapers became the main backers and he took over as chairman of the company running the Games. Maxwell himself said he was 'the saviour'. He even hinted as much to the Queen when, much to his delight, he was introduced to her in Edinburgh by his personal photographer and aide Mike Maloney, who had been on many royal assignments. Maxwell told her a joke and, when he handed over a gift of a set of coins in a magnificent display box, he said, 'Permit me to present you with a token of this great event that I have orchestrated.' Maloney said he was 'beaming like a corgi with three tails' on that occasion and was later very proud to have a private audience with Prince Charles and Princess Diana, who were also presented with a set of coins.

People were still arguing about Maxwell's role nearly three years later when the last of the bills was finally paid, though not by him. His name was still being discussed at meetings in the late summer of 1998, when the company in charge, Commonwealth Games 1986 (Scotland) Ltd, held its final meeting. By then the 'white knight' was long dead, his name blackened forever. In November 1991 Maxwell went overboard from his private yacht in the Mediterranean. It became clear after his death that he had fraudulently misspent hundreds of millions of pounds from his employees' pension funds.

Without him, though, Edinburgh 1986 would have been an even bigger mess, an embarrassment that Scotland, Britain and the Commonwealth Games Federation might never have lived down. When Mirror Group came to the rescue Maxwell told a gathering of reporters that there would have been no Commonwealth Games without him. The company set up to run the Games would have had to call in a receiver, he said, and that would have been a scandal. 'Not a scandal in that someone had put something in his pocket, but the damage to the good name of Scotland and Great Britain would have been untenable. Think of the humiliation to the country if Edinburgh had gone into receivership. I couldn't allow that.'

The Games would also have been a good deal less colourful without Maxwell, who liked to do things differently. On one occasion he invited a number of Commonwealth VIPs and their partners to dinner at his private suite. He sent out his staff to buy the meal, and served his guests Kentucky Fried Chicken straight from the bucket. At another function he introduced his friend Ryoichi Sasakawa to the press. He announced the Japanese businessman, who pumped in far more money than Maxwell himself, as a multimillionaire philanthropist who had 'single-handedly funded the eradication of leprosy'. That claim was strange enough, given that more than 200,000 were still suffering from the disease a quarter of a century later, but Sasakawa himself left reporters even more dumbfounded when he told them that he was 27 years old and would live to the age of 200. He was 87 at the time.

Why did Maxwell get involved? Maloney believes that somebody made a speculative suggestion to him about backing the Games, and he suddenly saw a great opportunity. 'He thought he could be the saviour, and he was,' said Maloney, who was with Maxwell for his six-week involvement in Edinburgh.

Several factors counted against the hosts before their own shortcomings forced them to turn to Maxwell, among them the ultra-conservative attitude of one unchanging sport, rugby union; Mrs Thatcher's intransigence, and how African leaders reacted to it; lack of government funding; and the state of the global economy. What a difference from Edinburgh 1970 when, for the first time, the event had been tagged 'The Friendly Games'. That was the start of a new era. The Queen attended for the first time, the races switched from imperial to metric distances and photo-finish technology was used. The party started when Scotland's Lachie Stewart won a memorable 10,000m on the opening day and Edinburgh 1970 was, unlike its counterpart of the 1980s, rated one of the all-time great Games. The overall budget was £3m compared to £17m in 1986.

With so much of what happened beyond the organisers' control it was hardly surprising that the 1986 Games left behind a pile of unsolved problems and unpaid bills. The spectre of a boycott was there from the start. The 1976 Olympics in Montreal, which cost the city a fortune, had lost 26 African nations who refused to compete because of New Zealand's presence. The problem was rugby: New Zealand's All Blacks were still happy to play against South Africa at a time when other sports, supported by the United Nations, shunned them because of apartheid. It led to the signing, in 1977, of the Gleneagles Declaration by Commonwealth nations who agreed it was their 'urgent duty to vigorously combat the evil of apartheid by withholding any form of support for teams or sportsmen from South Africa or from any other country where sports are organised on the basis of race, colour or ethnic origin'. They would also take 'every practical step to discourage contact or competition' with South Africa. In some cases, most notably in New Zealand and Britain, the words proved to be more meaningful than the actions.

The Soviet Union's invasion of Afghanistan in 1979 precipitated another boycott, led by the United States, of the 1980 Moscow Games. While Britain's athletes were left to decide for themselves, the government wanted them to stay away. Within a few years sport had become a prime target for politicians: it would remain so until the end of the 1980s when the Berlin Wall came down.

The announcement that Edinburgh would host the 1986 Games was made, coincidentally, in Moscow at a Commonwealth Federation meeting held during the Olympics. It was party time for the Edinburgh bid team even if it was hardly a champagne moment: there had been no other bidders. At a time of worldwide economic recession and great political differences, nobody else wanted the 1986 Games.

Peter Heatly, later knighted for services to sport, had first suggested Edinburgh should bid for a second time. He was a diver, three times a gold medallist at the Games in the 1950s, who became an accomplished sports administrator and eventually the top man in the Commonwealth Games Federation. He recalled that talk of a boycott had always been around, 'but when it hit, the extent and range surprised everybody. It broke 10 days before the Games and every morning you would wake up and another country had decided not to come. It was terrible. You died a little bit every day over those 10 days.'

Of all host cities for the Games only Delhi, in 2010, attracted bad publicity at anywhere near the same level as Edinburgh 1986. There was a long list of complaints in India: dozens of construction workers on Games-related projects died because of terrible working conditions;

bribery and corruption cases dogged the process, leading to jail terms and expulsions of senior officials; expensive venues were unused and abandoned after the Games; costs soared way beyond even the highest estimates; there was too much environmental damage; sanitation and hygiene was poor; and slums were 'screened off' so athletes and visitors did not have to see them. None of the problems in Delhi posed a threat to the future of the Games, however, and after the impressive opening ceremony Delhi did a good enough job to draw praise from the IOC and the Commonwealth Games Federation.

In *Unfriendly Games*, a book that detailed all the pitfalls and problems of Edinburgh 1986, the authors concluded that the Games might never have taken place had Heatly not persuaded Edinburgh to put their name forward. 'Is it too wide of the mark,' wrote co-authors Derek Bateman and Derek Douglas, 'to suggest that despite all the problems, the ineptitude, the poor management, the naive commercial deals, if Edinburgh had not taken on the task of organisation then the Games would have been cancelled? The answer is that in all probability this is exactly what would have happened.'

Edinburgh also had to contend with significant changes in sport that would have far-reaching consequences. First swimming, and then athletics staged new World Championships in the early 1980s. Before long they would become regular fixtures, prioritised by athletes ahead of continental and Commonwealth commitments. If these new events were one step towards a more professional, more commercial future in sport, there was another giant leap in 1984. Despite a retaliatory boycott by the Communist countries, the Los Angeles Olympics made a huge profit, largely through lucrative advertising and sponsorship deals negotiated by sharp businessmen. The Americans had shown the way: now the Commonwealth Games were up for grabs and the Scots could bring in sponsorship money. They failed dismally. When they needed professionals to negotiate deals, they relied on amateurs. Selling 'The Friendly Games' to British and Commonwealth sponsors was beyond them, hence the late call to Robert Maxwell.

If there was one sport that detested the very idea of money tainting or changing the way things were done it was rugby union. Until 1995 the sport would stay rooted in its amateur past, run by 'old farts', as the former England captain Will Carling famously called them. Rugby lived in a world of its own, with South Africa very much a part of it. South Africa's football teams had been exiled from the international game since 1957, and the nation had been effectively barred from Commonwealth and Olympic sport since the early 1960s. In rugby, however, New Zealand, Australia and the British Isles were happy to play the all-white Springboks.

Rugby fixtures against South Africa had led to talk of boycotts of the 1974 and 1982 Commonwealth Games. The warning to Edinburgh was issued starkly and swiftly within hours of that meeting in Moscow. Chief Abraham Ordia, the Nigerian president of the Supreme Council for Sport in Africa, told the *Herald*'s (Glasgow) Doug Gillon that continued sporting links with South Africa could lead to the destruction of the Commonwealth. Shortly before the Moscow Games the British and Irish Lions had played a series against the Springboks. 'The Lions tour was a great boost to apartheid, the Boers, and racism,' said Ordia. 'We have given a final warning to the Commonwealth Games Federation. If Mrs Thatcher had spent one tenth of the time trying to stop the rugby tour as she did trying to halt the Olympics here in Moscow because of Afghanistan then we might have got somewhere. Great Britain is now the greatest supporter of sporting links with South Africa.'

In 1981, after the Springboks toured New Zealand, a new Commonwealth Games code of conduct was introduced to avoid a boycott of Brisbane 1982. Under the code, proposed by Jamaica, nations could be banned from the Games if they failed to stick by the terms of the Gleneagles Declaration. It put a greater onus on national associations to take a stand against sports that were not part of the Commonwealth Games.

The first test of the new code came in 1984 when England's rugby team were to play in South Africa. Under the Code of Conduct the English Commonwealth Games Council were compelled to write a letter of protest to the Rugby Football Union. They refused to do so, saying it was none of their business. It appeared that the Commonwealth Games would go ahead without England. Edinburgh's organisers approached all sports affiliated to the English Commonwealth Council, telling them they would not be able to compete. The individual sports bodies made sure the letter of protest was written by their umbrella body. While this did nothing to halt the rugby tour in May it showed the African countries that the Code of Conduct was being taken seriously.

England tried to change the terms of the Code of Conduct when the Commonwealth countries next met at the Los Angeles Olympics. The Scots again held firm, successfully leading the opposition to England's plans. So confident were the Edinburgh team after this meeting that chairman Ken Borthwick wrote to the Nigerians to say, 'I for my part am very pleased that all the Commonwealth countries are now coming to the Games in 1986 … We look forward to having a very successful Games.'

Plans were announced for tours to South Africa by New Zealand in 1985 and by the Lions in 1986. When that 1985 series was called off in a New Zealand court the Edinburgh Games looked safe. The Lions' tour was cancelled too: suddenly, with so many teams having confirmed their intention to compete in Edinburgh, organisers were worried that there would be too many competitors and officials in the Games village. There was a late rush for tickets. But African politicians wanted more: they sought affirmative action from Britain, and specifically from Thatcher, against apartheid South Africa. Thatcher was unmoved, restating her opposition to sanctions. On 10 July, two weeks before the Games were due to start, newspapers across the world ran reports from press agencies in London:

> Two black African nations, Nigeria and Ghana, announced yesterday that they will boycott the 1986 Commonwealth Games later this month in protest of Britain's refusal to agree to major economic sanctions against South Africa.

> The boycott appeared to be an attempt to put pressure on Prime Minister Margaret Thatcher, who has long opposed economic sanctions. The Nigerian Embassy in London said yesterday that the boycott was meant to 'dramatise to the British government how strongly we feel about the matter'.

> David Dixon, secretary of the Commonwealth Games Federation, said that the boycott would keep away about 80 athletes of the 3,151 scheduled to participate. But Dixon said the move was significant because 'the unity of the games is lost'.

The final loss would be far, far worse: 32 teams and nearly 1500 athletes stayed away. When the focus switched to sport rather than politics, nowhere was the loss better highlighted than in the new super-heavyweight category in which Lennox Lewis won his boxing gold and an unknown Welshman took silver.

When the BBC cameras focused in on Aneurin Evans, Lewis's opponent in the final, the most famous voice in British boxing said, 'He really is out of his depth here. If I were him I'd be running for my life.' Perhaps Evans heard the remark by the great commentator Harry Carpenter, for he spent the next few minutes trying, unsuccessfully, to evade Lewis's brutal punches. 'It was clear from the first bell that Evans was only going to take punishment,' said Carpenter after Evans's corner had thrown in the towel after 23 seconds of round two. The title went to Lewis, arguably the best boxer ever to have fought in the Commonwealth Games. Because of the boycott Evans became the unlikeliest silver medallist in Games history.

George Foreman, a double world champion and great adversary of Muhammad Ali, said Lewis was 'the best heavyweight of all time'. Lewis himself, in his heyday as undisputed champion of the world, said, 'I am the master of the sweet science. There is not one heavyweight who can match my skill.' Aneurin Evans would never have said any such thing – even in his dreams. He should never even have been in Edinburgh, yet he took a place on the podium.

By 1986 Lewis had already fought at the Olympics and won a North American championship. Evans had fought only 20 times in his life and was not selected by Wales. Two days before the Games started there were only two entries in the superheavyweights, Lewis and the Englishman James Oyebola, who had beaten Evans earlier in the year. The boycott hurt boxing more than any other sport: Nigeria, Ghana, Kenya, Uganda and Zambia all had strong contenders who stayed at home.

A late rallying call by officials led to Wales nominating Evans, who was coached by the 1958 Commonwealth bronze medallist Don Braithwaite. The Welshman's luck was in: he zipped up to Scotland and drew a bye into the final. Lewis, representing Canada before his later switch to Britain, where he spent most of his childhood, made short work of the 6ft 9in Oyebola first, and then pounded Evans into submission. But for a rule change during the Games, Evans might still not have been on the podium. All three medals could not be awarded unless there was a minimum entry of five individuals in any contest – but because of the 'special circumstances' of the boycott, the Commonwealth nations voted halfway through the Games to award three medals regardless of the entries. Lewis went on to world fame, Evans returned to obscurity in Caerphilly and later moved to the English Midlands. 'A silver medal was his for just four minutes of understandable backpedalling,' wrote the *Guardian*'s Frank Keating.

Figuratively, the Games' organisers had been backpedalling and taking a beating, too, before Maxwell's late arrival. Their executives had undersold the media rights, failed to bring in sponsors and employed too many staff. Despite their best efforts they had been sideswiped by the boycott and by the Thatcher government's refusal, in the general economic gloom, to offer any financial support.

The massive success of the Los Angeles Olympics was largely down to one man, Peter Ueberroth. He worked for an airline before building up his own travel business, which, by the time he sold it, was the second largest in the United States. When he took over the running of the LA Games he created a committee of 150 'movers and shakers' – mostly business people and entrepreneurs – to generate ideas, among them the creation of the torch relay. He persuaded Coca-Cola and other sponsors to back the Games despite worries over the economy and the Soviet-led boycott. The Olympics produced a profit of a quarter of a billion dollars. 'Everything about the 1984 Games smacked of success, from the competition to the profits, and it all traces back to the man who ran them,' wrote the *Los Angeles Times*. Two weeks after the Olympics, Ueberroth became commissioner of Major League Baseball: his daughter, Heidi, is a senior executive in American basketball. He is said to be worth $100m.

In the same role in Edinburgh was Kenneth Borthwick, a confectioner and Conservative councillor who was Lord Provost of the city from 1977 to 1980. Borthwick was well respected, 'a real gentleman, a distinguished, imposing figure built like a flank forward,' said Gillon, the *Herald*'s top reporter on the Games. Alex Wood, the then Leader of Edinburgh Council who was brought on to the board, was less impressed. 'Borthwick was an old-fashioned small businessman, a conservative Conservative. He was, I believe, keen to achieve a knighthood. He neither had a "big picture" perspective nor a hard-bitten big business perspective: dithering inaction was his default position.' Malcolm Beattie, commercial figurehead of the Auckland 1990 Games and a leading name in New Zealand sports sponsorship, was even more forthright. 'Ken Borthwick was very old-school. He showed great deference to the Queen and the establishment but he didn't really understand anything about running a big sports event. We wanted to know about money, about accommodation, about sponsors – all he spoke about was the squirl of bagpipes at dawn. He was a thorough gentleman but by the end of the Games he looked terrible, as though he'd had all the stuffing kicked out of him. The whole team were a bunch of amateurs. What happened in Edinburgh set us back a couple of years.' Organising a Commonwealth Games, he said, was 'beyond nice people who are totally amateur and who are only finding out how to run the Games when the event is half-way through'.

Borthwick did what he could as chairman of the company running the Games, but it was not enough. The 1986 Games were a world away from the Olympics. Instead of connections with big business, with 'movers and shakers', the parochial Commonwealth Games had always been overseen by the local authority of the host city. The chief executive, Blair Grosset, was a pipe-smoking council official who was, in the words of the *Herald*, 'a chartered accountant by qualification and by nature'. Grosset described himself as 'an old-fashioned local authority man'.

When the city elections put Edinburgh in the hands of left-wing councillors in May 1984 – the month when England's rugby team toured South Africa – life became ever more difficult for Borthwick and Grosset, who had already been busy trying to ensure England would compete. Labour councillors had a manifesto that prioritised council-house repairs and public services, and some wished Edinburgh had never been awarded the Games: it had happened under the previous, Conservative, administration. The new political masters wanted a far bigger say in the running of the event.

Wood became a director. Many more jobs were given to local authority people, and, according to Bateman and Douglas, when the Duke of Edinburgh visited Games headquarters he saw a list of staff comprising 384 names. 'You could get rid of that lot for a start!' the Duke, president of the Commonwealth Games Federation, apparently said.

There was a good deal of self-inflicted damage. The television rights were sold to the BBC for £500,000 when others thought a fair price would have been at least three times as much. When West Nally, one of the world's leading sports sponsorship agencies, were asked to step in they declined. They could see the Games were heading for trouble, that the selling of sponsorship had been too localised and that too many bad deals had already been done. They did what they could to help, setting up their own giant screens in the stadium, but West Nally worked instead for Auckland 1990. 'Edinburgh was our launch platform for Auckland,' said the company's driving force, Patrick Nally. By the end of the 1986 Games Auckland had already raised one-third of its running costs: they incurred no losses as hosts.

Edinburgh's pride at becoming the first city to stage the Games a second time 'turned to humiliation', wrote Bateman and Douglas, when Maxwell had to be called in. One of his first pronouncements was that the early preparations had been 'appallingly amateurish'. The organisers had been upset by constant sniping in the newspapers but, Maxwell said, 'I told them it is their own bloody fault.' A preview to the Games in *The Times* blamed Borthwick, Grosset and Heatly for 'procrastinating over four years' and failing to raise money, or even trying to do so, from beyond Britain. Heatly, said chief sports writer David Miller, had been at fault in not working hard enough among developing nations to avoid the boycott. The amateurish attempts of Heatly, Borthwick and others 'in a sporting world now demanding professional relationships with sponsors, broadcasting and the competitors themselves' amounted to a dangerous crisis that threatened the future of the Games. Internal leadership was as big a problem as political interference, said Miller. Wood's view is that the boycott was going to happen come what may. 'I doubt if any lobbying would have averted it.'

No teams had withdrawn by the time Maxwell took over as chairman on 19 June. In the final fortnight before the opening ceremony, one after another, nations withdrew. It went on right up to the start of competition.

Eight teams arrived and checked in to their accommodation at the athletes' village only to discover that their governments had joined the boycott. Bermuda even took part in the opening ceremony before the athletes were ordered not to compete. All these teams were told they were welcome to stay in the village anyway.

A few days before the opening ceremony Chris Brasher, an Olympic champion and founder of the London Marathon, wrote in the *Observer* that Edinburgh 1970 had been 'the finest Games I have ever attended anywhere in the world'. His view on the forthcoming second Games in the Scottish capital was scathing.

> In those days of long ago Edinburgh opened its heart to the Commonwealth and was loved and admired. In these days when sport has become a tool of the politicians, the Commonwealth has rejected their invitation.

> The thirteenth Commonwealth Games are rudderless and hapless in a sea of discontent: discontent with Mrs Thatcher, with the Commonwealth leaders of African, Caribbean and Indian sub-continent countries, with the chairman of the Commonwealth Games Federation, Peter Heatly, and with the organising committee, ostensibly led by the embarrassing Ken Borthwick, one-time Lord Provost of the city and now a man who has an amazing ability to score own goals against his own team.

The races that would be most noticeably downgraded, Brasher said, were the men's 800m and 1500m, the 'two premier events of the Games' that had lost their African challengers.

'Have a thought,' said Maxwell, 'for the hundreds of athletes who will be suffering heartache and disappointment that all their years of preparation have been wasted because their governments have exercised their sovereign right to make politics supreme over sport.' He pledged to send a bill to all those who stayed away, deeming them responsible for £2m of the financial losses. He also said that if there was a further shortfall, he would bill Thatcher. 'She is a tough lady but I am a tough hombre,' he said.

Those athletes who did turn up left the fretting over the boycott and the bills to Games organisers, focusing strictly on the competition. Sally Gunnell was one of them. 'I was 20 years old and completely oblivious to all the boycott stuff, all the politics,' she said. 'I didn't expect to be in the team and I was just chuffed to be there. I wasn't reading all the papers. I had never been to a big event, and I was completely blown away by it.' Gunnell won the 100m hurdles, the first of her five Commonwealth golds, and has only good memories of Edinburgh.

The biggest hero for the Scottish crowds was, by some distance, Liz Lynch, who was on the dole when she won the 10,000m. It was the first time that the event was contested at the Commonwealth Games; it was Scotland's only gold medal in athletics. The host nation's biggest star on the track, the 1980 Olympic sprint champion Allan Wells, had, controversially, not been selected to defend his Commonwealth titles in his home city.

A year after the Edinburgh Games, Lynch married the Northern Ireland steeplechaser Peter McColgan, under which name she would win the BBC Sports Personality award in 1991, the year of her stunning 10,000m triumph at the World Championships in Tokyo. She was a silver medallist in the first Olympic 10,000m in 1988, successfully defended her Commonwealth title in 1990, won the World Half Marathon title in 1992, and numbered the New York, Tokyo and London marathons among her other notable victories – but that first gold in Edinburgh always meant more to her than anything she achieved later.

Lynch made it to the top the hard way, having been brought up on a tough Dundee council estate, living in a block of flats with 'filthy stairs and graffiti-scarred passages'. She and her father were both unemployed when she was offered an athletics scholarship in the United States, but she scraped together the money for her flight and was away for three years before returning to sign on again and train for the Edinburgh Games. Her biggest achievement in the States was helping her Alabama college to their first national track and field title in their 155-year existence, for which she received a letter of congratulation from President Ronald Reagan.

It was a gloomy Monday evening, with light rain falling and lightning in the sky, when the New Zealander Anne Audain, the Commonwealth record holder, set the pace in the big race. Everything went to plan for Lynch, who stayed with Audain until two laps out. The crowd roared as she moved into the lead, powering clear to win by the length of the straight. She beat her personal best time by more than a minute to set Commonwealth, UK and Scottish all-comers' records. She draped herself in a flag, kissed her parents, and ran a lap of honour.

Two of Lynch's fellow runners had bet her £75 that she would cry at the medal ceremony. She lost. 'I didn't think I would, but the crowd were something else and "Scotland the Brave" sounded so wonderful. It was so overwhelming, totally unbelievable.' She thought at the time that even winning Olympic medals would not make her feel so good, and she was right. 'I could never, ever relive that moment. They were still shouting my name an hour later in the pouring rain. It was the best moment of my sporting life.' She did not need to sign on the dole again after that.

Wells was the Commonwealth champion at 100m and 200m, yet he was not selected because he had not raced in the Scottish trials. 'I'd done the qualifying times, but they wanted me to prove my fitness,' said Wells. 'People couldn't understand why I wasn't in the team.' He showed the selectors what they had missed at a meeting in Gateshead shortly after the Games, where he caused a stir for two reasons. First, he was the first athlete to wear lycra shorts, a trend that soon went global; second, he defeated the Edinburgh gold medallists over 100m and 200m, the Canadians Ben Johnson and Atlee Mahorn. He would surely have been among the medallists had he not been overlooked.

Another champion who was born and bred in Edinburgh, the bowls player Willie Wood, was also denied the chance to perform in front of his home crowd. Wood, singles champion in 1982, was banned for 'professionalism'. He had indeed accepted prize money but, he said, so had all the other top players at a time when bowls was a popular televised sport. 'It was all nonsense,' he said. 'You could earn money but you had to put it in a trust fund. I didn't have the paperwork so the Commonwealth Games Council of Scotland wouldn't let me play. I was annoyed, especially after I'd been selected. I knew those greens like the back of my hand, and I was the defending champion. But that's how it was.' Wood flew more than a million miles during his playing career and appeared in a record eight Games, the last of them in 2010 when he was 72. The only one he missed, in a run of nine Games since 1974, was the one he could have walked to.

The prime minister of the host nation is traditionally invited to the Games for a 'meet and greet' visit. Thatcher's dinner with the Queen at Holyrood Palace on the night of her arrival would have featured some interesting discussions. The most recent edition of the *Sunday Times* had reported that the Queen was disturbed by Thatcher's attitude towards the Commonwealth and by some of her 'socially divisive' policies. The story was said to have been leaked by a high-level source at Buckingham Palace.

Thatcher would not agree to economic sanctions against South Africa, saying that they would hurt the general population. Edinburgh Council asked her not to come: she was not wanted. She was shunned on her visit to the athletes' village on 1 August, when the only competitor willing to meet her was a protester. Team officials said the other athletes were resting, training or unaware of Thatcher's arrival. The prime minister went on to the stadium where 500 anti-apartheid protesters were marshalled by nearly as many police. As she took her place in the VIP seating some of the 20,000 crowd cheered the announcement of her arrival but the majority booed.

There never would be any government support for these Games, which is but one reason why the losses mounted. There was, Wood believed, a political motivation behind Thatcher's refusal to support Edinburgh. 'She was not only avidly pro-South Africa – she did once describe Nelson Mandela as "a terrorist" – but by 1984 her government was on collision course with Edinburgh District Council over local authority budgets.'

At least Maxwell had made an immediate impact when he took over. He organised media committees in London and Edinburgh, placing Lord Stevens, of Express Newspapers, in charge of the former. A lunch at the Savoy raised £43,000, while the presence of newspaper owners and editors on the committees ensured favourable coverage throughout the country. 'His publicity machine was enormous,' said his photographer-aide Maloney. 'He was always shipping editors up to Edinburgh.'

Maxwell played a brilliant game, gaining millions of pounds worth of positive publicity. He pretended not to want to be the centre of attention, and laughed off as 'preposterous' any suggestion that he would want to present medals. But when Daley Thompson, the biggest star of British athletics, won the decathlon he received his gold medal from Maxwell, who earned maximum exposure for Mirror Group Newspapers. Logos for the *Mirror* and its Scottish sister paper, the *Record*, were everywhere – on the replay screen, on top of the main stadium scoreboard, the swimming scoreboard, at the diving pool, on the corner posts on the boxing ring. Officially the Games' main sponsors were Guinness. In reality it appeared to be Mirror Group. As Bateman and Douglas wrote:

> The real marketing value of the Games for Maxwell was something that all the professionals had missed. The biggest single bonus Mirror Group Newspapers had was the chairman himself, Ian Robert Maxwell. For six weeks his name and face were rarely off the front pages of the Scottish press. He appeared on national TV news, and for two weeks over the immediate period of the Games, the whole of the British media was talking about the man.

> The reaction of the newsmen went from antagonism to grudging respect. Here was a man commanding a multi-million pound empire in a cut-throat business, one whose dealings raised innumerable questions in the public mind, who had been officially pilloried on occasion and who engendered in the papers not under his control a professional animosity bordering on the obsessive. And what were the journalists doing? Writing about him, day in, day out. Like him or loathe him, there was no escaping him. It is doubtful if the Maxwell millions could

have bought the exposure he ultimately derived and no amount of money on earth could have paid to have the chairman of the board photographed amiably chatting with the monarch.

The accountants Coopers & Lybrand totted up all that exposure and put a value on it: £4.3m. By the final reckoning Maxwell had not even paid £0.3m. 'No one could guess at the time that the White Knight would ride off into the sunset leaving a £3.8m debt behind for someone else to pay,' Maloney said. 'He got worldwide publicity, which was his main aim. Even so, he *was* the saviour of the Games, and he loved it.'

'That whole time in Edinburgh was so fascinating, utterly unreal. He wanted the best hotel, and he wanted his team to look the part. So it was the presidential suite at the Sheraton, and he sent his entourage, about half a dozen of us, off to the tailor for new blazers, flannels and ties. We all wore the Commonwealth badge, and we had new shoes too. It was a pricy outfit.' Some of the most important people from New Zealand, including the prime minister and governor-general, were moved out of their rooms at the Sheraton to accommodate Maxwell's team.

'As soon as he arrived he just took over,' said Maloney. 'He was always at meetings, and whatever the subject, even if he knew nothing about it, he'd take control. On one occasion he came out of a meeting and wanted to go back to the hotel. He walked into the road and flagged down an official Games car and told the driver, "Take me to the Sheraton." The driver said he couldn't, as he was due to pick up somebody else, but Bob said, "I'm Robert Maxwell and I shall give you a letter of absolution to present to your boss." He even dictated it to me in the car.'

Maloney recalled an earlier visit to Tokyo, where Maxwell first met the businessman who donated so much money to Edinburgh, Ryoichi Sasakawa. 'That must have been when he asked him to put up some money for the Games. Bob always insisted on the best hotel, so he booked a suite at the Imperial Palace. I was paying the bills for him, and I know how much it cost – $8000 a night, and that didn't even include so much as a cup of coffee. Everything else was extra and it came to $80,000 in all when we checked out.

'Bob was a unique character. We became quite close friends but I have to say he was a bit of a pig when it came to eating. One evening he asked me what sort of food we should eat and I said I liked Chinese. So he got the best Chinese restaurant in Edinburgh and ordered a banquet meal for 14 people. They said they didn't do takeaways but he boomed down the phone, "Just tell the manager it's for Robert Maxwell of the Commonwealth Games." When the food arrived it was transferred to silver salvers on a giant table, with Bob at one end and me at the other. There was plenty of Dom Perignon too. When he said "Tuck in." I asked if we shouldn't wait for the other guests. There weren't any – there was enough food for another 12 people and he just got stuck in, digging in to the various dishes, sometimes with his fingers. There was curry sauce dripping down his shirt-front when he went off to bed.

'When he served the Kentucky Fried Chicken at another reception, it wasn't the first time. He would do it at the Labour party conference too. When he was offering round the buckets he actually took a bite out of a leg and said to one of the lady guests, "Tastes good, try this – you'll like it." And he put the chicken leg back in the bucket.'

Clearly, Maxwell liked his food. Did he enjoy the sport, too? 'He didn't have the attention span for that,' said Maloney. 'Even at football matches he'd always invent an excuse to leave, pretending he had to make a call. He could never have sat through the 5000m race, for example – far too long. The 100m would have been about his limit.'

Maxwell's preferred setting was not the stadium but sitting in front of the cameras. On the penultimate day of competition Maxwell called a press conference that was rated by some – among them Ian Wooldridge of the *Daily Mail* – as the strangest they ever attended. Maxwell told the press they had done 'a magnificent job', invited them for drinks at his own expense and welcomed Sasakawa, who would take questions through an interpreter. Sasakawa, it later transpired, contributed more than four times as much as Maxwell to Edinburgh's cause.

Sasakawa was introduced as 'a former politician who played an important role in the economic revival of his country after the War'. He had devoted himself to 'world philanthropy', had donated huge sums of money to the smallpox eradication programme that ended in 1980 (true), and was responsible for 'the eradication of leprosy' (false). Sasakawa, Maxwell said, was president of the Federation of World Volunteer Firemen's Associations, the World Union of Karate, the Japan Science Society and other bodies. He had held a private meeting with Thatcher, having responded to a plea for a donation to a British children's charity.

Sasakawa then spoke for five minutes, in Japanese, to explain what he was doing for world harmony, and to tell his audience: 'Sport is the path to peace.' His closing speech, as translated, was reported verbatim in *Unfriendly Games*:

> Finally, I would like to say my secret to keep youth for myself. I tell myself I should live up to the last moment of my life. So I tell myself I should live up to 200 years of age and because every year people feel they

get one year older, in my case I always throw away one year when the new year comes. So this is what I told myself when I was 80 years of age that I should throw 60 years out of my fiscal age. That is why I am still 27 years of age this year. So in order to attest to this, I can carry five or six years of age boy or girl on my back and march in front of you tomorrow.

He wished the royal family a long life, bowed, and let Maxwell return to the microphone.

Maxwell had glossed over some other facts about Sasakawa. Yes, he had given away $12 billion over 20 years, but no, he had not made his fortune from shipbuilding. A better picture of the man came after his death in 1995 – he did not quite make it to 200 – in an obituary in the *Independent* that said Sasakawa had been 'the last of Japan's A-class war criminals who stood out as a monster of egotism, greed, ruthless ambition, and political deviousness'. With his love of the limelight and because of his sensational private life – a string of mistresses – he was 'almost a lovable rascal', popular among Japan's non-liberals. Sasakawa was said to have had links with the Central Intelleigance Agency (CIA), which helped him to gain freedom after the war, and was involved in the opium trade. He made a fortune from gambling, built a business empire worth billions, and ran an island where prostitution was rife. He hated Communists and loved women, claiming to have slept with more than 500 partners. Sasakawa became, like Maxwell, a publisher and newspaper owner. In 1986, to enhance his image, he founded the Sasakawa Peace Foundation, an international education project, as well as putting money into the Edinburgh Games. The accounts showed that his donation, via the Japan Shipbuilding Industry Foundation, was £1.265 million.

The final deficit for Edinburgh 1986, before Sasakawa's donation, was about the same as it had been before Maxwell took over – nearly £4 million. The money from Japan made a big difference. Maxwell further reduced the losses by negotiation with creditors, among them two local councils. Those owed less than £100,000 were paid in full. There was still so much work to be done that the Games' administrative company did not clear up all its most pressing paperwork until 1989. There were still rumblings 10 years after that.

Alex Wood, who was company secretary of Commonwealth Games 1986 (Scotland) Ltd and who attended its final meeting in September 1998 received a letter from the Edinburgh office of PricewaterhouseCoopers in May 1999. The accountants' missive was the last official communication in the company's records. At the final, final reckoning, there was a small bonus. The interest on Sasakawa's donation had not originally been transferred across. This led many years later to a surplus of £10,825.05. It was sent by cheque to the Commonwealth Games Council for Scotland, on condition that 'no publicity be ascribed to it'.

The final letter from the accountants advised Wood that the company had been struck off the Companies Register and ended, 'Finally, may I take this opportunity to thank you all for your forbearance in bringing what was a difficult matter to a conclusion.'

Was it all worth it? In Alex Wood's opinion, no. His 'very personal perspective, and one reached retrospectively' was that the city should never have been involved. 'Robert Maxwell was a man of monstrous ego, devoid of any desire to serve the greater good but suffused with an urgent need for power, control and self-aggrandisement.' Those on the council, both Conservative and Labour, who pushed 'promoting the city' as a good reason for hosting the Games were more interested, in reality, in junkets, foreign trips and socialising with the rich and powerful. 'My view is that Edinburgh should never have become embroiled in seeking to host the Games.'

Despite all the failings and embarrassments, the Commonwealth Games Federation will be forever grateful that they did. Had there been no Games in 1986, who knows whether they would have made it back to Scotland in 2014?

Bibliography

Books

Achebe, Chinua, *There Was a Country: A Personal History of Biafra* (London and New York: Allen Lane, 2012).

Ademoyega, Adewale, *Why We Struck: The Story of the First Nigerian Coup* (Ibadan: Evans Brothers, 1981).

Agbogun, J. B., *Nigeria at the Commonwealth Games* (Unknown: Kwara State Sports Council, 1975).

Anyaoku, Chief Emeka, *The Missing Headlines: Selected Speeches* (Liverpool: Liverpool University Press, 1997).

Bannister, Roger, *The First Four Minutes* (London: Putnam, 1955).

Bascomb, Neal, *The Perfect Mile: Three Athletes, One Goal, and Less Than Four Minutes to Achieve It* (London: CollinsWillow, 2004).

Bateman, Derek, and Derek Douglas, *Unfriendly Games: Boycotted and Broke, the Inside Story of the 1986 Commonwealth Games* (London and Glasgow: Mainstream and Glasgow Herald, 1986).

Brill, Debbie, with James Lawton, *Jump* (Vancouver: Douglas & McIntyre, 1986).

Butcher, Pat, *The Perfect Distance: Ovett and Coe: The Record Breaking Rivalry* (London: Orion, 2004).

Connock, Marion, *The Precious McKenzie Story* (London: Pelham, 1975).

Dheensaw, Cleve, *The Commonwealth Games: The First 60 Years 1930–1990* (Victoria, BC: Orca Book Publishers, 1994).

Forsyth, Frederick, *Making of an African Legend: The Biafra Story* (Sutton: Severn House, 1983).

Fraser, Dawn, with Harry Gordon, *Below the Surface: Confessions of an Olympic Champion* (New York: William Morrow, 1965).

—, *Dawn: One Hell of a Life* (Sydney: Hodder, 2001).

Gbulie, Ben, *Nigeria's Five Majors, Coup d'Etat of 15th January 1966: First Inside Account* (Onitsha: Africana Educational Publishers, 1981).

Gordon, Harry, *Young Men in a Hurry: The Story of Australia's Fastest Decade* (London: Angus & Robertson, 1962).

Hadgraft, Rob, *Plimsolls on, Eyeballs Out: The Rise and Horrendous Fall of Marathon Legend Jim Peters* (Southend-on-Sea: Desert Island Books, 2011).

Harris, Norman, *Lap of Honour: The Great Moments of New Zealand Athletics* (London: Herbert Jenkins, 1963).

Hill, Ron, *The Long Hard Road: An Autobiography,* 2 Parts (Hyde: Ron Hill Sports, part 1, 1981; part 2, 1982).

Holt, Richard, *Sport and the British* (Oxford: Clarendon Press, 1989).

McKenzie, Arthur, *Marathon and Chips* (Morpeth: Alder Sports, 1981).

Maloney, Mike, and William Hall, *Flash! Splash! Crash! All at Sea with Cap'n Bob: My Astonishing Adventures with Robert Maxwell* (Edinburgh: Mainstream, 1996).

Mangan, J. A., (ed.), *The Cultural Bond: Sport, Empire, Society* (London: Frank Cass, 1992).

Ojukwu, Emeka, *Because I Am Involved* (Ibadan: Spectrum Books, 1989).

Ottah, Nelson, *The Trial of Biafra's Leaders* (Enugu: Fourth Dimension, 1980).

Peters, Mary, with Ian Wooldridge, *Mary P* (London: Stanley Paul, 1974).

Phillips, Bob, *Honour of Empire, Glory of Sport* (Manchester: Parrs Wood Press, 2000).

—, *The Commonwealth Games: The History of All the Sports* (Manchester: Parrs Wood Press, 2002).

Talbot, Don, with Kevin Berry and Ian Heads, *Talbot: Nothing but the Best* (Melbourne: Lothian Books, 2003).

Thurston, Tom, *Strongman: The Doug Hepburn Story* (Vancouver, BC: Ronsdale Press, 2004).

Webster, Jack, *The Auld Hoose; The Story of Robert Gordon's College* (Edinburgh: Black & White, 2005).

Wheeler, Tony, *Tony Wheeler's Dark Lands* (London: Lonely Planet Publications, 2013).

Newspapers and magazines

Aberdeen Press & Journal
Age (Melbourne)
Australian
Cape Town Post
Daily Express
Daily Mail
Daily Mirror
Daily Telegraph
Drum
Guardian
Hamilton Spectator
Herald (Glasgow)
Herald Sun
Independent

Mirror
Montreal Gazette
Morning Post (Lagos)
New York Times
New Zealand Listener
Nineteenth Century
Observer
Observer Sport Monthly
Sports Illustrated
Sydney Morning Herald
The Times
Toronto Star
Track and Field News
Vancouver Sun
West African Pilot

Websites (current and defunct)

la84.org
pullbuoy.co.uk
athleticsnigeria.org
geoffwattrun.com.au
thecgf.com
ishof.org
royal.gov.uk
gbrathletics.com
trove.nla.gov.au
bl.uk
natlib.govt.nz
fulltext.ausport.gov.au
islandsbusiness.com

British Library audio

Dorothy Tyler and Jim Peters interviewed by Rachel Cutler, *Oral History of British Athletics*, October 1996, British Library Sound & Moving Image Catalogue reference C790, © The British Library Board. Reproduced with permission.

All-time medals tables (1930–2010)

	Gold	Silver	Bronze	Total
Australia	803	673	604	2080
England	612	614	612	1838
Canada	436	459	493	1388
India	145	124	110	379
New Zealand	130	189	245	564
South Africa	104	102	106	312
Scotland	92	104	160	356
Kenya	71	59	65	195
Wales	51	78	107	236
Nigeria	50	55	71	176
Malaysia	46	52	63	161
Jamaica	42	34	36	112
Northern Ireland	27	30	44	101
Pakistan	24	21	20	65
Singapore	22	19	26	67
Ghana	15	17	22	54
Cyprus	13	8	10	31
Uganda	12	15	17	44
Nauru	10	9	9	28
Bahamas	9	10	11	30
Cameroon	9	7	11	27
Trinidad and Tobago	8	17	19	44
Zimbabwe	7	15	22	44
Tanzania	6	6	9	21
Sri Lanka	5	6	2	13
Hong Kong	5	1	9	15
Zambia	3	8	18	29
Guyana	3	5	7	15
Fiji	3	4	7	14

Samoa	3	3	10	16
Namibia	3	3	9	15
Isle of Man	3	1	6	10
Papua New Guinea	2	5	2	9
Barbados	2	3	6	11
Malaya	2	3	2	7
Bangladesh	2	1	2	5
Mozambique	2	1	1	4
Saint Vincent and the Grenadines	2	0	1	3
Mauritius	1	4	5	10
Botswana	1	3	7	11
Guernsey	1	3	2	6
Bermuda	1	2	2	5
Lesotho	1	1	1	3
Jersey	1	0	3	4
Cayman Islands	1	0	1	2
Saint Kitts and Nevis	1	0	0	1
Seychelles	0	3	3	6
Malta	0	1	3	4
Swaziland	0	1	3	4
Grenada	0	1	0	1
Malawi	0	0	3	3
Tonga	0	0	3	3
Saint Lucia	0	0	2	2
Gambia	0	0	1	1
Norfolk Island	0	0	1	1

Ghana tally includes medals won by Gold Coast before independence; Zimbabwe includes early years as Southern Rhodesia, Rhodesia, and Rhodesia and Nyasaland; Zambia includes early years as Northern Rhodesia; Sri Lanka includes early years as British Ceylon and Dominion of Ceylon; Guyana includes early years as British Guiana.

Top six in athletics

	Gold	Silver	Bronze	Total
England	184	182	167	533
Australia	175	148	124	447
Canada	75	90	121	286
Kenya	58	45	41	144
Jamaica	40	29	28	97
South Africa	36	31	27	94

Top six in swimming

	Gold	Silver	Bronze	Total
Australia	258	183	160	601
Canada	94	110	113	317
England	84	113	127	324
South Africa	21	26	20	67
Scotland	17	24	26	67
New Zealand	13	29	35	77

Top six in weightlifting

	Gold	Silver	Bronze	Total
Australia	57	49	44	150
England	41	44	21	106
India	35	41	25	101
Canada	26	28	38	92
Wales	18	12	20	50
Nigeria	14	16	19	49

Top six in boxing

	Gold	Silver	Bronze	Total
England	49	26	36	111
Canada	24	21	34	79
Scotland	15	16	28	59
South Africa	15	8	10	33
Australia	13	14	32	59
Nigeria	13	6	14	33

Picture credits

The photographs in the plate section come courtesy of Burlington Historical Society (page 1), Precious McKenzie (page 2, top left and right), Steve Rowe/Sports Journalists Association (page 3), Ron Hill (page 6, bottom), Gert Potgieter (page 7, bottom left), Mike Bull (page 8, bottom), Norm Scott-Morrison (page 9, bottom), Adewale Ademoyega (page 10), the White House (page 12, top) and Paul Coffa (page 12, bottom). Other photos in the plate section, pages: 2 (bottom) © S&G and Barratts/EMPICS Sport/Press Association Images; 4 (top), 5 and 9 (top) © Tony Duffy/Getty Images; 4 (bottom) and 11 (bottom) © Hulton Archive/Getty Images; 6 (top) and 13 (top right and bottom) © Fox Photos/Hulton Archive/Getty Images; 7 (top and bottom right) © Keystone/Hulton Archive/Getty Images; 8 (top left and right) © Chas Sime/Hulton Archive/Getty Images; 11 (top) © Tony Feder/ALLSPORT/Getty Images; 12 (bottom) © Paul Coffa; 13 (top left) © William Vanderson/Hulton Archive/Getty Images; 14 and 16 (top and bottom) © Popperfoto/Getty Images; and 15 © Getty Images.

Index